P9-DBQ-437

Books by Carl J. Friedrich

Europe: An Emergent Nation?
Trends of Federalism in Theory and Practice
Constitutional Government and Democracy
Impact of American Constitutionalism Abroad
Introduction to Political Theory
Totalitarian Dictatorship and Autocracy (*with Zbigniew K. Brzezinski*)
Transcendent Justice: The Religious Dimension of Constitutionalism
Philosophy of Law in Historical Perspective
Man and His Government
Constitutional Reason of State, the Survival of the Constitutional Order
Age of Power (*with Charles Blitzer*)
Age of the Baroque: 1610–1660

Edited

Nomos: Yearbook of the American Society for Political and Legal Philosophy (Vols. 1–8)
Public Policy: Yearbook of the Graduate School of Public Administration, Harvard University
Politische Dimensionen der Europäischen Gemeinschaftsbildung
From the Declaration of Independence to the Constitution (*with Robert G. McCloskey*)
Studies in Federalism (*with Robert Bowie*)
Totalitarianism

EUROPE: AN EMERGENT NATION?

This study has been prepared under
the joint sponsorship
of
The Center for International Affairs
at Harvard University
and
Institut für Politische Wissenschaft
University of Heidelberg
and
Implemented by Funds of
the Ford Foundation

Europe

AN EMERGENT NATION?

Carl J. Friedrich

Things won are done; joy's soul
lies in the doing.

—SHAKESPEARE, *Troilus and Cressida,* I, 2.

The mode whereby the inevitable comes to pass is effort.

—OLIVER WENDELL HOLMES

Nous ne coalisons pas les Etats, nous unissons les hommes.

—JEAN MONNET

1817

HARPER & ROW, PUBLISHERS

NEW YORK AND EVANSTON

FIRST EDITION

LIBRARY OF CONGRESS CATALOG CARD NUMBER: 70–83592

To the memory of
ADRIANO OLIVETTI,
seeker after community and beauty

Contents

Preface — xi

Map—The European Community — *(facing page 1)*

1. The Background of European Community — 1
2. European Consensus and Community Structure: A Federal Potential? — 24
3. The Business Community: Enterprises — 47
4. The Business Community: Associations — 69
5. The Agricultural Community — 90
6. The Labor Community in the Factory and the Guest Worker — 114
7. The Trade Union Labor Community — 133
8. A Community of Communities: Grass-roots Integration — 151
9. The Academic Community — 175
10. Trends and Prospects — 196

Notes — 217

List of Abbreviations — 245

Index — 251

Preface

It is now over forty years since Coudenhove-Kalergi published his *Paneuropa* (1924), following upon his article in the *Neue Freie Presse* (Vienna) in 1922. Ever since then, I have been a partisan of European unification. This needs to be said so that the reader may know where my heart is. But as a student of European politics, my mind has watched the ups and downs, and the accumulation of knowledge has increasingly impressed me with the enormous obstacles in the way of the goal, no matter how desirable in itself. Even if politics is not merely the art of the possible, but at least at times the art of making the seemingly impossible possible, the skill and dedication of quite a few master-politicians from Briand and Stresemann to Schumann and Adenauer, not to mention those now at work in this stony vineyard, have been expended in achieving very limited results. Europe is moving—it is *en marche*—but the march seems at times more nearly at a snail's pace than at the required speed demanded by the problems Europe is facing.

Over the years, I have been impressed, and especially since the first Congress of Europe in 1948 which it was my privilege to attend, by how many nameless people of deep devotion have contributed to these results. All their doings will never be told. But it has seemed to me for some time now that the political implications of many of these small undertakings were increasingly vital to the progress of the European Community toward a viable political framework. Many are the studies devoted to this framework and to the overall policies which have issued from these emergent institutions. But we have had relatively much less knowledge of the informal community growth which has set in since this framework was created. The increasing contacts between businessmen and workers, between farmers and journalists, and between universities and communes have accumulated a certain weight over the years; they have developed a momentum of their own which it seemed worth exploring in fuller detail than was readily available.

Hence I am very grateful that the Center for International Affairs and its director, my good friend Robert R. Bowie, were interested and willing to enable me to set up a rather extensive research project. This project is still continuing, and further studies are in the making. But five of them have been completed and were published in 1967 under the title *Politische Dimensionen der Europäischen Gemeinschaftsbildung*. They were authored jointly under my editorship by Richard Grauhan, at present a *Privatdozent* at the University of Konstanz; Karl-Heinz Neunreither, permanent secretary of two committees of the European parliament; Hans-Viktor Schierwater, deputy director of Haus Rissen (Hamburg); Henri Schwamm, Lecturer at the Institut des Hautes Etudes Internationales (Geneva) and a staff member of the Centre Européen de la Culture (Geneva); Dusan Sidjanski, Professor of Political Science at the University of Geneva. I have benefited greatly from their studies, as will be shown more clearly in the chapters to follow. Their studies were developed in accordance with a "research strategy" that involved all available techniques, but concentrated upon the kind of evidence which in modern literate societies usually provides more reliable clues to the actual behavior of social groups than attitudinal inquiries, even when reinforced by computer analysis of the results. All these studies concentrate as a primary focus upon the Franco-German relationship. But there are others now nearing completion, notably a study of the migratory Italian workers by Stefano Passigli, a lecturer in political science at the University of Padua; a study by Rudolf Steiert of the German trade unions' reaction to the crisis of the Common Market; and a study of the French agriculturists' behavior toward European integration by Hélène Delorme Louët and Yves Tavernier, both of the Fondation Nationale des Sciences Politiques (Paris). The last will soon appear in French and an English translation is being prepared for the Center; similarly, the publication of Passigli's study is insured in Italian and an English translation is planned; Steiert's work will probably be published in German. Other studies are in the making, especially in the field of mass communications and on Franco-German intermarriage. We are also planning to extend this work into Benelux, Italy, and Great Britain. At the same time, related studies are being published by others, such as the one by Meynaud and Sidjanski on business interest groups.

A very large number of friends, colleagues, students, and officials have, over the years, helped me in developing and refining my thoughts and research on European integration. It would be both presumptuous and impossible to undertake their listing here. Many of them know better than I can say what they have contributed. My thanks to all of them is heartfelt. I should, however, acknowledge specifically the help of M. J.-R. Rabier, deputy director of the Press and Information Services of the CE and chairman of the International Political Science Association's Research Committee on European Integration, which is actively engaged in sponsoring work in this field. Special thanks are also due to my research assistant, Miss Edith Kaiser, and to my secretary, Miss Rosalind Cummings.

CARL J. FRIEDRICH

EUROPE: AN EMERGENT NATION?

1. The Background of European Community

There always has been a European Community. It is the community which has been the carrier of what is called European culture or civilization. It has included different peoples and different territories at different times. Neither Russia nor America nor the British settlements of European stock can be excluded from it. In spite of the colonial revolution against these Europeans, they still dominate the world at large; for beyond the reach of "little Europe," the United States, and the Soviet Union and the British Commonwealth of Nations, there are many people, but not much power. India and China speak the language of Europe in arguing their case for independence and neutrality; their rival ideologies are Western.[1*]

It is not this world-wide European linkage that concerns us in these pages, but rather that core of "little Europe" which is constituted by the so-called Continent—a limited, but densely populated promontory of the continent of Asia—which centers in France, Germany, and Italy. Actually, the relationship between France and Germany, for so many generations a community of fighting rather than of cooperating, in many ways constitutes the actual (as well as ideological) core of the communal problem of Europe.

* Notes begin on page 217.

This Europe of the Six—Belgium, France, Germany, Italy, Luxembourg, and the Netherlands—constitutes the "heartland" of that European culture which developed after the so-called Dark Ages over approximately a thousand years into what is the greatest concentration of industrial production in the contemporary world, especially if the closely linked Europe of the Seven—Great Britain, Austria, Denmark, Ireland, Norway, Portugal, and Switzerland—are seen as the partners of the Six they in fact are. Greece and Turkey also are associated with the Europe of the Six. It is these lands which together constitute Europe proper; although a very real problem is presented by the relationship to them of Spain, Poland, Czechoslovakia, Yugoslavia, Hungary, and Rumania: both in cultural and political terms they have a real claim to be included in this definition of Europe. But political obstacles which at present appear of long duration, except possibly in the case of Spain, would make it appear the pragmatically sensible thing to exclude them from a demarcation of Europe for the time being.[2]

It is this Europe of the thirteen—a baker's dozen—which has shared a common culture and has constituted a political community since the days of Charlemagne. Indeed, the Europe of the so-called Middle Ages—that is to say, of the centuries from A.D. 800 to 1450—was a rather close-knit cultural community. It was considered quite proper for men teaching at the universities to move from country to country—for Albert Magnus, the German, and Thomas Aquinas, the Italian, to teach at Paris, to mention only two of the most famous.[3] By contrast, as we shall have occasion to explore in Chapter 9, the academic community even today is reluctant to see itself as one, and great efforts are required to overcome the national particularism of the academic world which forbids anyone but a Frenchman or an Italian to hold a permanent professorship at one of their national universities. Germany is in a somewhat more tolerant posture, perhaps in part due to the fact that its universities are not national, but local (*Land*) institutions.

The medieval cultural community of Europe was, of course,

characterized by a common language and a common religion. It was very incompletely organized, though trade relations were reasonably lively, and was centered in the cities, which in Italy became the very focus of political as well as cultural and intellectual activity. "City air makes free" (*Stadtluft macht frei*) was the slogan which expressed this localism which attached itself to Empire and Papacy in its desire to maintain a measure of independence. (In Chapter 8 we shall show how such a communal Europeanism manifests itself today.) Empire and Papacy, the *Sacrum Imperium*[4] which inspired the dreams of a Dante, though no modern organizations, provided some measure of structural unity, at least in the center; they were politically ineffective and became increasingly so as the nations, goaded on by the power politics of ambitious princes, began to form in linguistically cognate lands. Nations partly grew and partly were made; the development of political organization and of common culture took place in a process of continuous interaction. They did so within the weak but, at least in aspiration, universal framework of Church and Empire. Both believed themselves to be "world-wide" because the "world" was that of Europe. It was a world dramatically set off against the Arab antagonist, from the Holy Land to Spain, and uneasily related to the Eastern Empire and Church—the Greek world in contrast with the Roman West. As the Middle Ages wore on, the imperial bond became more and more feeble, being restricted to Germany and the lands immediately adjoining it, while the emerging national monarchs each claimed to be an emperor within his own realm. Hence the unity of the European community had to be maintained and structured by the Church. Toward the end of the Middle Ages, the Church underwent an abortive effort at federalizing and constitutionalizing itself in the Conciliar Movement. After its failure the Church's universal claim was shattered by the Protestant revolt.[5]

The emergence of the national states, especially England, France, Poland, Sweden, and Spain, and the response in non-national terms expressed in the rise of similar states in Austria,

Bavaria, Prussia, Saxony, and elsewhere, did not completely shatter the unity of Europe.[6] Notions and practices such as the balance of power and the concert of Europe, of international law and of the intermarriage of princely houses as well as of their aristocracies, provided a looser, but nonetheless a real, structural bond of a vague confederal type. In the intellectual sphere, Leonardo da Vinci, Dürer, Cervantes, Shakespeare, Rembrandt, and Descartes, to mention only a few of the most celebrated, were more European than Italian, German, Spanish, English, Dutch, or French. The intellectual history of Europe resembles in a sense a great and ever-renewed conversation among the great and near-great of all the nations; though increasingly divided by their vernacular tongues, they nonetheless speak a common language, the language of Christianity and humanism, inspired by the heritage of Greece and Rome—of Homer and Virgil, of Plato, Aristotle and Cicero. It was and has remained a true community of language and religion, of values, beliefs, and convictions, if not of interest. Hence the broad movements of cultural development are all European movements which engulf the common folk of all the nations, continent-wide, into a new feeling for life and man's aspirations. Gothic and Renaissance, Baroque and Rococo, Romanticism and Materialism are all European in scope, if not in origin. But wherever the particular movement originated, the influence and effect of creative work was often greater abroad than in the place where it was first created. Thus even in this age of rising national communities, the nations remained subcommunities of the all-inclusive European community; hence they thought of themselves as a family of nations, large and small, who, even while they fought bloody wars and felt bitter hatreds among themselves, worked together in developing and shaping a common culture through the rivalry of their thinkers and poets, and building their sciences and the industrial civilization which resulted from them.

The bloody wars and bitter hatreds could not fail to suggest to some of the more thoughtful Europeans the need of re-creating a common structure, a political organization, as soon as the medieval order was shattered. From the Grand Design (1610) of Henry IV of France's great minister Sully—he himself sought to credit it to his king—to the deeply philosophical essay *On Eternal Peace* by Immanuel Kant (1795) proposals were advanced for the effective organization of the European political community.[7] The most widely discussed of these plans was that issued by the Abbé Saint-Pierre in 1712–17, following the Peace of Utrecht (1713–1714). He had been secretary to the French delegation, and hence was an experienced diplomat. His *Projet pour rendre la Paix perpetuelle en Europe* was essentially a plan for a perpetual league of the monarchs of Europe. It is a kind of draft treaty, worked out in considerable detail and recommending itself to the princes as "enlightened" men of good sense. The good Abbé, a characteristic eighteenth-century optimist, thought that the advantages of such a union were so real that rational rulers would not hesitate to adopt it forthwith. His league was to provide the foundation for a permanent international organization to maintain a rule of law between nations; the states would renounce war, establish arbitral procedures for the settlement of disputes, and maintain a common police force. Although at the time he was laughed at and sardonically commented upon by men of such different outlooks as King Frederick II of Prussia and Jean-Jacques Rousseau, his ideas correspond so closely to what has been the conception of the League of Nations and the United Nations that we can only agree with Immanuel Kant who defended the Abbé's scheme in very sensible terms:

> Even though this idea may seem utopian, it is the inevitable escape from the want into which human beings bring each other [by war]. It must force the states to the resolution (hard as it may seem) to which savage man was forced equally unwillingly, namely to surrender his brutal freedom and to seek rest and security under a lawful constitution.[8]

The League of Nations and the United Nations have been seen as attempts at realizing this idea. But of course the League and the UN are global in concept, whereas the *Projet* was conceived in European terms and was based upon that cultural and convictional community which at the time manifested itself in the Enlightenment. In point of fact, this community continued to function on the basis of the balance of power, international law, and the intermarriage of princes and aristocracies until the French Revolution challenged it.

This great and Europe-wide upheaval forced a radical rethinking of the traditions upon which the European community had been based. Both monarchy and church were replaced by the "third estate"—the triumphant people who constituted themselves the nation. This turn posited entirely new questions for the maintenance of European community because the divisive principle of nationality seemed to destroy its viability. For the revolutionary movement itself the matter was simple. The ideology of the Rights of Man being conceived in all-human, universalist terms, the French nation and its leaders had a *mission civilisatrice*, a civilizing mission, to convert the reactionary heathen to this new faith. Sympathizers were encouraged to set up regimes based upon this new belief system, and the effective collaboration and communal unity of Europe would thus be secured.[9] A free federal organization such as Kant envisaged would crown the revolutionary enterprise. As Kant put it in his essay in 1795:

> If good fortune should bring it to pass that a powerful and enlightened people develops a republican form of government which by nature is inclined toward peace, then such a republic will provide the central core for the federal union of other states.[10]

Obviously he thought of the French nation as constituting this core—though it was in fact provided much later by the American Republic. But the European Community continued. In France, as in the rest of Europe, the revolutionaries and their ideology were, after the bloodbath of the *Terreur,* swept away by the dictatorship of Napoleon Bonaparte. He saw himself as the executioner of the Europe-wide aspirations of the French

Revolution. Inspired by Rousseau's oratory, Napoleon liked to imagine himself to be the lawgiver of all Europe. His *Code Civil* was meant to be the lawbook of the European community.[11] The mass armies of the revolutionary *levée en masse,* originally raised to repel the invading armies of the monarchs who had banded together to suppress the revolution, became the instrument of Napoleon's blatant imperialism. Eventually, when the great Corsican was a prisoner at St. Helena, he described this imperialism as an effort to unite Europe under his imperial banner. Napoleon's ruthless destruction of the shadowy remnants of the universal order of Europe by the *Reichsdeputationshauptschluss,* or "Main Agreement of All the Reich Deputies," immediately raised the issue of what new order was to take its place. Whether Napoleon's was a nebulous dream or a rationalizing afterthought of his imperial ambitions, the idea of a united Europe apparently expressed a deep need. Indeed, the very fact that Napoleon could consider such an explanation as a good way retrospectively to legitimize his imperial aggressions would seem to prove that the idea of a European Community had broad appeal. Even in Germany, Italy, and Spain, where Napoleon's aggressions had precipitated resistance movements of radical patriotic outlook, European unity was argued by the fighters for freedom against the foreign usurper.[12]

The peace of Vienna which concluded the wars unleashed by Napoleon's ambition was inspired by the idea of the "concert of Europe." Emperor Alexander I of Russia sought to institutionalize this concert by the Holy Alliance, which in a sense was an attempt at putting the Abbé Saint-Pierre's ideas to work. At the core was a league of the main rulers of Europe with whom were associated such lesser ones as might be willing to cooperate. Britain never formally joined the Holy Alliance, though she "supported" it. Regular meetings were held for quite a few years, and peace was in fact maintained for a considerable period. Metternich and others skillfully employed the Alliance for concerted action against the rising democratic and popular forces and movements, converting it thereby into an instrument of reaction. But its basic conception was European, even if conservative; it intended to maintain the *status quo* in the name of European and Christian civilization.[13] It slowly disintegrated as its protagonists yielded to new conceptions, including a rampant nationalism associated with the unifications of Italy and Germany, as well as the empire of Napoleon III.

The second half of the nineteenth century down to the outbreak of war in 1914 saw the emergence of a new "balance of power." While novel means of mass communication and transportation served to knit Europe ever more closely together, this balance of power proved a deceptive form of structuring the relations of the European powers. Riddled by the world-wide imperialist rivalry for colonies, it failed to provide adequate machinery even for minimal peace requirements. Hence, once again upon the initiative of Russia, conferences were held at The Hague, in 1899 and in 1907, to discuss means of organizing Europe more effectively. The practical results were negligible, except in the field of international law wherein a code of conduct of modern warfare was elaborated.[14] While the United States, other American states, and the British Dominions played an important role in these gatherings, the Hague Conferences were still dominated by the European powers and their illusion of a common destiny to rule the world. The community of Europe in cultural terms was still taken for granted and the superiority of its civilization treated as a matter of course. These were the days of such slogans as "the white man's burden," understood as the civilizing mission of European peoples throughout the world.

The First World War changed all that. The common destiny was affirmed on the bloody battlefields, where many of the finest young manhood of the European nations died for reasons which were at best confused and superficial. To many of the survivors it became clear in the course of this senseless slaughter that an organization must be found to "end all war." President Wilson's proposal for a League of Nations was therefore greeted enthusiastically by many, even though the political leadership in Britain and France, not to mention the U.S., remained sceptical. Within a few years the world-wide aspirations of the League, and the failure of the United States to join it, led to a reassertion of the more limited objective of European unification. Even though the League was predominantly a European organization, led by the British and French,[15] it was felt that it failed to provide Europe proper with that close-knit union which was needed in a world threatened by bolshevism and increasingly emancipating itself from European control. The question of European community organization now came to be the problem of insuring the survival of a culture which had been so long taken for granted.

The leading spokesman of this new and defensive conception of European union was Count Coudenhove-Kalergi, who in a prophetic book called for the effective federal organization of Europe. The title of the volume was significantly *Pan-Europa*.[16] In this book Coudenhove-Kalergi argued for a federally united Europe which would not include Great Britain and the Soviet Union. Its publication was immediately followed by the founding of the Paneuropean Union, which provided the organizational kernel for the Paneuropean movement. In his preface to the second edition, the author reported that leading statesmen and political leaders of a number of states and parties had proclaimed themselves in favor of such a program of uniting Europe, and that the movement was spreading rapidly. He had hopes that the movement would become so massive that it would force the politicians to decide in favor of it. The words of the preface seemed to be on the way to becoming reality: the book was meant to awaken a great political movement. It formulated the European question thus: "Can Europe preserve its peace and its autonomy in the face of the growing non-European world powers, if she remains politically and economically divided, or is she forced to organize herself as a federation of states in order to save her existence?"[17] Coudenhove-Kalergi felt that this question, the European question, was at least as important as the social question which everyone was then arguing and fighting about, sharpened as the class conflict had become after the Russian Revolution and the establishment of the Soviet Union.

Coudenhove-Kalergi envisioned the unity of Europe essentially in confrontation with four world forms, namely the British Empire, the Russian Empire, the emancipation of Asia, and the ascendancy of the United States. It is a vision still dominated by conceptions of power (including the notion that Japan would be the leading Asiatic power) which have since disintegrated. His notion that the empires would become federal unions was mistaken. But his basic starting point, namely the conviction that Europe's world dominion was at an end and that Europe was facing a problem of self-maintenance, was nonetheless sound. Only it must now be placed within the context of an emergent world of great cultures which are in the process of organizing themselves into politically viable entities. This trend has become more pronounced in recent years, in spite of some ups and downs. Whether one considers Asia, Latin America, Africa, or the Arab world, movements for cultural integration, so-called pan-movements,[18] have made their appearance and have spread. They all employ the idea of federalism as offering a potential solution to the problem of how to achieve a measure of unity while retaining a great deal of diversity. Nationalism, regionalism, localism—they are involved in these goings-on just as they are in Europe.[19]

There are of course great obstacles standing in the way of a realization of these dreams, such as the local pride of newly won independence and statehood, and the lack of experience in operating a constitutional system without which federalism remains a facade. But in spite of these obstacles, the emotional and ideological appeal of these pan-movements has been so strong in various parts of the world that most politicians have found it politic to support or at least to render lip service to these efforts at integration. Integration is, to be sure, a process which fills an urgent need of any political or social order.[20] In traditional societies, such integration may be largely accomplished by symbol, ritual, and the persistence of values and beliefs embodied in them. In rapidly changing societies, and more especially in revolutionary situations, such as confront a large majority of mankind today, integration has to be achieved by determined efforts on the part of many people, governors (rulers) and governed alike. It produces a broad basic consensus without which there can be neither legitimate rule, nor genuine authority.[21] Integration may therefore be defined as "the process of unification of a society"[22] which is never-ending, because the numerous subgroups which all social life, but more markedly modern industrial life, begets engender divisive propensities which a process of integration overcomes or rather transcends. It is evident that something more is meant when men undertake to integrate hitherto independent states, as is the case in these movements of cultural integration. The integer here is the common culture—its values, beliefs, and the interests derived therefrom. It does not operate automatically and by itself, but requires politically organized human agents to set it under way. It is a striking fact of the contemporary world that in many different contexts such leadership is springing up and making determined efforts at cultural integration. Leaders have done so regardless of whether their confidence in the realizability of such integration is widely shared by their community or not. There can be no question that very definite progress is being achieved in many areas. Not only Pan-Africanism, but Pan-Arabism and Pan-Americanism are on the march. In spite of the many setbacks resulting from personal and group ambition, consolidations are going forward from year to year. The study of comparative federalism documents this universal trend; even where definite failures have occurred, as in the Caribbean, the forces making for integration—namely the inspiration which the idea has for imaginative leaders and followers—are so great that efforts at federalizing the particular area are forthwith resumed.[23]

The world-wide movement for large-scale cultural integration suggests an emergent world structure composed of a limited number of rather large units, running from 100 to 700 million people each. They are basically held together, each of them, by a common culture and tradition, reinforced by religious ties which, in spite of great subdivisions, provide significant integrators: Christianity, Mohammedanism, Confucianism, Buddhism. It will be many decades before these large cultural entities are really effectively organized in a political and economic sense. Yet there is reason to believe that in terms of modern technology and the world situation which mankind finds itself in, these large units will eventually become organized; although the possibility of widespread anarchy may accompany these efforts for many years.[24] There is, however, a countertrend of what one might call an interference factor of major importance—a fundamental challenge to this cultural consolidation. For what has been said about it does not hold for either the United States or the Soviet Union.

The communal basis of these two middle-sized units, which at present are predominant in the world, contrasts sharply with the cultural wholes. Though different in many respects, the United States and the Union of Soviet Socialist Republics rest upon a convictional, rather than a cultural, basis. That conviction is expressed in a more or less explicit creed which, in the Soviet Union, takes the form of a carefully elaborated ideology. Claims to the effect that this ideology was no longer significant have been belied by recent Soviet party history; indeed, there has been a dramatic revival of ideological preoccupation in the United States in the sixties.[25] Characteristically, it is possible to "become" an American or a Soviet citizen because it is quite within the capacity of any human being to become converted to the particular creed upon which these communities rest, and by adopting it to become a full-fledged member of that community. In fact, such a convert may well be a better American or Communist than those born under their respective flags; whereas it is not possible to become a "good" Frenchman, Englishman, or Chinese without being part of that cultural community through the ties of "blood."

Cultural units, or building blocks, tend in spite of some countertrends to be turned inwards—that is to say, they are primarily occupied with themselves, with their own cultural past, present, and future, and with the meaning that can be attached to life and the world in terms of their cultural tradition; its established values, interests, and beliefs. This is partly due, no doubt, to the exclusiveness of each cultural whole, constituting as it does a creative effort and inspiration of a very distinctive kind. Just what caused these particular unities to form and to become literate in the sense of self-understanding and self-consciousness, we do not know. Efforts at comparative philosophical interpretation, such as Spengler's and Toynbee's, have simply accepted them as given, in all their multiplicity and originality. Both the biological and the morphological approach, tracing with much learning the recurrent patterns of the growth and development of cultures or civilizations, have been unable to produce any insight into the reasons why men produced such a variety of cultural manifestations.[26] All we know is that they exist, with all their creative achievements and limitations, and that human beings are passionately attached to these several ways of life.

By contrast, the creedally based political communities of the U.S. and the U.S.S.R. have a markedly outward-bound propensity toward missionary activity and expansiveness. Cultural communities have known such phases, especially at the height of revolutionary enthusiasm, such as the French conceit of a *mission civilisatrice* already mentioned. But such periods are of short duration in culturally circumscribed communities, and their own adherents come to laugh at such notions as the German one that "the world will be cured by the essence of German-ness."[27] It is different in the case of the Soviet Union and the United States. Like the world religions which they resemble in many ways, they are not only eager to make converts, but depend upon conversion for their self-understanding, their feeling of identity or self-identification. To be sure, the sharp lines of conflict which since the Second World War have tended to divide the world into three camps—one inclined toward the U.S., the other toward the U.S.S.R., and a third trying to remain uncommitted—are at present increasingly blurred by the reassertion of cultural self-identity, nationally and culturally. De Gaulle, Tito, Ceausescu, Dubček, and the Latin Americans—not to mention Vietnam—all are speaking that same language of cultural autonomy and selfhood. These trends tend to obscure the important insight that the missionary expansiveness of the U.S. and the U.S.S.R. is not simply another version of imperialism. Like the Christian missions of old, such ideological and convictional thrusts may well be serving as pathfinders of imperial undertakings. Yet their hard core is of another, nonexpedient sort. Its primary concern is not empire. The expansiveness is felt by its protagonists to be convictional and to a degree "unselfish." For the community's resources are being expended in the service of "ideals" which may contribute little or nothing to the well-being of its members, may indeed jeopardize these interests to a very dangerous degree. This lesson is most dramatically manifest in America's experience with the conflict in Vietnam; but the Soviet Union's is not far behind. The universalist thrust, since there exist two rival centers, leads inevitably to conflicts of the sharpest kind. The European states, caught in the middle, have every reason to remember their own cultural identity and to unite under its symbols in order to escape from both sets of claws—the bear's and the eagle's.

The dramatic confrontation of these two giant powers, convictional rather than cultural in their base, which lasted from 1945 to 1965, and in a measure continues, contained the danger of a most destructive cataclysm. There was no balance of power system available to modify the impact. The confrontation has been modified and moderated in recent years by an internal loosening within the blocs the superpowers had built, a process which provides retrospective evidence in support of the contention that the advent of this polar confrontation was a fortuitous historical coincidence. There was nothing in the past of these two powers themselves which necessarily propelled them towards such a confrontation. Nor was it intrinsically predetermined that the two powers evolving into creedal organizations would control the two largest arsenals of the earth's resources. But it was in the nature of things political that once it should have occurred, and the threat made lethal by the invention of weapons of total destruction—this invention being in the longer perspective itself a gratuitous additional coincidence—the emergence of these two powers should elicit determined efforts to counterbalance their sway by effective consolidations in other areas. It provided the occasion for European unification, the causes of which lie, as we have indicated, much deeper, but which needed an initial consensus. This confrontation of the U.S. and the Soviet Union, so misleadingly misnamed "cold war" when it was neither cold nor a war, amply provided incentives for all those who were firmly rooted in their national cultural past, yet came to realize that only through pooling their resources could they hope to provide adequate security. Partly as a result of these efforts the danger implicit in the confrontation has so far been avoided. There were of course other factors at work, notably in both convictional systems the creedal commitment to "peace" between nations. The commitment was reinforced by a firm belief in the eventual prevalence of its own scheme of things. The world-revolutionary thrust seems on the face of it to contradict this statement, since it breeds tension, conflict, and hence war. But to the extent to which it restrains and restricts itself to assisting autochthonous Communist movements, it loses much of its war-begetting potential.

The emergence of Communist China, perplexing enough in itself, has, in the perspective of the contrast between cultural and convictional consensus, a novel significance. For China belongs naturally to the great cultural units. As a result of the Communist victory on the mainland, it became the one component of the world today which is both cultural and convictional in its origin. To be sure, some would claim this for the Soviet Union, insisting upon its being Russian.[28] It is a view that was dear to Churchill and other conservatives, deliberately cultivated by Stalin during the Second World War, but quickly abandoned afterwards. As occupation authorities from the West were pointedly reminded by their Soviet colleagues, theirs was not a Russian army, but the Soviet or even the Red Army composed of many nationalities. As its official title—Union of Soviet Socialist Republics—makes amply clear, the Soviet Union wishes to think of itself as the "socialist fatherland." Its consensus rests upon Marxist-Leninist ideology. That ideology may be to some extent ritualized or, as Max Weber would say, become an everyday routine (*veralltaeglicht*), but it continues to be the vital bond, as even oppositional writings show.[29] "Stalinism," a recent striking statement by Andrey Sakharov remarked, relied upon "a progressive, scientific and popular socialist ideology."[30] But under Stalin it was a "subtle kind of hypocrisy and demagogy," whereas in fact "we have demonstrated the vitality of the Socialist course. . . ." All the evidence points to the conclusion that the basis of political consensus in the Soviet Union is Socialist values and beliefs, serving to unite a great many distinct nationalities.

China, by contrast, is an ancient cultural community with the world's longest continuous political history to date. It is culturally united to an extent unique for so large a unit; both linguistically and religiously (and that in China meant tradition and folkways) China possesses a degree of homogeneity that provides exceptional opportunities for a wholesale convictional conversion. In the present context, the observation may be ventured that the "cultural" revolution of the recent past represents a gigantic effort on the part of Mao and his followers to destroy the cultural basis of Chinese existence, more especially Confucianism and Taoism, and substitute for it his own ideological creed, as derived from Marx and Lenin. It is not possible at the present time to diagnose with any confidence the outcome of this struggle. What is clear from it, it seems to me, is inner contradiction between a cultural and a convictional consensus which is rending Red China. It has been accompanied by a specific ideological conflict with the Soviet Union that revolves around the problem of violence and war in connection with the class struggle and the liberation of colonial peoples.[31] Thus a bipolarity is injected into the aspirationally universalist Communist camp.

Yet in a way the conflict was foreshadowed by the breaking away of Yugoslavia, and has its parallel in the more recent efforts of Poland, Rumania, and Czechoslovakia to claim an independence from the Soviet Union which is partly ideologically motivated, and partly nationally—that is to say, culturally. For these countries, except perhaps Yugoslavia, resemble China in that their consensus is based upon national-cultural homogeneity. This means that they too labor under the difficulties which such a national-cultural consensus causes for those who are determined to ideologize their country in Socialist terms. The block-formation upon an ideological basis is proving as fraught with contradictions on the Socialist as on the capitalist side. The Soviet Union and the United States find themselves thereby encouraged in seeking ways of cooperating. It is striking that beyond the familiar and somewhat hollow formulas of coexistence, voices are now heard on both sides which proclaim the possibility of convergence. "Both capitalism and socialism are capable of long-term development, borrowing positive elements from each other and actually coming closer to each other in essential respects."[32] Europe, in the opinion of many of its most sophisticated advocates, has a vital role to play in such a development.

In any case, Europe is bound, in this world of emerging cultural and convictional federal unions of continental dimensions, to go forward in the direction of unification. For such unification is the ineluctable condition for its survival as a major factor and force in the world that is emerging. We shall, in the next chapter, explore more fully the general problems facing European consensus formation before turning to particular phases of informal community formation in the chapters that follow. The dynamism of Europe's juxtaposition to the United States and the Soviet Union is reinforcing a convictional commitment to the basic humanism of Western Europe from which both the American and the Soviet creed sprang. European humanism is therefore in a measure reconfirmed. It is at the same time somewhat troubled by the perversion of its core through materialism and scepticism. In that perspective Europe is seen by many of its ablest and most devoted representatives—and by no means only by General de Gaulle, but by political and literary men alike—as a bastion to be defended for cultural reasons; its values are to be protected against a "barbarian threat," not only from the East, but from across the seas.

Actually that barbarian threat is indigenous to Europe itself. Europe has its own barbarians, as the wave of fascism and Hitlerism and related movements have made amply clear. Its competitors, and more especially the United States, have produced quite a few of the standard bearers of European humanism. Indeed, did Europe during the entire nineteenth century bring forth a statesman who could be called the equal of Abraham Lincoln in his combination of poetic depth and political sagacity, or a writer who could be compared to Tolstoy in the strength and passion of his humanism and pacifism? Hence the defense of Europe, in its spiritual tradition, is against its own perverters, wherever found. The movements for the unification of Europe were born or rather reborn in the underground against Hitler's empire.[33] They draw the strongest inspiration from a consensual conviction that only a united Europe can withstand the totalitarian lure.

Europe, thus seen as one, would appear to be on the road to becoming an operating part of a world composed of Africa, Arabia, China, Great Britain and the Commonwealth, India, Latin America, the United States of America, and the Union of Soviet Socialist Republics. Such a polycentric world is apparently in the making.

There are of course bound to be in such a system—if the present semianarchic conglomeration of emergent cultural wholes can be called a system—some odd elements which do not fit into the rational pattern. There would be Turkey and Iran, Pakistan and Burma, as well as Cuba if it continues on its present course. And there are other deviant Socialist states, such as Yugoslavia and Albania. The Indonesian and the Caribbean world may or may not succeed in forming federal unions. Islands, with their natural insularity, seem always to have very special difficulties in cooperating with others, especially with other islands. Japan is an island which might, perhaps reinforced by Korea, become a cultural whole by itself. Japan's teeming millions have passed the hundred mark and are therefore already exceeding Arabia in size; furthermore, Japan's industrial development appears to be more advanced than that of any other nation, except the U.S. and the U.S.S.R.[34] There would also be Israel, another deviant member of the family of nations, creature of the United Nations and distinguished in its welding of cultural and convictional bonds. Israel illustrates well why and how these a-systemic elements are likely to survive: they result from special situations deeply rooted in the cultural and convictional past. Such a situation is not without precedent: the free city of Hamburg was a full-fledged member of the German Empire, as were two other city republics. Experience has shown that such a-systemic entities do not prevent a system from operating. Quite the contrary, the free Hansa cities of the German Empire showed, as did Switzerland, Belgium, and the other small states in Europe, that such entities have a distinct role to play as mediators between surrounding larger states. Reflections of this order should encourage partisans of a united Europe and dissuade them from being too concerned about outsiders.

It is within the context just sketched that the formation of a European community acquires a new fuller meaning. The decision has been made by many people in the Common Market area, if the kind of process that is going on can properly be called a decision. Many contemporary authors dealing with political studies exaggerate the importance of "decision-making." In many highly developed political orders political action does not imply genuine decisions, but embodies a repetition or an adaptation to a reasonably familiar context. In any case, decisions must be seen in the context of policies and institutions, and community formation is compounded of all three. What this means is that the "responsible electorate" is just that, within reason. Thought and opinion of the "common man" are, where this community context is democratic, in the last analysis of decisive importance.[35] Institutions develop as a result of decisions and policies which rest upon the explicit or tacit assent of a community's constituency. Hence the long-range importance of consensus formation, which will be explored more fully (Chapter 2). The protest of the "silent partners" from time to time causes an actual reversal of decisions and policies, as happened in 1965 (Chapter 5); but what is often forgotten is that where such a reversal occurs even once, the rule of anticipated reactions teaches us that many other decisions are more or less continuously influenced by guesses as to what the reaction might be of those who could bring about a reversal, if they would.[36]

To return now to the macroanalysis, let us recognize that at the time Coudenhove-Kalergi took the initiative, stressing as he did the Franco-German partnership,[37] only a brief flowering was its lot. The ardent hopes aroused by the Locarno Treaty and the Franco-German rapprochment under Briand and Stresemann, epitomized in the "spirit of Locarno,"[38] were dashed when the rival nationalisms in France and Germany proved stronger than the two remarkable statesmen who had embraced the new vision.[39] The rise of Hitler and his seizure of power led to a renewal of the effort to unite Europe by conquest and under the overlordship of a hegemonial power—this time Germany rather than France. Nazism's ferocity and violence testified to its leaders' subconscious realization that the enterprise was hopeless from the start and destined to fail. But its very bestiality awakened in many a sense of urgency. Indeed, a certain amount of inter-European personal comradeship was formed in the very concentration camps in which Hitler and his minions hoped to crush forever the liberal and international, the pacific spirit which had fostered the voluntary and hence federal unification of the old Continent. It was probably due to the vigorous opposition of Stalin, who in fact imposed a veto upon Roosevelt, that the unification of Europe did not become a part of America's war aims.[40] Soviet opposition has continued to this day and by its explicitness has served to reinforce the recurrently flagging interest in carrying forward the political and institutional community formation.

At the same time, the rise of Communist China to world power status, alongside the shaping of the other great cultural communities, has given Europeans a distinct sense of self-identity combined with a fear of eventual obliteration. In the face of this radically altered setting Count Coudenhove-Kalergi has called for the creation of a European nation.[41] Rightly drawing an analogy to such modern "nations" as India, the Soviet Union, and Switzerland, he insisted that linguistic and cultural homogeneity are not necessary elements of the concept. It is important, however, not to allow oneself to be drawn into maintaining that "first there must be a nation and then there can be a state." State and nation grow up together: a state, if created, will be seeking to form a nation, as a nation will be making every effort to bring into being "a state of its own."[42] They are the Siamese twins which Western culture has begot and which in turn have molded modern politics, not only in Europe but throughout the world. The great problem of European unification is whether state and nation can be projected beyond the framework of the old and established nations, and that is what the argument of Coudenhove-Kalergi is really addressed to. All human beings with political aspirations want to build states and nations.[43] The national "will" has at times been overemphasized; it cannot become operative until a national being has come into existence. Hence the crucial importance of community formation. Only such community formation will produce a cohesive group of persons whose conduct is motivated by a set of common values, interests, and beliefs. It is a mistake to stress only the *building* of such a community; it is equally one-sided to insist only on *growth.* Nations have grown through building, but nation-building has not infrequently been done by men who did not realize what they were at or who even intended to do something else. I raised some years ago the question whether the men who are unifying and integrating Europe might not be engaged in the task of "nation-building" just as much as the Indians and others who seek to weld tribes into nations, often with sword in hand as had the European monarchs. The answer depends on what is understood by a "nation." Usually the building of a state has set the stage for the growth of a nation, but this is not always true, even in Europe; both the German and the Italian nations grew into self-conscious entities before they were able to achieve statehood. There are also instances, such as Poland, in which the interaction is very complex.

It is clear, however, that the growth of a political community and its sense of shared values, interests, and beliefs needs studying. This process may be approached with the tools of quantitative inquiry.[44] It is, however, also possible, and perhaps in some contexts more feasible, to explore such community development in studying the actual structure and functioning of the human contact points. In highly structured, pluralistic societies such an inquiry may yield telling results, especially if the problem is that of gauging the political implications. The mere fact of the multiplication of communications, while highly significant, is unrevealing for such political implications as long as the contents of such communications are disregarded. Again, a relatively small number of intensive contacts with high political incidence may, in a structured situation with strong elite formation, be more significant than many more casual contacts. Thus the change in outlook of key trade union leaders may over considerable periods be the actually operative part of emergent community formation.

It is with this method in mind that the following studies were undertaken. But before we plunge into the concrete detail of our findings, it seems desirable to outline the growth of consensus formation as it relates institutions to community formation in general terms, since the tendency has been to focus attention upon the development of these institutions rather than the diversified behavior of the human beings living under them. If a political community, as implied in our topic as well as in general discussions on European community, is to be characterized realistically, it must be seen as a togetherness of persons who are united by having in common some of their values, interests, ideas (including ideologies), myths, utopias and their symbols, religion and its rituals. Such uniting will be partly by emotional attachment and partly by subjection to common rules, responding partly to organic need and partly to conscious purpose, expressing both what already exists and what is explicitly willed.[45] There is nothing either impossible or inevitable about this. It is to be assumed, then, that such a political community will come into being as a result of a complex interaction of many factors, and the following chapters are devoted to exploring some of these. There is nothing definitive about the findings and interpretations, except that existing trends and prospects permit one to conclude that this community formation is an ongoing process. What is not admissible is the often heard assertion made by impatient writers who in the fashion of the day, especially in this country, proclaim the political community dead. It is very much alive and kicking, and indeed growing, if the "political" is understood in its communal dimensions. To conclude with Oliver Wendell Holmes: The mode whereby the inevitable comes to pass is effort.

2. European Consensus and Community Structure: A Federal Potential?

All political order rests upon political community. Hence its institutions reflect, to the extent to which they are adequate, the social structure of the community. They are permeated by the values and beliefs prevalent in the community and, at the same time, provide a framework for the realization of interests through conflict and compromise. The reason for repeating these generally acknowledged empirical truths is that they call for a patterning of values, beliefs, and interests in which common and complementary values, beliefs, and interests are balanced against conflicting ones. There must, in other words, be a consensus on some values, beliefs, and interests in the community at large, as well as territorially well-delimited values, beliefs, and interests within it to provide the basis for a viable federal order. That the latter exist in Europe is obvious; the nations have been territorially defined units for a long time.

The real problem is that of the inclusive community. As we showed in the last chapter, Europe has "existed" for a long time, in the sense of having a distinctive consciousness of its identity and being. But such consciousness has been built and focused upon the cultural self-consciousness of a particular nation. There exists in this sense an English, a French, a German, and an Italian Europe—in each case a Europe which revolves around the cultural identity of the unique experiences and achievements of the particular subdivision: Magna Charta and Shakespeare in the first; *Le roi soleil,* the French Revolution, and Descartes in the second; Luther, Bismarck, and Kant in the third; Dante, Leonardo da Vinci, and the Risorgimento in the fourth. It is, of course, a question of emphasis. The European significance of each of these events and persons would be acknowledged by all. But the crucial question is whether the common ground which has supported European culture for so long is capable of expanding to the point where a sufficiently solid basis of common values, beliefs, and interests can be identified and accepted by a sufficiently large part of Europe's population to support common institutions and policies. For a time, many participants and observers were inclined to stress the Communist threat as the common interest which would provide the basis for European community.[1] As the threat has faded, or is believed to have done so, this incentive for unification has become weak; yet integration has gone forward. It probably never was as important as people believed. Anyway, it has been a recurrent experience in the genesis of federal orders that outside pressure provided the occasion for the start of the process of federalizing rather than the basic cause. The foundation of federal unity lies elsewhere.

Before we consider the specific problem of federalism, the notion of a "federal spirit" needs to be explored. In successful federal systems, a new spirit develops which is highly pragmatic and yet also rather sophisticated in its approach to political institutions, policies, and decisions. Such a federal spirit is manifest in political behavior that avoids all insistence upon "agreement on fundamentals" and other kinds of doctrinaire inflexibility. Rather it proceeds and thinks in terms of compromise and accommodation. It is molded by a strong sense of tolerance for diversity, combined with a capacity to differentiate between distinctive selves: there are many rooms in the house that federalism builds. Failures of federalization, such as the Nigerian and the Caribbean federations, are traceable to the lack of a federal spirit in the communities to be federalized. Such a lack may be demonstrated either by a preoccupation with local concerns—in the case of Europe this would be nationalism—or by too great an insistence upon the central concerns which may be due to a variety of pressures, especially economic ones. It may also result from a decline in the local cultures. Unless there is present a firm determination to maintain both diversity and unity by means of a continuous mutual adaptation, a federal order cannot last. Such determination presupposes a "federal spirit."

The federal spirit engenders two significant behavioral peculiarities of a working federal order. These are federal loyalty and federal comity. They tend to overlap and hence are not always clearly distinguished.[2] Federal loyalty (*loyauté fédérale* or *Bundestreue*) is asked of the component units, their officials and representatives. It calls upon them to demonstrate in their actions a basic commitment to the overall needs and requirements of the federal order. Such commitment involves a sustained readiness for cooperation with federal authorities in matters of common concern. The breakdown of such federal loyalty occurs in secession; if the secession is not accepted, civil war results from it.[3] But quite a few stages must be passed before these extremes are reached. There is, for example, administrative sabotage, at present rather common in the southern states of the U.S. when the rights of Negroes are involved. Such sabotage has often had wide political support among dissenting elements; and when this happens, it leads to the nullification of federal policies.[4] It is to some extent found in all federal regimes, as indeed in many administrative setups. Nullification may go beyond connivance at disobedience and take the form of outright counterlegislation. It is an open question how much such lack of federal loyalty a functioning federal system can stand; the tolerance level has not been determined and probably varies in connection with other factors.

Federal *comity* consists in the practice of fair play by *both* federal and local officials. It presupposes, or rather implies, a readiness to give the other side in a conflict situation a chance to present its case or otherwise to make its claims felt. Comity means that both federal and local officials are prepared for and skilled in reaching a compromise whenever serious strains develop. The pragmatism of the federal spirit manifests itself here in the approach to problems and policies on which the federal and local authorities are divided or on which their interests clash. One of the main arguments for such a body as the Council of Permanent Representatives in the European Communities is that such a group can develop the kind of face-to-face human relationship which makes for federal comity. Comity is, so to speak, the oil on the complex machinery of a federal regime.

All three—federal spirit, federal loyalty, and federal comity—are vital behavioral features of a working federalism. Without them, federal orders become unworkable. Together, they constitute what might be called federal behavior. It is the microcosmic aspect of the macrocosm that is a federal regime. In them is focalized and made operational the consensus that a federalizing process presupposes. But before we can effectively analyze the makings and workings of such a federal consensus, it is necessary to sketch briefly the dynamic concept of federalism which is implied in such a statement.

The rapid expansion of federal regimes and proposals has led to a steady broadening of the theoretical scope of federalism.[5] Thirty years ago one could write that "from an empirical standpoint, an effectively centralized government, a federation, a confederation or league of governments (states), an alliance, an alignment, a 'system of independent' governments (states) and finally completely unrelated governments—all these could be represented as differences of degree in the relation of governments to the persons subject to their rule. . . ."[6] This was the beginning of the end of the traditional juristic notions which were oriented toward and preoccupied with the problems of sovereignty, and hence with the distribution of functions and the structure of institutions. These issues are not without importance and they continue to play a big role in political oratory. Yet, the emerging functional and behavioral view recognized that a federal system could be characterized simply by the fact that its structure "resembles a league in one or more of its organizational features...."[7] It does; but such a characterization remains at the structural surface, at the design of a federal order. It is decisive that one grasp the dynamism of its functioning: federalism calls for and implies a *process of federalizing;* it is an ongoing process in which the mutual relation and adaptation of clearly differentiated component communities and an inclusive community is continuously at issue.[8]

It is the core of such an understanding of federalism that a federation is seen as a union of groups, united by one or more common objectives rooted in common values, beliefs, and interests, but retaining their distinctive character for other purposes. A federation or federal union unites distinctive *selves* without destroying them; its purpose is to strengthen them. In other words, it is the structured, organized cooperation of groups as groups. As such it is much affected by the nature of the particular groups which are federating. This very general characterization implies that the federalizing process involved in the building of a federal order may be operating both centrifugally and centripetally—that is, it may be intended to achieve greater differentiation as well as greater integration. Thus the major part of the British Empire became the British Commonwealth, the Tsarist Empire became the Union of Soviet Socialist Republics, and Prussia was transformed into a federal entity within the Weimar Republic before it passed out of existence at the collapse of the Hitler regime.[9] But the more usual process is that of integration, and it is this process one is concerned with when discussing the integration and unification of Europe.

Many have seen this integration dogmatically in terms of the establishment of a United States of Europe in the sense of a close-knit federal state. But the extension of the range of vision which sees federalism as not only implying a federal structure and design, but also, and perhaps more important, a federalizing process, leads to the recognition that this process may well in its initial phase start from an international league loosely joined together by treaty or charter.[10] Whether such a league is the beginning of an integrative federalizing process depends upon many circumstances. K. C. Wheare has laid great stress upon the "desire" of the population in the federalizing units, and has related such a desire to a variety of factors. Cultural and linguistic diversity, different social and economic structure and stage of development, religious diversity, and so forth, are said to have reinforced the inclination to retain local autonomy: foreign policy and defense needs, economic development and related matters have, he argues, produced a desire for uniting. It is evident that the combination of these desires, or at least some of them, forms the basis of what we have called the "federal spirit."

The need to organize a political order in response to such a federal spirit produces specific federal structures of governance. These structures are necessarily of a certain complexity. This complexity involves considerable "costs." These costs have seemed in the United States in recent years particularly high in the field of civil rights. The chances which a federal system offers to regional minorities to block the will of the majority are often great. In the United States the question has become more insistent as to whether traditional, judicial methods of enforcing human rights guaranteed by federal law are going to be adequate. It has rightly been pointed out that as contrasted with past approaches in terms of the personal rights of individuals, the rights of larger groups of people, notably the Negroes, require firmer methods of enforcement. "The loss of faith in law—the usefulness of federal law and the fairness of local law—is gaining very rapidly among Negro and white civil rights workers." It is certainly possible to argue that "civil rights issues cut into the fabric of federalism."[11] The fabric of the American federal order is being put to a severe test. That test is more apt to be met if the discussion will turn toward how to restructure American federalism. The situation is a recurrent one, and men when confronted with such tensions and breakdowns unfortunately often develop a general antagonism toward federalism, instead of asking for the reform of a particular federal structure.[12]

European discussions about the federalizing of their state system have been beset by unreal issues of this kind. The political leaders of a number of key countries, notably Great Britain and France, have had no experience in operating a federal system. They are consequently weak in the federal spirit, and at every turn, when difficulties arise, cry out against it, or act contrary to it. A recent striking instance was the French government's unilateral action in meeting the crisis which arose in May and June 1968. It is part of the same propensity to make federalism the whipping boy of whatever seems objectionable to a particular party or segment of the electorate to claim that the competitor has the better of it. Thus both French and German industrialists are in the habit of asserting that the other is favored by the Common Market and that their government in order to reach agreement sacrificed their interest to assumed political advantages. Similarly, it is popular among trade unionists to talk about a "Europe of Businessmen" (*L'Europe des Affaires*), while businessmen like to claim that the Commission at Brussels is partial to the workers. Similar assertions have in all seriousness been made time and again in the United States and other established federal systems by responsible scholars.[13] These observations raise anew the question of the kind of consensus required for the establishment and operation of a federal system.

On this score, a variety of disputable claims have been set forth in recent years. Count Coudenhove-Kalergi, the renowned early advocate of European Union,[14] some years ago developed the thesis that Europe must first become a "nation" before it can be federally united.[15] His view is basically shaped by the experience of such federal enterprises as Germany's and India's, and neglects other ones such as the United States where demonstrably the nation developed after the establishment of the federal framework. So acute an observer as Alexis de Tocqueville could, after fifty years of American government, still believe that America would not last because of a lack of national consensus. He was, as everybody knows, much impressed with the American experiment. In line with the federal spirit, he claimed "the Union is as happy as a free and small people, and as glorious and as strong as a great nation."[16] Yet he misjudged the future profoundly. Thinking in terms of European nation-states, and of the peoples of the component states as nations, he refused to believe in the duration of "a government which is called upon to hold together forty different peoples." Rightly guessing that the American population would reach 150 million before another hundred years had passed, he asserted that "where there are a hundred millions of men, and forty distinct nations, equally strong, the continuance of the federal government can only be a fortunate accident."[17] It is hard to believe that de Tocqueville did not appreciate that a nation was in the making, and that he should have continued to agree with his great countryman, Chateaubriand, that an American nation could not come into being. Chateaubriand, two generations earlier, had thought that the several national origins of the American settlers would make them crystallize into distinct nations—in the premises a more reasonable, even though erroneous, hypothesis than de Tocqueville's far-fetched notion of the "peoples" of Massachusetts, Connecticut, and Virginia being in the process of becoming nations like the French, the Dutch, and the Swedes. I cite these dramatic misjudgments at some length partly because they demonstrate how easy it is to misjudge consensus formation. They also illustrate the difficulties of assessing accurately the relation between federalism and nationalism, which is involved here.

Nationalism has played a decisive, if not always a helpful, role in the federalizing process. The interaction of the two, both in theory and in practice, is a complex one. The powerful emotional appeal of nationalism, its crucial role in building a community basis for the modern state, and its capacity for providing strong secular consensus are universally acknowledged. Federal relationships may be utilized to provide a political order for a nation to be united out of separate and distinct states, governments, or tribal entities, as was the case of Germany in the nineteenth century and that of India in the twentieth. Or federalism may serve as a means of combining several nations or nationalities into one political order, as was the case in Switzerland, in Belgium, and in Canada, and is the hope of those who are seeking to achieve the integration of Europe. In the one case, nationalism reinforces the consensus on the federal level; in the other, on the local level. In either case it may help to create and maintain the federal spirit; it may also disrupt and undermine it.

It all depends upon how the cards are stacked. Nationalism is generally acknowledged to be probably the most potent political emotion of the contemporary world. Hence Coudenhove-Kalergi would like to see it reinforcing the European Union. But nationalism, because of its emotional intensity, is also one of the most unmanageable forces of the contemporary world. Political leaders have had occasion to discover this, often in the most unexpected situations. There has been a good deal of discussion and argument over its nature, a discussion we shall not enter here.[18] One of the major obstacles to European unification has been that the emotionalism of nationalism is ranged against it. Federalism has no comparable appeal. Peace, on the other hand, has; and a great deal of the more emotional support for European integration, especially in France and Germany, has come from this source.[19]

Emotional appeals are especially important when trying to reach youth. They tend to be on the side of nationalism in many of the newer countries. But they are also increasingly on the side of peace and pacifism. In consensus formation, the younger generation is often providing the challenge of the future. Europe is no exception to this general observation. Careful studies have been able to show that while the more radical forms of demonstration, such as burning border barriers, have passed away with the early moves of establishing European unity, there is a persistent trend toward greater support for integration on the part of the younger generation in Europe. As a careful recent investigator has noted, "The response by a majority (of young people) is overwhelmingly favorable to European unification; it swamps all differences of social class, sex, religion, etc."[20] His statistics, based upon many hundreds of questionnaires, are shown in Table 2–1. But it might be ob-

TABLE 2–1. OVERALL PERCENTAGE "STRONGLY FOR" OR "FOR" EUROPEAN UNIFICATION

	Netherlands	France	Germany
Adults			
1962	87%	72%	81%
Youth			
1964–1965	95	93	95

SOURCE: Ronald Inglehart, "An End to European Integration?" in *APSR*, Vol. LXI, No. 1 (March 1967), p. 92.

jected, and often is, that these figures tell little because of the vagueness of the terms of reference, especially that of "European unification." It is therefore highly significant that the same author secured comparable percentages on specific measures of European unification, notably the abolition of tariffs (I), the free movement of labor and business (II), a common foreign policy (III), and the use of taxes to aid poorer European countries (IV). The average percentage for the four measures is shown in Table 2–2, from which it can be seen that in both France and Germany youth is sixteen percentage points more favorable to unification measures; even in the Netherlands with its very high general percentages, youth is five percentage points higher. Table 2–3 shows the breakdown for the four measures.

It is evident from these figures that youth, ages 13 to 19, are

TABLE 2–2. AVERAGE PERCENTAGE "FOR" FOUR MEASURES

	Netherlands	France	Germany
Adults	73%	56%	62%
Youth	78	72	78

SOURCE: Ronald Inglehart, "An End to European Integration?" in *APSR,* Vol. LXI, No. 1 (March 1967), p. 92.

TABLE 2–3. PERCENTAGE "FOR" FOUR PROPOSALS: ADULTS V. YOUTH

	Netherlands	France	Germany
I			
Adults	79%	72%	71%
Youth	87	83	89
II			
Adults	76	57	64
Youth	64	65	75
III			
Adults	67	50	60
Youth	80	71	74
IV			
Adults	70	43	52
Youth	82	68	72

SOURCE: Ronald Inglehart, "An End to European Integration?" in *APSR,* Vol. LXI, No. 1 (March 1967), p. 92.

definitely more "progressive" on European integration, with the one curious exception of Dutch youth on the freedom of movement for labor and business (II), for which the explanation may well be lack of appreciation of the significance of such a policy. The general progressiveness, however, may also be in part related to such inexperience, and it would be uncritical, to say the least, to assume that their enthusiasm would last and that one could therefore count on a steady increase in pro-European sentiment. Such increase may nevertheless occur.

Our studies will show that a general consolidation of pro-European sentiment is to be observed in the various cadres of the countries of the Common Market. It is accompanied by a more hardheaded and practical attitude toward Europe. That such a change has occurred is very clear; it has led to serious misinterpretations. That youth should be more enthusiastic about the general idea, while adults are concerned with and keen about the concrete working out of so massive a social transformation as is engendered by the integration of the old and traditional national cultures of continental Europe, should not occasion any surprise. Indeed, it would seem the very core of lasting consensus formation, as contrasted with the straw fire of idealistic enthusiasm.

The most serious challenge to this view has come from four American scholars—Karl W. Deutsch, Lewis J. Edinger, Roy C. Macridis, and Richard L. Merritt—who, in a study entitled *France, Germany and the Western Alliance—A Study of Elite Attitudes on European Integration and World Politics,* have argued that "European integration has slowed down since the mid-50's, and has stopped or reached a plateau since 1957–58," and they have predicted accordingly that "the most likely pattern for the next ten years, therefore, will be a Europe of national states, linked by marked but moderate preferences for mutual transactions, in contrast to transactions with countries outside Europe, and with little growth—and possibly some decline—in the intensity of those preferences as expressed in actual behavior of the populations and business communities of the European countries."[21] The data they gathered led them to conclude that "the mid-1960's find Western Europe in a critical state of flux," and they added that "the prospects for any form of political integration—prospects that had seemed so bright at the outset of the decade—appear to be fading rapidly, as the Common Market encounters major obstacles. . . ."[22] These sentences, presumably written in 1965/66, have already been proved in error by the actual course of events. Since that time the crisis of 1965 has been overcome, an agricultural policy has been hammered out, and the customs barriers between the six countries of the Common Market were completely eliminated on July 1, 1968, ahead of schedule. This epochal event was, however, not accompanied by much fanfare and mutual congratulation. Rather it elicited much sober comment to the effect that the customs' union must now be transformed into an economic union (see pp. 69 ff., below), and that many details needed careful attention. In light of this record, it might be simplest just to lay the analysis of the four distinguished authors aside as mistaken and ill-advised. However, it seems to be more in keeping with our basic purpose in this study to explore their analysis more carefully in the hope of determining where the sources of error lie and how they might be corrected. This is the more true since their analysis raises a number of interesting methodological questions.

The first concerns the emphasis on what the authors call "elite" opinions. The second question concerns the evidential value of what the authors call "transactions," and more particularly what they call the "relative acceptance index." Thirdly, there is the question of whether European unification and national sentiment can properly be treated as necessarily antagonistic, so that the strength of one can be assumed to mean the weakness of the other. That appears to be the hypothesis underlying the above-quoted prediction, although in fact the trend of actual behavior runs quite counter to this prediction. I suspect that part of the error has its source in the fallacious assumption that a leveling off of the increase in transactions means a decline in community consensus. Actually, as an arguable optimal situation is reached, the leveling off in the increase carries no such implication. We shall return to this point presently.

The elite concept is very equivocal. As the authors note, "the term 'elites' means many things to many people." They define their own meaning of the term as referring to both formal and informal decision-makers at a society's national level. Admittedly political decisions are the primary focus of their interest.

There are two difficulties with such a concept in a democratic context, such as that of Western Europe. In the first place, it is wellnigh impossible to identify the "decision-makers" in such a context. Due to the prevalence of consensual power, politically relevant decisions are made by everybody. To use recent American examples: the decision to seize Columbia University's main administration building was made by a small group of revolution-minded students; the decision to shoot Martin Luther King was made by an obscure individual with a criminal record; that to kill Robert Kennedy was made by a nationalist fanatic; and the decision not to serve in the armed forces of the United States, when called to do so, has been made by hundreds of humble folk who consider the war in Vietnam unjust. These illustrations can readily be duplicated from the Community of the Six; the students and strikers in France and Germany have made the most significant "decisions" of recent months.

The second serious objection arises from the fact that no such statistical classification as "decision-makers" suffices to establish the existence of a governing elite. Unless there is definite group cohesion and group-consciousness in the sense of self-identification, we have no more than statistical sums when we analyze what such aggregates "think," "opine," or "will."[23] The study of French and German "elite" opinion as presented in the study of Deutsch and his collaborators does not give us more than the sum of the opinions of those interviewed or assessed. The reason this is serious lies in the fact that there may be striking differences in the leadership potential of particular individuals. If a comparable "elite" survey had been made in the American colonies in 1770, it would have provided a very misleading impression of what was in store; and in 1784 or 1785 a "leveling off" of integration could have been demonstrated by treating every Tom, Dick, and Harry as the equivalent of Washington, Jefferson, and Hamilton. Consensus formation in such a context cannot be gauged by consulting the "elite"—now frequently referred to as the "establishment"— because it is the very context of revolutionary transformations which offers chances of leadership to particular individuals who may be quite obscure as far as their position in the established order is concerned. But it may also happen, and does quite frequently, that an individual wields an influence in consensus formation far in excess of that of many of his equals; he molds the opinion. What is going to happen in a democratic context can often be gauged more safely by consulting such an individual than any conceivable elite. The thoughtful and self-questioning sophistication displayed by the authors does not eliminate this fatal flaw in approaching the problem of consensus evolution in the context of the Common Market.

As for the evidential value of what the authors call "transactions," which they proudly refer to as actual behavior, it is more than dubious. As later chapters in this study will show, there are more reliable indices of actual behavior than these "transactions." But let us examine the evidence on its own merits. These transactions are juxtaposed to the results of elite interviews, mass opinion polls, and the content analysis of a few elite papers. They constitute, according to the authors, the "aggregative statistics of actual behavior."[24] A mass of trade statistics is put forward to show that in Europe "there have been no increases—and there have been some marked decreases—in the observable preferences of the Six, particularly France and Germany, for dealing with one another rather than with other countries."[25] The actual statistics show, on the contrary, that intercommunity trade has increased much more rapidly in the past decade than has trade with outsiders. The figures for the Federal Republic, the economically most important member, with the largest foreign trade of the three major members, show the following picture: the percentage of imports from Common Market countries from 1957 to 1965 rose from 23.4 to 37.8 percent, while those from the European Free Trade Association (EFTA) countries dropped from 20.2 to 17.2 percent, those from the U.S.A. from 17.8 to 13.0 percent, and those from other countries from 38.6 to 32.0 percent. For exports the picture is quite similar: to Common Market countries exports rose from 29.2 to 35.2 percent, while those to EFTA countries fell from 28.4 to 27 percent, those to other countries from 35.5 to 29.7 percent, and only those from the U.S. rose from 6.9 to 8.1 percent—a 15 percent increase not quite as much as the increase of roughly 20 percent within the Common Market. The trend is continuing, and should be seen in the perspective of a rise in the social product of 5.5 percent for the European Economic Community (EEC) between 1953 and 1964, which compares with a rise of 316 percent for EFTA, and 3.1 percent for the U.S. These figures speak by themselves an eloquent language. How then do the learned authors manage to construct a diametrically opposed conclusion? They do it on the one hand by constructing what they call a "relative acceptance index," and then, on the other, extending the analysis far back into history. Both of these procedures are highly questionable.[26]

The relative acceptance index (RA Index) measures the percentage by which the volume of actual transactions, such as trade between two countries, exceeds or falls short of the hypothetical amount that would be proportional to the overall share of each of these two countries in the total flow of transactions *among all the countries of the world*. This index therefore "seeks to give a realistic measure of the extent to which the distribution of trade among two or more countries deviates from the level which could be expected from the mere size of the total trade of each." Whatever may be the value of this index for other purposes, does it, by its complicated computations, provide any measure, realistic or not, of the increase of political community between two or more countries? Why should this be a function of world trade? It seems obvious that on the one hand such increase might increase at a great rate, because many underdeveloped countries are becoming independent, thereby adding to "international" trade, while a group of highly developed countries are establishing close ties. It seems equally obvious on the other hand that the world community might be becoming more close-knit at the same time that the European community is developing. As compared with the statistics offered above, the RA Index is therefore of little, if any, value.

The same can be said of comparisons with trade growth in remote periods, such as 1890 and 1913, or with such culturally homogeneous areas as Scandinavia and the United States/Canada.[27] For the significance of these figures all depends upon the built-in hypothetical assumptions which are involved for different periods and places. That the particular index should show higher scores for the two groups just mentioned is not to be wondered at. Even so, the authors admit that "in 1928 and thereafter, integration was stronger among the six than it was among the four English speaking countries." What importance attaches to the further comment that "integration among the six was at all times much weaker than it was among the Scandinavian countries" or "between the United States and Canada"? For in both these cases there has been extended consensus for generations, and hence political community has flourished even without institutions to reinforce it.

Similar criticism must be leveled at the comparison of RA Indexes concerned, besides trade, with mail, travel, and the exchange of students. They are once again supposed to prove that "the structural unification of a Europe of the Six has *halted*" since 1955–57. We cannot here reproduce the tables which are supposed to support this assertion, but they fail to prove this because of the purely external and hence artificial nature of the data used for comparison. Take mail: the mere number of communications is quite inconclusive. Two business concerns, closely cooperating across national boundaries—say, between France and Germany—may correspond more frequently at a lesser stage of integration, and usually do so, when cooperation is just getting under way. Afterwards a standard operating procedure has been worked out, and what problems arise are, under an efficient management, solved by personal encounter.

Travel likewise may spurt at the start, but may thereafter

hit a level which persists over a long period, it may have its ups and downs in connection with economic conditions, the lure of novelty may wear off, and so forth. We badly need a careful empirical analysis of the role of travel in consensus formation, and we are projecting such a study at the present time.[28] Not only quantitative, but many qualitative and attitudinal factors call for more detailed exploration. Travel between Vermont and Mississippi is quite limited; yet is the consensus less than between Georgia and New Hampshire, or between Oregon and Florida? Scenic attraction may or may not be decisive; thus travel from Germany to Italy was heavy even in pre–First World War days, whereas travel from Italy to Germany was limited indeed. Today, due to the large number of guest workers (see Chapter 6 below), travel from Italy to Germany has greatly increased; whereas travel from Germany to Italy, though still at a high rate, has been falling off. In any case, such work-related travel surely has different implications for consensus formation than tourist travel. In this connection, the acquisition of real estate by many Germans may mean that many of the travelers are no longer considering it an excursion into a foreign country, but a return to what has become a second home. We need to know much more about this dispersion of real estate ownership throughout Europe. It unquestionably is not restricted to the Common Market, but may contribute greatly to consensus formation because of an increase in common interests. We shall not comment further here on the exchange of students, because this question is treated at greater length below, where it is shown that the RA Index figures are almost meaningless.

Truly puzzling is the argument that a slowdown in the increase of organizations shows that the establishment of European institutions "has not been matched by any corresponding deeper integration of actual behavior."[29] Our later chapters show in depth how erroneous this conclusion, derived from questionably interpreted statistics, appears in the light of empirical evidence. After all, once organizations have been founded, there is little sense in going on founding them. That is as true in the sphere of business (Chapter 4) and labor (Chapter 6), as it is in the field of education (Chapter 9). In short, quantitative curves are bound to flatten out, though they may at a later date resume a slow rise in connection with a determined rate of expansion. One must therefore question severely the proposition that "much then may depend on whether there is any strong desire among the elites and masses of France and Germany to increase quickly the level of practical actions and commitments for European integration well beyond its present level." On the contrary, a slow but steady growth rate, such as is actually prevailing, would more definitely argue for the presence of substantial consensus; though it by no means would prove it. In this connection the decline in the ratio of foreign trade to national income of which the authors make so much at one point[30] actually reinforces the argument for trade between France and Germany; this trade rose from less than 5 percent of all German foreign imports in 1957 to 11.2 percent in 1965; in short, it more than doubled and therefore moved dramatically countertrend[31] (the figures for exports are 6.3 percent and 10.8 percent, respectively, and hence also close to double). It therefore goes to prove the exact opposite of what the authors allege when they say that "the preference of the French government for a less closely-integrated 'Europe of the Fatherlands' . . . may not be due wholly to the unique personality of General de Gaulle." It surely is not; but the statistics presented do little in the way of supporting this point. In this connection, comparisons with the curves that have been worked out for the United States 1735–75 should be treated with the utmost caution. For the integration process of primitive colonial territories containing not one city of more than 50,000 inhabitants is bound to "resemble a learning curve" which one could not possibly expect in the case of the European Community, with its dozens of large cities and a predominantly and increasingly urban population at an advanced stage of economic development.[32]

Consensus formation clearly cannot be determined on the basis of such data as were criticized on the foregoing pages. It requires a very different approach to a very different set of data. In the following chapters such an approach has been taken. It undertakes to study the actual informal community formation and its political implications, where they can be discerned. The approach is selective in view of the mass of data to be assembled and explored. Emphasis is upon France and Germany (Federal Republic) because they were farthest apart and removed from any sort of effective political community in the past. Certain organizational dimensions have been omitted, such as the churches in whose activities the European community thinking is incidental to a world-wide (ecumenical) outlook, or the political parties on which relevant and interesting work has been done.[33] It may, however, at this point seem appropriate to report and comment briefly upon a broad-gauged opinion study which was undertaken by a number of polling organizations at the request of the Press and Information Section of the European Communities.[34]

The study entitled "Enquête Internationale" and published in *Sondages,* 1963, is concerned with the attitudes of the public in the six community countries toward European unification. About half the material presented concerns French public opinion. The inquiry found that there is widespread acceptance of the "European idea" but little passionate commitment or curiosity about the steps required in the construction of a united Europe, that information is fairly widespread but superficial, and that the prime motivations are security and an increase in the standard of living. It also found, and this may be surprising to some Americans, that there is no animosity and little sense of rivalry between the several populations of the Community. In evaluating the EEC a very much larger percentage sees it as advantageous, although in both France and Germany nearly as large a percentage feels that there is not much change.[35] The small percentage which sees disadvantages talked largely in terms of specific economic losses suffered by limited groups. The inquiry identified four major advantages as seen by those questioned: (1) economic advantages, (2) improvement in the standard of living, (3) intensification of cultural exchange and the consequent better human relations, and (4) the facilitating of travel and tourism. Evidently, there is widespread consensus in terms of major value orientations of Western liberal industrial society. At the same time, there is no excessive optimism about the probable rate of progress: only approximately 20 percent thought it would be achieved in ten years, 25 percent that it would take up to thirty years, while the percentage of those who were utter sceptics and did not expect it ever to come to pass was somewhat over 10 percent—curiously enough double the number in Germany and the Netherlands than in France and Belgium. To make these figures a bit more concrete and specific, let me cite the results when those questioned were asked about the desirability of particular measures to be taken[36] (see Table 2–4).

These data tend to show that there existed in 1963 a powerful sentiment in favor of advanced measures of European integration, at least among the Six; for the deviation of the maxima from the average is never very great. At the same time, the data also suggest that this sentiment was least strong in France and most strong in the Netherlands. The Federal Republic of Germany apparently occupies a middle position; it does not appear once among the maxima. Similar findings of a more recent date confirm these figures.[37] That measures of foreign aid found much less support is no indication of a lack of consensus in Europe; on the contrary. Europeans generally are much more sceptical about foreign aid, especially those who have had colonial experience. It is also noteworthy that this sentiment has increased since that time and as experience has accumulated from the association of a group of African states with the Common Market.[38] In any case, by no means are all the elements of European community consensus part of an international outlook; there are considerable strands of exclusivity, and the saying about "the barbarians from the East and the bar-

TABLE 2–4

Measure		%	Extremes (Maxima)	%
Eliminate customs, that is, facilitate the sale of home products and permit foreign goods to enter	For:	81	For: N	91
	Against:	6	Against: F	8
Freedom of movement for labor and capital throughout the Common Market	For:	68	For: I	78
	Against:	16	Against: F	32
Making academic degrees equivalent in the six countries	For:	72	For: N	91
	Against:	4	Against: F	15
Common foreign policy	For:	60	For: N	75
	Against:	9	Against: F	15
Common research facilities	For:	75	For: N	84
	Against:	3	Against: F	4
Common agricultural policy	For:	69	For: N	83
	Against:	8	Against: L	12
Common social security policy	For:	77	For: N	88
	Against:	4	Against: B	6
Use of tax resources for aiding poorer regions of Europe	For:	49	For: N	76
	Against:	28	Against: F	44
Use of taxes for aiding African countries	For:	35	For: N	65
	Against:	40	Against: F	56
			L	54
			B	53

SOURCE: *Sondages, Revue français de l'opinion publique,* 1963, pp. 23–24.

NOTE: B = Belgium; F = France; I = Italy; L = Luxembourg; N = Netherlands.

barians from across the sea" is not only a rhetorical slogan.[39] In the chapters which follow we shall, however, concentrate on the positive sides of European community development and consensus as the political dimension of such development.

It remains to indicate briefly what is to be understood by consensus. For, if it is alleged that what "Europe lacks in order to constitute a political community is a consensus of Europeans,"[40] such a judgment would appear to result from a mistaken notion of what political consensus is. It is not necessarily the kind of close-knit syndrome which characterized European national states in the nineteenth century. These states themselves no longer possess it, General de Gaulle notwithstanding, who was quite mistaken when he proclaimed that only these states are a political reality and that "il n'y a que les Etats qui scient valables, legitimes, et en outre, capables de réaliser."[41] For while these states certainly continue to be major focal points of power, and hence of consensus and decision-making, there are other groupings competing with them.[42] Wherever consensual power is wielded, consensus and consent are at the base of it. A number of empirical researches confirm that value and belief consensus is partial and fluid, that it is always associated with dissent and opposition. There is a measure of consensus in any political order, but it may be structured in a highly pluralistic fashion.[43] Such consensus may be integrating, if it steadily increases; or it may be stationary and purely traditional. In the case of Europe, a common cultural tradition of rather static nature has in this century been reinforced by ideological positions which have dynamized and dramatized consensus formation. Since these dynamic positions have created a framework for effective political cooperation and power-sharing, further consensus has been generated in all those life situations where formerly nationally isolated individuals and groups have come together and learned to work with each other. It is with some of these informal processes that we are here concerned. This growing consensus is molding all those who live within the boundary of the Common Market into a community possessing legitimate authorities engaged in governing and defending it.[44]

3. The Business Community: Enterprises

"Business circles," commented a careful student of economic integration some years ago, "after initial reactions ranging from cautious support to outright hostility, had accepted the Common Market as a *fait accompli* and jumped in with almost breathtaking speed to form a network of agreements within the Six."[1] This "jump," in its political implications, will be the topic of our next two chapters. The French call it: *L'Europe des Affaires*, the Europe of the Businessman. For it is the businessman-enterpriser who has had the largest share in building the new European community after the framework of institutions had been erected by the politicians. It began with the coal and steel masters under the European Coal and Steel Community (ECSC) in 1950 and it has been continued on a broad front ever since 1958, when the Common Market came into being. But how much community is there? Is there a noticeable change of attitude and outlook? It is a question which one might try to answer by the time-honored method of sending questionnaires to a more or less complete sample of European businessmen in the Common Market and then analyzing the results by a variety of statistical techniques. The results, while doubtless interesting, would be subject to serious objections from a realistic standpoint, in a political perspective. For all these techniques proceed by the highly questionable assumption, presumed to be democratic, that each businessman is equivalent to every other businessman and that if 90 out of 100 answer that they do not know much about the EEC, while 5 say that they are much opposed, and 5 others that they are much in favor, this provides a portrait of communal sentiment. Perhaps from a psychological standpoint it does, but political analysis is ill-served by such computations. For the business community, and more particularly its associational life, is highly structured and indeed informally hierarchical. One businessman like Louis Armand or Hermann Abs will count for at least 100 other businessmen; not only is his authority (in the refined sense)[2] much greater, but he will decisively influence the actions taken at crucial points in the shaping of economic policy. It is therefore necessary to study the actual behavior of businessmen in their enterprises and in their associations and groups, including, of course, their speeches and other more or less formal communications.

The other possibility would be to identify the leaders (elite) and inquire into their view. There are, however, great difficulties in this approach, some of which were already dealt with in the preceding chapter. Here we might add that a group of researchers using this approach found that "the selection of French and West German leaders proved a thorny problem."[3] Discarding a random sample for good and sufficient reasons, the "elite" of businessmen were selected by writing to established scholars and experts on French and German politics and thereby compiling a panel of 441 French and 650 West German leaders; but only a limited number of these were actually interviewed (147 French and 173 West Germans), among whom there were in turn only 17 businessmen in France and 36 in Germany. Considering the range and complexity of modern industry and business, this surely constitutes a rather inadequate sample—the German daily *Die Welt* publishes the profile of a business leader as an almost daily feature!—especially if one's concern is the actual behavior of businessmen in response to the challenge of European integration, rather than the elusive notion of "influence upon policy" which these researchers made the focal point of their inquiry.

Our study is methodologically based upon the notion that what businessmen *do* in their businesses is a more dependable empirical basis for judging their response to integration than what a small handful of them say about it. There are two fields of such major activity: their own business, and the associations in which they cooperate with other businessmen. In both fields their response to European integration has been massive and sustained. Let us examine this in greater detail. In a recent poll of the attitude of Frenchmen toward European unification, undertaken by the French UNESCO Clubs with the assistance of the French Institute of Public Opinion and the Information Service of the Communities, it was found once more that businessmen and their administrative personnel led the public in holding views favorable to integration. To the question: Would you say that your attitude toward the Common Market is (1) very favorable, (2) rather favorable, (3) rather unfavorable, (4) very unfavorable, or (5) indifferent?, 34 percent replied affirmatively to the first alternative; 55 percent (employees) and 52 percent (*cadres et industriels*) affirmatively to the second alternative; in short, an overwhelming 86/89 percent of the group were more or less favorable. To the obverse question: If the Common Market were dissolved for some reason, would you consider this (1) a catastrophe, (2) a rather bad thing, (3) of little importance, or (4) a good thing?, 27 percent and 29 percent, respectively, answered affirmatively to the first alternative, 62 percent and 51 percent, respectively, replied affirmatively to the second; that is, again 80/89 percent of the group were found to be strongly on the side of unification. That one in four French businessmen should judge the cessation of the Common Market a catastrophe suggests the extent to which the *actual conduct of business* has come to be intertwined with the existence of the Common Market; for only the realization of such interdependence would make businessmen willing to make so radical a judgment. It is therefore not surprising that 76 percent of all French (and in light of the foregoing presumably an even higher percentage of French businessmen) judged a political organization either indispensable (17 percent) or desirable (59 percent), and of these 39 percent thought that it should be undertaken immediately, and 22 percent that this should be done in five years.[4] But there are other indications, more solid than opinion polls, which provide evidence for the rapidly developing consensus among businessmen and its political implications. It has seemed best to present this evidence in two separate chapters, since the entrepreneurial and the associational life and activity of businessmen are quite separate and distinct. But before we enter into the details of the first of these subjects, some further general introductory remarks which provide the setting for this evidence are in order.

In presenting the evidence for the business community of the Common Market, it is important not to allow oneself to become myopic and to forget that there is also growing a wider European business community including the countries outside the Common Market. For there are many French and German businessmen to whom their relations with Great Britain or the Scandinavian countries are at least as important as those with countries in the Common Market. At the same time, the statistical picture of the change that is occurring is quite clear and unmistakable; on an overall basis the growth of the Common Market community has far outdistanced the growth of relations with the rest of Europe and the world at large. The basic facts for the EEC as a whole, as well as for France and Germany, are shown in Table 3–1. The same trend continued, as more recent statistics furnished by the Brussels authorities clearly show (see Table 3–2); they are on a percentage evaluation for the year 1965/6.

In short, while trade, as measured in exports, increased two and one-half to three times within the Common Market, it increased only about 50 percent beyond the Common Market.

TABLE 3–1. INCREASE IN EXPORTS OF EEC COUNTRIES TO (A) COUNTRIES WITHIN THE EEC, AND (B) TO COUNTRIES OUTSIDE THE EEC
(Figures in billions of DM; $1 = 4 DM)

		1958	1959	1960	1961	1962	1963	1839	Relative Approximate Increase 58–67
EEC (as a whole)	(a)	6.86	8.18	10.25	11.89	13.56	15.93	18.39	3 times
	(b)	15.91	17.05	19.48	20.43	20.63	21.63	24.16	1/2 times
France	(a)	1.14	1.52	2.04	2.42	2.71	3.09	3.49	3 times
	(b)	3.98	4.08	4.82	4.80	4.65	4.99	5.50	1/2 times
Germany	(a)	2.41	2.73	3.37	4.03	4.51	5.45	5.91	2 1/2 times
	(b)	6.40	7.07	8.05	8.66	8.75	9.16	10.30	

SOURCE: Data furnished by the Statistical Office of the EEC.

TABLE 3–2. GROWTH RATE OF TRADE BETWEEN MEMBER COUNTRIES FROM 1965 TO 1966 (IN PERCENT)

Importing Country / Exporting Country	Germany	France	Italy	Netherlands	B.L.E.U.	EEC
Germany	—	+14.0	+14.5	+7.5	+12.5	+12.0
France	+14.0	—	+23.5	+9.0	+15.0	+15.5
Italy	+11.5	+27.0	—	+9.0	+11.0	+15.5
Netherlands	+ 4.5	+10.5	+12.0	—	+ 8.0	+ 7.0
B.L.E.U.	+ 9.5	+16.5	+15.5	+5.0	—	+10.5
EEC	+10.0	+16.5	+16.5	+7.0	+12.0	+12.0

SOURCE: European Economic Community Commission, *Tenth General Report on the Activities of the Community (1 April 1966–31 March 1967)*, Brussels, June 1967, p. 136.

NOTE: Computed on the basis of average import and export figures in the member countries.

Since the figures are merely to show the comparative growth, purchasing power and related problems can be neglected; the dramatic way in which intra-Common Market trade has outdistanced European and world trade is very evident. In the course of this development, France and Germany have become each other's largest customers; each heads the list of foreign trade partners of the other. Even so, it has been pointed out that there is also observable a "certain sentiment of a world community" while at the same time "the class struggles of the nineteenth century have become transformed into struggles between the economically secure and the proletarian nations."[5] By contrast, the business community of the Common Market finds itself confronted by a labor community which openly recognizes the new situation. "We know perfectly well," the representatives of organized labor have stated, "that we are above all called upon to appear before public opinion as the representatives of well-defined interests: the interests of millions of workers who wish to live in peace and the well-being of a united Europe."[6] What the Europeans call rather euphemistically the "social partners" (*partenaires sociaux*) are to some extent stimulating each other into Europeanizing their respective activities.

It should also be mentioned at the outset that national governmental activity in the economic sphere has responded to the challenges emanating from the Common Market, as well as from more general, world-wide economic collaboration. Yet the Common Market has been predominant in providing this general impact of international activity upon national economic administration. Not only are there governmental units, like a French interministerial committee to deal with questions of European economic cooperation, but there is in France also a special presidental committee, called *Comité de l'Elysée*, which meets with the President of the Republic quite regularly to deal with the problems of the Common Market. As one researcher has put it, its purpose is to "réaliser une constante confrontation entre les aspects politiques et les aspects économiques des problèmes soulèvés par la mise en oeuvre de l'intégration européenne."[7]

There is no doubt that a European business community of some sort would exist, even if there were no Common Market. Indeed, it always has existed, just as there exists a world community. But its bonds were tenuous and the hurdle of the boundaries very high. To put the change into a formula, one could say that whereas the world community and the European business community outside the Common Market manage to operate in spite of the impediments imposed by sovereign national states, the business community within the Common Market is promoted by the EEC. It is so promoted because the radical changes in economic relationships between the national economies—the disappearance of tariff boundaries now accomplished and the gradual reduction of fiscal, administrative, and other differences which is in process—has forced many businessmen to rethink their operations. The large number of new competitors practically obliges every firm to engage in new entrepreneurial undertakings. These undertakings have called for a great deal of complex forecasting and planning, productionwise and marketwise, raising the prospect of large additional profits or losses. They continue to do so. One is justified in saying that the Common Market brought a new epoch to a large number of enterprises; in the years ahead skill in manipulating their adaptation to the new situation will spell success or failure for a goodly number of them.

This has produced considerable discussion, and the challenge of American business in seizing the opportunities here offered has been a prime focal point. We shall discuss this aspect more fully below.[8] Among the innovations that entrepreneurs had to consider and potentially to undertake were not only expansion, but modernization, to rationalize as well as to increase production. It is evident that for quite a few the solution to at least some of their problems lay in the direction of entering into joint operations of one kind or another with similar and complementary enterprises in countries of the Common Market other than their own. In the following analysis we shall give particular attention to those producers and enterprises which had hitherto been protected by tariffs and other means against competition from their likes in other countries. For it is these enterprises which show the change in political and business mentality in a particularly marked degree.

A rapid adaptation of all sorts of enterprises to the new conditions of competition which are being created by the Common Market has been taking place since 1958. This statement holds true, of course, not only for industry within the Common Market but also for other countries, including the United States. For so profound a change in so important a production and consumption area as is represented by the more than 180 million people who live and work in the area of the EEC cannot but affect business calculations in all countries who trade with them. But in this study we shall deal exclusively with business in the Common Market area, and primarily with enterprises in France and Germany (Federal Republic). We shall also leave aside, for reasons of research design, actual fusions of enterprises, the establishment of joint subsidiaries, and agreements for cooperation on the national plane. Our primary attention will be directed toward agreements between enterprises and groups of enterprises which seek to cope with the new production and marketing conditions existing in the Common Market, and more especially within France and Germany.

Lindberg noted that besides a greatly accelerated rate of mergers and forms at the national level for which statistics are lacking, "the Common Market has also given rise to an ever-expanding network of various kinds of agreements between firms of the several EEC countries."[9] Yet, actually less has happened than enthusiasts expected in view of the conditions which have been created. What is more, American entrepreneurs have been more aggressive in seizing the advantages which the Common Market offers than the Europeans themselves. Even the Germans, though more active than the others, have failed to respond to the challenge to any striking degree. A leading French engineer and business leader, Louis Armand, has commented upon this failure as follows:

> A l'heure actuelle (1965) en France comme dans chacun des six pays, on continue la plupart du temps à distinguer d'un coté les entreprises nationales, de l'autre les entreprises étrangères qui englobent à la fois celles qui sont européennes et les autres. . . . Il faut changer cette approche. . . . Il faut promouvoir l'industrie européenne. . . .[10]

It seems that Americans are more inclined to think of Europe as a whole; they see the big market which for most Europeans remains divided. Their position is, of course, strengthened by the financial resources of large American firms. In a recent study concerned with the problem of American investments in Europe,[11] the author notes at the outset that American investments in Europe have increased 183 percent between 1958 and 1964—at an annual rate of about 20 percent—while in the Common Market, American investments constituted about half of the foreign investments, within the context of this overall development; it continued unabated until the American government intervened. This was part of its policy of protecting the dollar by reducing the dollar deficit in America's balance of payments.

The facts about an individual firm may be illuminating. The Standard Oil Company of New Jersey, one of the American giants, considers Western Europe as Jersey's largest market, accounting for more than a third of the company's total sales. "Jersey's investment in Europe," so their *Quarterly* Report of September 1966 stated, "amounts to more than $2.5 billion . . . employing some 41,000 people." Nearly all of these (99 percent) are citizens of the country in which they work. The report then goes on to give details about the various phases of their activity, and concludes that "in an energy market so large, so fast growing, and so competitive as Europe, national boundaries are becoming anachronistic as far as the efficiency of the oil industry is concerned . . . the task of Esso Europe is on a continental scale." Since total revenues of Standard of New Jersey (Esso) in the first six months of 1966 were over $6.5 billion, an investment of $2.5 billion might not appear sizable; the figures illustrate, however, the vastness of the financial resources which American firms can bring to the task of doing business in the Common Market, as in the rest of the world. The customs and other barriers which surround this and other European markets are an important incentive for making these investments.

A rather elaborate study of these several kinds and degrees of interpenetration in manufacturing industries has been presented by Michel Falise. It covers the year 1959–1960.[12] He concentrated his research upon the establishment of new factories and lines of business. He found that the fastest development occurred in the chemical industry. Next came metallurgy and related industries (except in the Netherlands, where they were first). Much more slow development occurred in the food-processing industries and textiles. In short, consumer industries lagged behind others, which is natural enough in a period of rapid industrial expansion.[13] It is noteworthy that these new factories and establishments more often owed their coming into being to American and British than to intra-European capital sources: of 303 new enterprises 182 owed their establishment to "foreign" capital, 82 to "national" capital, and only 39 to "mixed," i.e., to a combination of both. Without going into the further details which show that in that year the largest number of new establishments went to the Netherlands and the fewest to Germany, it is obvious that foreign investors are much more active than European ones. On the whole, the range of foreign capital investment is of limited scope. The Deutsche Bank, in a study of 1965,[14] was able to show that foreign capital was involved in only 5 percent of the enterprises and that in these enterprises foreign capitalists held about 16 percent of the capital. In other words, in the field of manufacture only less than 1 percent were capitalized from abroad, so even a rather rapid increase such as was noted above does not signify a great deal of interpenetration in absolute terms.

For it deserves to be noted in this connection that in one sense the Common Market does not encourage, but rather discourages, the entrepreneur to make investments in other countries under EEC. Tariff walls serve to encourage foreign investments, because only thus can the tariff be avoided. The Swiss, for example, started many subsidiaries in Imperial Germany which had surrounded itself with high customs barriers. Switzerland has since generalized and expanded this system in France and in Germany. Since there is now (in effect since 1968) one great customs union, a French firm can hope to manufacture its goods in France and sell them throughout the six countries of the Common Market more readily than when customs barriers had to be surmounted. Therefore, whatever additional capital it can secure for expansion, it will be tempted to employ in enlarging its production facilities in its established locations and merely expand its sales setup in the other countries. However, as already mentioned, there are numerous other impediments yet to be removed. Among the nontariff barriers administrative and fiscal differentiations play a major role, especially different taxes. Work is going forward to reduce these differences; thus Germany has introduced the "added-value tax" which has been an important part of the French system, but a great deal of work remains to be done. Besides, there are the external tariff problems; e.g., the difficult question of customs classification. An ashtray may be listed as a household item, a glass product, or an art object; each of these listings might mean a different duty. The completion of the customs union requires that these classifications become uniform. There remains also the very difficult problem of how to divide the revenue from duties among the Six.[15] But even if all these problems were satisfactorily solved for the businessman, he might still have good reasons for dispersing his production, one of them being nearness to markets. Thus the French tire manufacturer Michelin controlling a predominant position in the French market, when confronted with the task of entering the German market, preferred to build a large factory (near Karlsruhe) to merely developing a sales organization; this may in part be due to his desire to enlist German participation. American firms often do the same in spreading their manufacture far and wide. There may also be differential advantages in the supply and cost of available labor, or the general cost differential may provide a chance to provide additional production facilities at less cost per worker; for such differentials recur in national economies, so they are bound to remain a factor in European business for a long time. After all, they have remained important in America after generations of a common market economy and effective economic union. Capital is, generally speaking, more mobile than labor, though here again there are exceptions. As will be shown later, the statistics confirm this general hypothesis: commercial affiliates are much more common than are production branches in adjoining countries of the Common Market, whereas outsiders are more prone to establish production facilities. In this respect, the Scandinavians and the British, as well as the Americans, seem inclined to "join the Common Market" indirectly through large-scale expansion of individual firms.

The then director of the Franco-German Chamber of Commerce, H. J. von Hake, summed up the situation rather well in November 1965; noting that the economic interpenetration between France and the Federal Republic had only reached 6–7 percent as compared with the 20 percent prevailing between the Benelux countries, he added:

It shows how difficult is the integration of two economies. Mere commerce is slowly implemented by investments. This change is reflected in the daily work of our Chamber at Paris. Ten years ago questions of customs legislation, of "contingents" and of foreign exchange were in the foreground; today they are questions about establishment of subsidiaries, the forming of branches or the value of investments. It is impressive with what frankness and mutual confidence the partners of two countries cooperate today.[16]

This business leader thought that it showed that the business community was often more advanced in its outlook and point of view than the governmental and administrative apparatus. He also felt that the political crises had not particularly affected business relations. Integration proceeded apace. The same observation was made by quite a few businessmen individually and can be demonstrated by the statistics. After these introductory observations, we must now turn to these "hard facts."

Generally speaking, there are two primary forms of economic cooperation and interpenetration: direct investments and agreements. Direct investments are, as just mentioned, involved in the creation of branches and subsidiaries in another country, in mergers, in concentrations and the acquisition of capital participation, whether minority or majority, and finally in the outright purchase of another firm. Although still not very extensive, these operations are steadily increasing between France and Germany, as well as generally in the Common Market. Whether they exceed what they might be without a common market is difficult to say, but in light of the foregoing reflections would not prove any lack of communal development.

Agreements may be concerned with various aspects of industrial activity, of course. Joint research may be organized, engineering know-how may be exchanged, licenses and patents shared, production divided according to specialized tasks, purchasing and selling combined, and financial requirements coordinated through joint insurance, joint credit, or mutual guarantees. For all these agreements, examples can be found in the relations between French and German business firms.[17] They are, of course, not restricted to France and Germany, but have played a very great role in relations between other foreign, especially American, and European business firms. But they have been facilitated within the area of the Common Market, and increasingly so as the Customs Union neared completion. Its consummation now places into the foreground the further steps toward an Economic Union, which is getting under way. In fact, the consummation of the Customs Union on July 1, 1948, had been so long anticipated that it passed without much fanfare and most of the commentaries one heard from businessmen, as reported in the leading journals of France and Germany, were preoccupied with what was still lacking before there would exist a complete customs union and how one could now proceed toward implementing it in order to achieve an economic union. A typical comment was:

> Landmark that July 1 promises to be, ushering in conditions which a generation ago would have seemed totally unbelievable, its impact should not be overrated. Goods will not as yet be shipped as freely from Paris to Milan, or Brussels to Stuttgart as they now are from one Belgian province to another or from New York to New Orleans. Their flow will remain hampered by a multitude of restrictions . . .[18]

Hence agreements remain very important.

The various kinds of agreements all presuppose a very large number of personal contacts, and a consequent shift in attitude due to greater familiarity with "the other side." This change is, however, not uniform for the economy as a whole. Wide variations occur. Many foodstuffs are, because of their perishability, local eating habits, and so forth, sheltered from European competition; yet the extent to which, for example, French and

Italian wines and cheeses are seen in German stores is impressive. Where the government appears as the purchaser, local producers are still in a preferred condition; e.g., while the percentage of German cars in France and French cars in Germany is increasing rapidly, it will be some time before the respective governments will purchase them for their official duties. Similarly, the production and sale of drugs is still largely localized. On the other hand, in the fields of chemistry, textiles, mechanical and electrical equipment, and so forth, the general international competition has been further intensified as a result of the Common Market. This may take inter-European forms. A major German rubber manufacturer, after acquiring control over a French rubber shoe producer, is now abandoning the German lines and bringing the presumably better and cheaper French shoes into his German market.[19]

In these latter industries and businesses the interpenetration has gone forward rather rapidly as manufacturers have adapted themselves to the new situation. Such interpenetration proceeds from the top down and from the "bottom" up. For along with capital and management the customers are the most immediately affected, and in many instances in their intimate spheres of personal living, such as food and clothing. Reinforced by a vastly increased amount of travel, the intracommunity pattern of living is being both Europeanized and internationalized. European interpenetration is in this perspective a more intensive form of transcending the former national boundaries. It involves exchange of know-how, joint use of selling organizations, agreements for each partner's specialization in a particular line of production and, closely resembling this specialization, a combination of lines of production (NSU and Citroen, for example), often spoken of as "joint production."[20] As in the case of capital investment, so even more continuously in the field of all these different agreements, the multiplication of human contacts is very great. If the director of a firm like Nelle (Netherlands) states that for them the EEC is considered their internal market, then the sales organization has to be developed on a binational basis; for the local man is needed on account of his knowledge of buyers and their habits, the Dutch member of the team for his knowledge of the product. It has been found that the more intensive the actual collaboration the better the commercial result: interpenetration is good business. It is often a question of making a particular item known to merchants and buyers through elaborate sales efforts, including advertising. All this is, of course, again, in no way peculiar to Europe or the Six, but placed within the framework of European institutions, it has political implications which in other cases remain vague and ineffectual. In times of political crisis, these relations have shown a remarkable stability and resilience.

The range of agreements to cooperate is naturally very great, and runs all the way from a short-range verbal agreement to permanent fusion of two or more enterprises. M. Schwamm cites the observation of a French engineer on such agreements, which is worth quoting: "After the conclusion of an agreement, whatever its form, the enterprises involved, while preserving their individuality, change their orientation. They seek to obtain the agreed-upon harmonization and complementarity, but all with the understanding that the relation can be ended."[21] It is very different, of course, in the case of mergers where the managerial line of command is made one; but it is incorrect to say that the fusion necessarily extinguishes the distinctiveness of the merged enterprises. It depends a great deal upon the attitude of the controlling groups. If a French or German firm acquiring control over a firm in the other country desires to maintain its individuality by retaining the pre-existing managerial staff or part of it, and more generally decides that the locally controlling personnel shall belong to the nationality where it is located, the firms can be merged without being absorbed into each other. All the evidence at hand suggests that this procedure of strongly decentralized operations gives superior results and therefore is apt to persist and spread. A former French firm, now a German subsidiary operating in France under management personnel who are all Germans is almost certain to experience very great difficulties. Quite a few American firms which have tended in this direction have found this out at their expense.[22]

The reason for the vigorous response of some businessmen to the challenge of the Common Market is not only a matter of increased profits—though this motive remains paramount—but also is due to the realization that cooperation means an expanding market and a fuller participation in technological advance. This latter consideration is of increasing importance and is decisive in coping with the problems that the cost of modern scientific research poses for any number of industries. This need is being stressed by businessmen and it finds expression in any number of official and semiofficial publications. Thus we read in a report of the European Communities: "More than ever is research the pre-condition of modern industrial development. The tasks which are facing Europe—building of large computer centers, utilization of atomic energy, . . . communication by satellites—can only be solved by cooperation, because no single European country can raise the needed funds."[23] In a major effort at evaluation, made by Euroforum in January 1968, this task is made one of the key principles (VII) on the basis of a resolution of the Ministerial Council of EEC adopted on January 31, 1967. (See below, Chapter 9.) It is seen as involving the joint financing of major research projects, coordination and division of labor between the member states in their national research, and promotion of cooperation by industry with the aid of tax and economic policy.[24] In this matter of joint research, as in that of defending themselves against American investment initiative, consensus among European businessmen is very widespread. A similar consensus is developing in the field of industrial relations, more particularly the problem of workers' participation in management. Long a distinctive feature of German business life, where a law for the internal order of industrial and other business enterprises (Betriebsordnungsgesetz) provides for workers' participation in management through elected representatives, both in the direction (Vorstand) and the supervisory council (Aufsichtsrat),[25] it has now become a battle cry in France, although primarily in terms of participation in profits rather than management.[26] Businessmen in both countries are, if not outright opposed, disinclined to favor the extension of the system, as recently demanded by the trade unions. In Germany the argument is reinforced by pointing out that such a system makes German industry unattractive to foreign investors and weakens it in competition with non-German European manufacturers.[27] It is noteworthy, however, that the seizure of French plants by rebellious workers in May 1968 did not produce *Schadenfreude,* but rather led to a strong manifestation of group solidarity.[28]

A characteristic development today in large industrial units is to have one of the top personnel specialize in European integration problems. Interviews disclose that these men become hard-bitten partisans of Europe. They are, however, *sans phrase*. The glowing rhetoric of the fifties leaves them cold. These industrial "specialists" on European matters usually are preoccupied with the way the evolution of the Common Market affects their specific business. Frequently men who already possess an intimate knowledge of the countries concerned, and speak the language, spend extended periods in sales offices or factories linked by agreement to the firm. The formation of this European personnel inside a good many business enterprises, paralleling the general development of international business, gradually changes the political mentality of these businessmen.[29]

All the aforementioned developments have led to the demand for creating the legal basis for European corporations.[30] It is mentioned in all the commentaries, critical and constructive, which were made on the occasion of the realization of the Customs Union on July 1, 1968. The creation of such a corporate form, subject to uniform taxation, is a problem familiar to American business, where after nearly two centuries of economic development there still does not exist the legal basis for an American corporation—all corporate units being incorporated in one of the states. This situation is, in part at least, acceptable because all the states accept the principles of the Common Law and are subject to one set of federal courts. In Europe, though the countries all recognize the civil law in principle, the laws of France and of the other Common Market countries display great differences. Hence, the creation of a European corporation seems more urgent. Thus a leading official of the EEC Commission, Claudio Segré, has commented that

> ... the formation of multinational corporations and the conclusion of agreements of cooperation and of specialization between enterprises on a national and even more on an international (European) basis constitutes an essential element in the adaptation of the industrial structure to the requirements of the Common Market. Indeed, it is urgent that the legal and financial framework within which these transformations are to work is furnished in order to avoid a localization of activities which is preoccupied, not with the basic economic givens, but with the greater or lesser strictness of each country and with the available facilities for financing their operations.[31]

Similarly Hilde Claessens, the secretary general of UNICE (see next chapter), declared when asked in what field action was most urgently needed after July 1, 1968: "The creation of the European company ... we have heard a lot of talk about the American challenge, but nothing is being done about forming companies that can compete in the very fields where the Americans have the edge ..."[32] If a law establishing such a corporation is not at present possible, there exist other methods, two of which would seem to be available for accomplishing this task of establishing the legal framework for European corporations. One would be to seek to harmonize the legislation dealing with corporations in all the six countries. This would be an extremely slow and uncertain process and many years would surely pass, as the experience with codification of corporation law in the United States demonstrates. The other, proposed by the French government, and considered preferable, would be to work out a model law for a European corporation (*société commerciale*) which each of the member countries would adopt and make part of its law. Such a law would satisfy the objectives of the Treaty of Rome (Art. 100) while at the same time encouraging the concentration of economic activity. It is in any case highly significant that businessmen throughout the Common Market area are inclined to favor the adoption of laws which would make the establishment of such corporate entities possible. This tendency is greatly enhanced by American competition.[33]

But the inherent development of corporate giants raises serious problems of overconcentration. The Common Market Treaty is greatly concerned with this possibility and has made explicit provision against all combinations in restraint of trade. American influence was powerful, as was the philosophy of neo-liberalism, shared by quite a few of the businessmen interested in the promotion of Europe in such organizations as CEPES and ELEC. Article 85 ff. of the Rome Treaty embodied essentially the philosophy of American antitrust legislation; that is to say, legislation which prohibited agreements in restraint of trade. Such restraint is defined as having "as its object or result the prevention, restriction or distortion of competition within the Common Market." Price-fixing, limitation or control of production, markets, and technical development or investment are among the practices thus outlawed. The Commission, and the Coal and Steel Authority before it, have devoted a great deal of effort to the implementing of these treaty provisions, and generally speaking have had substantial support from businessmen in these efforts to prevent the integration of Europe from becoming a prime opportunity for the development of big trusts. This seems somewhat in contradiction to the professed desire to promote effective cooperation and indeed even the merger of business enterprises across national boundaries. The establishment of a special office or bureau by the governments of France and Germany for the purpose of studying ways for French and German businesses to work out relations seems to be at variance with such a prohibition. But the Treaty itself in its next article explicitly exempts from its antitrust provisions agreements and practices which do not eliminate competition and which contribute to the improvement of production or distribution or to the promotion of technical or economic progress, provided the consumers are allowed to share in the benefits accruing from them. In short, whenever agreements are in keeping with the functioning of a competitive market economy, they are welcome, and indeed are considered worthy of support.[34] As a result, European businessmen have come to support in increasing measure the economic policies involved; the Common Market has in a way promoted a widening consensus on a liberal economic policy; the same can be said for social policy, which is discussed below, in Chapter 6.

A word should be added here on the consumer who remains "voiceless" largely because of the difficulty of representing so diffuse a group—many businessmen being themselves the consumers of the products of other businessmen. If the European parliament had adequate powers of control comparable to those of the Swiss legislature or the American Congress (for it is not necessary, as so often assumed in European discussions, that such a parliament should have the power to overturn the government in order to be an effective controller), and if it were popularly elected, consumer interests would presumably be more adequately represented and protected. In the absence of these changes, which only the establishment of a political union could bring (see below, Chapter 10), most of the protection is provided at their discretion by the Community's authorities. An interesting instance is provided by the Grundig-Consten (radio and television instruments) case. Grundig (German) products were to be sold in France by Consten at a high profit. Thereupon a competitor bought these products in Belgium and Germany and undersold Consten. So a suit was brought before the Court of the European Communities. It ruled that the agreement between Grundig and Consten was incompatible with the provisions of the Common Market Treaty.[35] This case and others like it show that a certain amount of consumer protection is provided by the antitrust provisions of the Treaty. At the same time, the student of politics will have to add that such inhibitions necessarily act as a brake on entrepreneurial initiative in building European business, lured by exceptional profits in certain kinds of cooperative agreements. The Court, by adopting a moderate position on these treaty provisions and not giving full effect to the antitrust provisions of the Treaty met "the needs of many economic groups." A more doctrinaire interpretation of these provisions "would have created many problems and a great deal of legal uncertainty."[36] When a European parliamentarian sermonizes that "we in the Community have to find ways of bringing the Common Market closer to the consumer . . ."[37] she is basically also admonishing businessmen not to forget the consumer as the basic constituent of any market.

Let us conclude this discussion of the entrepreneurial or business community by citing a social psychologist's thoughtful study whose anticipatory comments have been confirmed since he wrote them in 1960. He argued, on the basis of his findings, that experience had not decreased the faith of German businessmen and union leaders in European union and the Common Market. "Once the institution is established," he wrote, "evaluations of it are not greatly determined by ideology . . ." and he added, "new patterns of behavior and resulting values and beliefs [will] develop."[38] That businessmen's community-oriented behavior has gradually been strengthened in spite of the decline in political tensions and in face of General de Gaulle's recurrent hostile acts is evidence of the slowly evolving political implications of European community formation in this sector of economic life. As the next chapter hopes to show, that conclusion is further reinforced by the findings in the field of businessmen's associational activities.

4. The Business Community: Associations

The general secretary of the important *Union des Industries de la Communauté Européenne,* Hilde Claessens, voiced a widespread worry when she declared upon the coming into being of the Customs Union on July 1, 1968: "Our main concern [over the fact] is that this operation is not being accompanied by complete tariff harmonization, the disappearance of technical obstacles to trade, and uniform anti-dumping legislation."[1] Hers is a highly characteristic voice in the babel of proclamations by interest groups accredited to the European Communities in Brussels. Businessmen and women work and fight with each other, as we have already noted, not only in their enterprises, but also, like everyone else, in their associations. A vast network of such interest groups exists in all the countries of the Common Market. These associations have been increasingly involved in all kinds of informal community formation. Their activities are among the most striking political results of that formation. In the next chapter we plan to explore this range of the European business community.[2] However, a complete picture of these associations cannot, of course, be drawn here. There are the associations for particular industries, and even quite a few of their subdivisions, and there are the federations of special associations in the overall groupings, such as the Federal Union of German Employers Associations (*Bundesvereinigung der Deutschen Arbeitgeberverbaende–BDA*) and the Federal Union of Germany Industry (*Bundesverband der Deutschen Industrie–BDI*) as well as the corresponding National Council of French Employers (*Conseil National du Patronat Français–CNPF*) and the General Confederation of Italian Industry (*Confederazione Generale dell'Industria Italiana–CONFINDUSTRIA*); there are also the Chambers of Commerce and Industry, the Chambers of Handicraft (*Artisanat, Handwerk*), and other assorted professional organizations.[3]

These bodies have since 1958 (or even before) formed Common Market–wide organizations of varying scope. Thus the Council of Federations of Commerce (*Conseil des Fédérations Commerciales d'Europe–CFCE*) has come into being alongside the Union of Industries of the European Community (*Union des Industries de la Communauté Européenne–UNICE*) and the League for European Economic Cooperation (*Ligue Européenne de la Coopération Economique–LECE*), and the Union of the Handicrafts of the CEE (*UACEE*).

All the evidence suggests that within these European organizations a definite community spirit is in the process of developing. At the same time it is equally clear that these European organizations are weak compared to the national constituent bodies. Just as in the entrepreneurial field, the massive activity within the confines of the several national states is only thinly overlaid by a slowly growing European sector of activity and sentiment. Generally speaking, it is probably right to consider these European organizations as loose confederal entities whose very existence depends upon the support of the national organizations. In some cases, such as UNICE and COPA, this fact finds organizational expression in the predominant role which the Council of Presidents of the national association has played. (Some further details will be offered later in this chapter.)

It must be remembered that these organizations did not come into being without some preparation. When the EEC was started in 1958, several major sectors of the French and German economies, namely steel and coal, had already had an opportunity to gather experience. It is only natural that this experience should have, to some extent, shaped the original attitudes of the associations of French and German industry. It is well to remember this, although in the sequel different experiences produced considerably different attitudes and viewpoints.[4] A remarkable transformation had occurred in the course of the experiences with the Coal and Steel Community. At the outset there was very great hesitation and general suspicion, but this soon yielded to a more realistic appraisal of the situation. The French coal and steel industry had been afraid of a powerful offensive by their competitors in the Ruhr, but this offensive did not materialize; in fact, French industry achieved some success in exporting its own products. German apprehensions, especially the fear that the French might try to block their development, proved similarly incorrect. At the same time, the consumers of coal and steel increasingly felt the beneficial effects of the establishment of a Coal and Steel Community. Thus even in the short span of four years the affected industries learned to live with the new authorities. They took advantage of the new opportunities and at the same time found it possible to counteract measures which seemed unacceptable. Major points of such a counterattack were the hostility to cartels, the control of mergers, and in part, price-fixing as well as taxation. One can sum up this experience in terms of a sober appreciation of the extent to which business interests are being served, and hence practical cooperation is indicated, even though no particular enthusiasm for Europe is generated. Various forms of European cooperation were developed and a fairly firm organization was in fact created in the coal industry as well as a cartel of the dealers in scrap iron. The state of mind in the limited organizations that had come into being just before 1958 had been summarized fairly well by Ernst Haas as follows:

> These associations will band together supranationally and cooperate practically on issues on which their interests naturally converge and they will organize accordingly, but they will not immediately out-

grow their separate national ideological experiences and habits. No doubt a much longer period of tactical cooperation is required and a much more intense series of stimuli must be injected into the scene before any mass ideological cohesion will develop.[5]

This stronger experience has, of course, taken place; but on the whole (as will be shown presently) the attitude has continued to be pragmatic rather than ideological, which would seem to be all to the good.

In terms of such pragmatic appraisal of their interests many industries in both France and Germany were inclined to assess their common or complementary interests more optimistically than had been the case with coal and steel. Heavy industry, like agriculture, tends to be more inclined toward national and parochial views than manufacturing industries at large. Therefore the overall reaction to the proposed Common Market was at the outset more favorable. It is necessary to recall also that the economic situation had further improved since 1953, and hence there was greater confidence in the ability to cope with foreign competition. The experience under the Coal and Steel Authority had also borne fruit in the elimination of some of the provisions which had been particularly irritating to business in the treaty dealing with coal and steel. Therefore the businessmen were inclined to look upon the Rome Treaty as more friendly toward business and less inclined toward "technocracy." Generally speaking, French industry was more reserved than German industry. The CNPF stated its general readiness to go along, but at the same time formulated so many reservations that the document almost could be considered a negative one.[6] At the outset French industry was very reluctant to accept the automatic reduction of customs tariffs because it so radically conflicted with their traditional protectionist outlook. German industry, which had already gone through the crucible of a neoliberal reform, was ready, by contrast, to see the Common Market as "a realistic road," although it qualified that proposition by suggesting that the treaty "in its present form is no ideal solution."[7] For this reason it urged the High Commission to collaborate closely with industry and to seek its participation-advice, which was afterwards followed. At the same time, German industry demanded the unification of the several authorities—a demand which has since been realized. This was no doubt partly motivated by the desire to eliminate the more restrictive provisions of the Coal and Steel Treaty in favor of the more liberal outlook of the Common Market Treaty. In this connection the regulation of competition played an important part. German business associations insisted that they welcomed the proposed unification; but they misjudged what was coming by believing that an increased intra-Common Market trade would be compensated for by a drop in trade beyond its boundaries—a development which did not take place.[8] Without dealing in detail with the somewhat similar and similarly differentiated reaction in Italian and Benelux business circles, it can be said by way of a summary that European businessmen said a qualified "yes" to the proposed creation of the Common Market, the qualifications being largely dictated by what were believed to be distinctive national situations and interests. On the whole the affirmative views predominated. In spite of apprehensions about the impending changes, businessmen found the courage to accept the proposed experiment—a courage which was to be rewarded by a remarkable degree of forward movement and industrial progress.

Once the Common Market structure—institutional and otherwise—had come into being, rapid development of intra-European trade served materially to increase the affirmative attitude of businessmen and their several associations. Happily, the starting phase of the Common Market coincided with a broad upswing of the international business cycle; the Common Market emphasized, and to some extent perhaps even exaggerated, this upswing. Since much business activity at the top level consists of planning and anticipation and, if need be, some speculation, the basically favorable attitude of business constituted an important factor in the initial success of the Common Market. For as businessmen proceeded to restructure their own enterprises—a process we have explored to some extent in the preceding chapter—the work of the Common Market organization was facilitated to such a degree that the original schedule for the elimination of tariff boundaries was shortened and the process of mutual accommodation stepped up. U.S. industry played an important part in this development. For American businessmen proceeded, as we have already seen, to seize the prospective chances of the Common Market and to shift investments in Europe to that area so that already by 1960 investment in the Common Market area exceeded that in the rest of Europe. As we have seen, this trend has continued.[9] Naturally, the attitude of businessmen could not but be reflected in the views and positions displayed by their associations. As the Common Market became a success, the associations proceeded to play an increasingly active role. Thus the BDI stated in 1961 that "critical remarks of the BDI concerning particular measures or proposals of EEC offices must be seen in this perspective (namely a general overall firm support of the Common Market); they never are directed against the EEC as such."[10] As contrasted with industry, German trade interests were inclined to stress the desirability of merging EEC with the free-trade organization that Britain had sponsored,[11] but this viewpoint did not prevail.

Throughout the past ten years industry in France and Germany has never wavered in its support of the Common Market, and its associations have become more and more articulate in stating this position. At the same time, the progressive views quoted at the beginning of this chapter indicate a general inclination among businessmen to demand the more energetic implementation of the Customs Union and its transformation into an Economic Union (see Chapter 10). The poll among French businessmen reported in the preceding chapter (see pp. 49–50, above) is readily duplicated in all the Common Market countries, with even higher figures than in France. At the same time, there are, of course, considerable differences among businessmen in different sectors of industry and commerce, but also in response to various policies. Thus the antitrust policy is more likely to find support among small and medium-sized businesses than among the giants of industry. These differences lead to protracted discussions inside the associations; hence we shall now describe the functioning of these associations in greater detail.

It is noteworthy how rapidly European interest groups have increased in the course of the Common Market's existence. The figures offered in Table 4–1 overlap and cannot therefore be

TABLE 4–1. NUMBER OF EUROPEAN (CM) ECONOMIC ASSOCIATIONS (Exclusive of agriculture[a])

	1961	1965
Industry	88	135
Trade	40	69
Handicraft	7	11
"Free" professions	19	22
Services	—	4
Transport	7	7

SOURCE: Karl-Heinz Neunreither, *Politische Dimensione*, p. 401.

[a] See Chapter 5 of the present book.

simply added together. Dr. Neunreither estimates that by the end of 1965 about 290 to 300 such associations had come into being; this figure includes, however, over a hundred such groups in the agricultural field, so that the total of nonagricultural business groups at that time was more nearly 200. With the forward march of plans for an Economic Union and the completion of the Customs Union the trend has continued unabated, but no more recent estimate of their approximate number has been given. By no means are all of these associations very active or able to exert pressure upon the authorities of the EEC; they merely serve as channels for communicating to their membership basic information about the developing Common Market. Such information-gathering and transmitting is altogether one of the important functions of all interest groups. It is particularly crucial in a field of such extensive innovation as European unification.

A rapidly growing amount of general information is continually being distributed to every kind of business and professional group. Much of this information is very concrete and practical and devoid of all general rhetoric about Europe.[12] An addict of quantitative "evidence" counting the number of times words belonging to the vocabulary of this rhetoric occurred in such publications would be sorely disappointed and misled into very erroneous conclusions. For the commitment is taken so much for granted that the "Europeanization" of the mentality of the readers of these communications occurs indirectly as a result of the relevance of the implications of the information for the readers' immediate and continuing business and professional concerns.

These organizations make, however, a more conscious and elaborate effort through various forms of "adult education." Congresses, round tables, courses—all such and similar devices have been increasingly employed by many of these groups for the education of their members. They may engage in such activities themselves or they may engage other organizations or special institutes to undertake these tasks. Dr. Neunreither reports as an illustration and example that the German Union of Industry and Trade presented a number of European themes in about a hundred local branches as part of their discussions of economic policy. They also held a Franco-German seminar and meetings of the junior chambers.[13] Similar educational efforts are sponsored by many other organizations, which frequently enter into cooperative arrangements with the numerous university research institutes (see below, Chapter 9). There is less of this sort of activity to be found in France; but on the other hand there exist undertakings like the *Centre International de la Formation Européenne* (CIFE—see p. 183, below), which are supported by French industrialists; *Patronat Français*, the periodical publication of the CNPF, contains much informational material which has an educational impact through its continuity and the extent of its readership. It demonstrates at the same time how difficult it is to draw a hard-and-fast line between information and education on a subject of this kind.

Equally important is the extent to which interest groups participate in the process of informing and educating the general public. All such groups nowadays are more concerned with public relations activities than with old-fashioned lobbying.[14] Such public relations activities, in the case of Europe, naturally involve the issuer of the required publications in a discussion of the federalizing process. The desire to explain and promote not infrequently clashes with the older tradition of secrecy and confidentiality of such political information. Neunreither comments that this conflict seriously impedes the public relations activity of so important a body as the Federal Association of German Industry (BDI), which communicates its views to the public only in a monthly and an annual report, types of communication which are ill-adapted to catching the mass communication media.[15] The aforementioned German Union of Industry and Trade (DIHT) has been somewhat more successful in this respect, whereas the CNPF is even more conservative than the BDI in its approach to the public; its publications do not reach the public to any extent. As a consequence of more recent conflicts with the government (see p. 97, below), French businessmen have become more aggressive, and as the statistics quoted in Chapter 2 show, also more committed to the European liaison of its organizations.

The activities just sketched are, of course, closely related to the more specific task of influencing public policy by means of pressure. Such pressure presupposes a certain degree of unity, and much work has been devoted to developing common positions in the various organizations.[16] In all the different fields of economic activity—industry, trade, agriculture, handicraft, free professions, and so forth—federated European bodies have sprung up, as mentioned before. The most important among these are UNICE (*Union des Industries de la Communauté Européenne*) for industry, COCCEE (*Comité des Organisa-*

tions Commerciales des Pays de la C. E. E.) for trade, UACEE (*Union de l'Artisanat de la C. E. E.*) for handicraft, but no overall organization for the free professions. All these and many others are formally represented in the Social Council of the EEC as provided in Article 165 of the Rome Treaty. Before discussing their activities in relation to the EEC authorities, their internal structures ought to be compared and analyzed.

We have, in our analysis so far, repeatedly referred to what such organizations as BDI and CNPF are doing. The justification is that the European interest groups are to a very large extent federations of national interest groups. Occasional attempts to organize such associations on a strictly European basis, and without any national units supporting them, have met with the opposition of the High Commission of the EEC on the ground that they lack representativeness. Thus when the International Chamber of Commerce tried to set up a European Chamber of Commerce, the Commission did not recognize it,[17] but preferred to accept a body which the Chambers of Commerce of the Six had organized as the "Permanent Conference" of these chambers at the suggestion of the French Minister of Commerce and Industry.

The Commission's preference for having European interest groups rest firmly upon national interest groups is in a sense a reflection of the relatively loose structure of the EEC itself. The strongly federalistic structure of the European associations may be illustrated by the way the Union of Industries of the EEC (UNICE) is organized. According to its bylaws of April 1, 1959, the core authority is the Council of Presidents (of the constituent national bodies), which meets every two months. It is clearly the parallel to the Council of Ministers of the EEC; like it, UNICE also maintains a Committee of Permanent Delegates. These delegates meet every fortnight and select the issues which the UNICE should deal with. A permanent secretariat headed by a secretary-general, with its seat in Brussels, provides the administrative continuity and coordinates the activities of the committees of experts and of the working parties which have been organized for particular questions, the general political questions being handled by the Committee of Delegates itself. Over all this organizational network a chairman presides who is elected for two years by the Council of Presidents. There seems to be little competition for this post. The first president was M. Bekaert, a Belgian who offered the advantage of being near at hand. He was followed by H. J. de Koster of the Netherlands, who is reported to have sought the office. When he became a high Dutch official, the presidency devolved upon Fritz Berg, the long-time president of the BDI, who apparently agreed to serve only for the prescribed two years and only on condition that he would be elected unanimously. These procedural details suggest a relatively harmonious cooperation within UNICE.

It is striking that no such body as a general assembly is provided in the statutes of UNICE, in contrast to a number of other organizations, such as COPA (the European overall organization for agriculture; see Chapter 5, pp. 93 ff.). These general assemblies have proved, however, to be rather an adornment than operationally significant, except where, due to the structure of the economic group, there is need for a broad response among the membership, as is the case with farmers. Generally speaking, there is a tendency to rely upon some such organ as the Council of Presidents of UNICE.

It is, therefore, quite important for such a group which meets only intermittently to be provided with a well-functioning administrative setup, such as the secretariat of UNICE. However, most of these European interest groups—like most pressure groups in Washington—can consider themselves lucky if they have a full-time secretary and a stenographer. In the case of UNICE, six senior staff members, corresponding in rank to higher government officials, divide the work among themselves: the general secretary handles the top-level political contacts with the Commission, as does his deputy. Besides these, there is one specialist for social and farm questions; one for atomic, tax, and transport problems; and a fourth serves as secretary of the employers contingent in the Economic and Social Committee of the EEC. Such rather startling intertwining of official and pressure group activity is not limited to this group; it exists also in agriculture, the trade unions, and consumer interests. The general problems of this Committee are comparable to those of national economic councils, and are discussed below (Chapter 7). That the "independence" provided for in the Treaty is virtually unattainable in that kind of body should have been known to those who included it in the Treaty. In any case, it is not without significance for the "European" spirit of UNICE, and for these groups generally, that for quite some time five of the six officials of the secretariat were Belgians. In the case of the smaller secretariats, the Belgian member association frequently takes care of the business of the European body.

How is consensus achieved within these European interest groups? On the face of it, such consensus should be very difficult to bring about, considering the highly competitive nature of the several national positions. The task is further complicated by the fairly general practice of requiring at least formally unanimous decisions; majority decisions would obviously be difficult even to define. For what constitutes a majority in such a grouping as UNICE or COPA? The unanimity rule is formally required by the statutes of UNICE (Article 15 provides that decisions of the Council of Presidents be taken unanimously). But informally positions, particularly on economic issues, can be and are taken by a majority, while the views of the minority are stated explicitly. However, in political matters, usually unanimity is sought and frequently it is achieved.[18]

The process by which such decisions and positions (*prises de position*) are arrived at is not very well known. It is a complex and time-consuming process, because not only do the interests and outlook of the several national associations clash, but there is often sharp disagreement within the national associations which must first be ironed out; and the later coordination of the several national positions may be affected by the fact that a particular interest group, say, the chemical industry, shares across national boundaries a common interest divergent from other industries, as happened in connection with the Kennedy Round negotiations vis-à-vis the American system of calculating customs duties.[19] In the long run such interindustry cooperation seems more nearly in keeping with the concept of a uniting Europe than compromises on the national level which tend to become too rigid. Neunreither tells us that "in the formation of an associational will to be represented toward outsiders" several factors play an increasing role: "the increasing familiarity with European problems, precedents on similar questions, and the considerable potential of a known atmosphere of personal acquaintance."[20] The ever greater inclination of the national associations toward seeing their problems within a European framework—to which their reports clearly testify—constitute a telling response to the challenge of the Common Market, primarily in terms of concrete interests and problems. The national associations are learning more and more to adjust their national positions to European requirements; they have learned by experience that "the best way to protect their separate interests is to sacrifice a part of their position for the sake of joint action."[21] But such a consensus exists *ad hoc* and for the time being; it must not be confused with a stable type of homogeneity. Agreement of this sort may gradually turn into the more stable and persistent homogeneity, however, if it becomes in course of time habitual and more or less the expected behavior pattern. Increasingly, European thoughts and approaches are replacing the older national preoccupations, even though the latter remain a powerful residual element (see Chapter 5, below, for further detail). When confronted by a common crisis, agriculturists in France and Germany responded in similar ways. It is therefore doubtful whether one is justified in claiming that "a large majority of the [interest] groups place primary emphasis on routing demands through national governments and assign secondary priority to the direct approach to community institutions."[22] It all depends upon the particular situations, including variations among the several countries. It often may be important to "play" the national government in collaboration with the Commission. The general strategies that national economic interest groups employ may work either way in the complex decision-making process that is involved in the evolving policies of the Common Market.

How, then, do these associations behave in their relations with European governmental authorities, and more especially the High Commission? Like all interest groups, their concern is to influence the decisions of these bodies. The general insight into the operation of influence as a particular form of political power has brought to light that its presence can be detected with the help of the rule of anticipated reactions.[23] This rule teaches that whenever a formal decision of an authoritative body is reversed as a result of criticism or protest, it can be presumed that the behavior of such an authoritative body is influenced continuously by those whose criticism or protest has been effective in reversing a formal decision. In the case of the High Commission (and the same holds for the High Authority and Euratom), recurrent instances show the influence of European business to be very great. They also show that on the national level the European outlook of these associations influences the behavior of their national governments vis-à-vis Europe. This will be demonstrated in greater detail below (Chapter 5) in connection with the crisis of 1965/6 and the French presidential elections; but it is quite obvious in the case of the High Commission, which openly and avowedly seeks the advice and counsel of these associations, realizing that their support is apt to provide significant support for any positions that the High Commission may wish to adopt. The Council of Ministers apparently is less concerned; but this may be the result of the fact that the several ministers are subject to substantial pressures on the national level and do not care to have to go through the same crucible twice.

It would, however, be a mistake to imagine that this influence is primarily a relation between, say, UNICE and the High Commission. Actually the largest part of such influence is exercised on the lower level of the several administrative subdivisions, called "general directorates," of the Commissions. Their organization used to provide for seven such directorates, namely (1) external relations, (2) economy and finance, (3) internal market, (4) competition, (5) social affairs, (6) agriculture, and (7) transport and communications. But since EEC, ECSC, and Euratom have been consolidated into the European Communities (EC), a new organization setup has been created.[24]

It is evident from Figure 4–1 that a representative of one of the associations, for example, UNICE, cannot limit himself to dealing with one of these directorates. It is of very great importance to know where what decisions are being handled. This task is made easier for such a representative by the inclination of the administrators to seek the advice of the interested parties. There is nothing unusual to be observed here; the very same trend has for many years marked the operation of interest groups in the United States, Britain, France, and the Federal Republic, to mention only the most important. Such initiative on the part of EEC officials also has the great advantage for the interest groups that they learn what is "in the air," or rather more precisely what the Commission is considering proposing. Even so, it would be very unwise for such groups to depend upon official initiatives. Continuous and close contacts are vital indeed. It is interesting that these contacts have been free of corruption to date. Neunreither attributes it to the high income, prestige, and corresponding independence of the Eurocrats.[25] For the rest, he stresses the marked differences in the degree of cooperation between directorates and interest groups, and notes that it is closest in agriculture and social policy—again paralleling the situation in the United States for good and sufficient reasons: the minority status of the interests represented by both associations and officials leads to an identification of one with the other.[26] These differences affect to some extent the work of the High Commission. The more popularly based directorates may "play" the interest groups via the national government and parliament and thereby manage to outmaneuver the Commission—again a process familiar on the Washington scene.

As already mentioned, associations like UNICE and COPA

EUROPEAN ECONOMIC COMMUNITY

First phase of the Commission

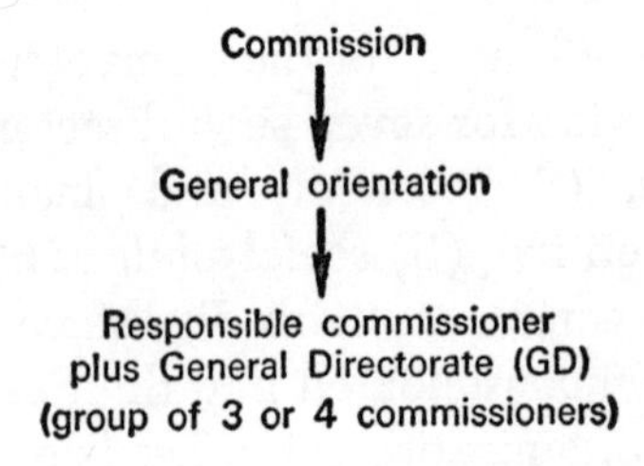

A) *Preliminary work*

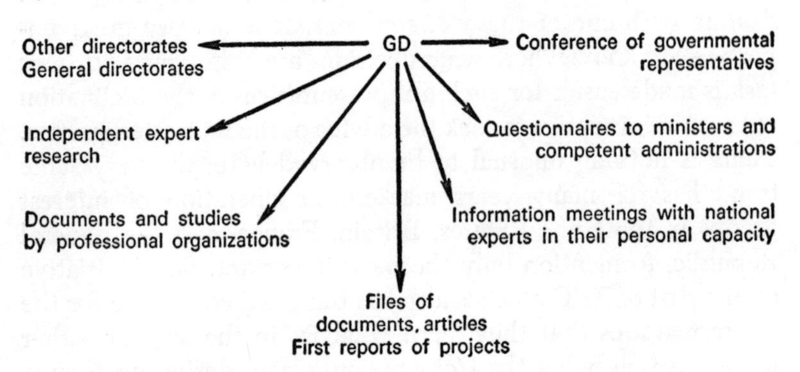

B) *Consultations*

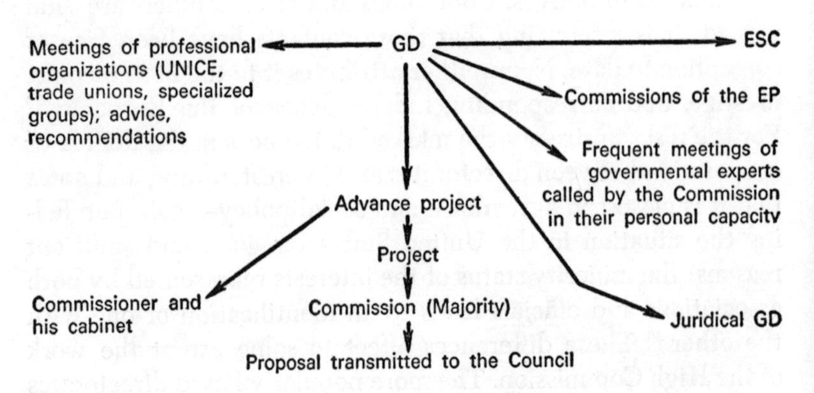

Sources: Treaty basic statutes, proposals and initiatives of the Commission, initiatives of the Council, government of private organizations.

Figure 4–1. European Economic Community–Diagram Illustrating How Basic Decisions Are Made. (After D. Sidjanski, "Pressure Groups and the European Community," *Government and Opposition*, Vol. II, No. 3 [April–July, 1967], p. 401.)

do not, or perhaps it would be more nearly correct to say cannot, maintain very close contact with the Council of Ministers; though their relation with the Committee of Permanent Delegates is pretty good, or at any rate better than it used to be. A good deal of secrecy surrounds the proceedings, and the interest groups have a tough time keeping themselves informed about what is going on. Since propositions of the High Commission are subject to alteration by the Council, and are as a result often changed, the fact that interest groups are practically excluded from participation obliges them to have recourse to their national capitals and parliaments for pressing their position. Thus the procedure favored by the Council reinforces the "confederational" insistence on the predominance of national politics. Even so, it no longer appears accurate to say that "most national interest groups do not seem to perceive European-level umbrella organizations as very effective in attaining their objectives and fear a dilution of their individual goals in the process of bargaining."[27] The crisis of 1965 and the developments since that time have, however, obliged these groups to shift their weight, depending upon the particular situation and the policy their government is pursuing vis-à-vis the Community at the time.

Whereas access to the Council of Ministers, and even their Committee of Permanent Representatives, is accessible largely via the national capitals, almost the obverse is the situation of the interest groups vis-à-vis the European parliament. Here all doors are wide open, but the interest group representatives rarely enter through them. Since the parliament is only a consultative organ, and is furthermore elected by the national parliaments, European interest groups have less reason to try to influence it, and can do so readily via the national parliament. Even so, one might wonder why they do not more fully exploit the opportunities which the parliament's right of initiating proposals and of interrogating members of the Commission would offer to an enterprising interest group representative. Neunreither speaks from personal experience when he deplores this situation.[28] Yet he recognizes that the extent to which particular interests are already represented in the various parliamentary committees makes it less important for them to develop effective contacts.[29] Hearings are unknown, and there exists no discernible tendency to strengthen parliamentary contacts. That might change if the often repeated demand for popular election of the European MP's were accepted, for a popularly elected parliament would contain quite a few members who would not be nearly as much integrated into national parliamentary life as are the present members.

The Common Market regime contains, as remarked above, also an Economic and Social Council. In its Article 193, the Rome Treaty provides that this Council (*Conseil*) "shall consist of representatives of the several groups of economic and social life, more particularly the producers, the farmers, the transport enterprises, the employees, the merchants and the draftsmen, the free professions and the general public." It contains 101 members, proposed by their governments and appointed by the Council of Ministers by unanimous vote; they are, of course, drawn from the several interest groups and therefore do not constitute an independent body, but rather an integrating device through which these groups are brought into continuing contacts and cooperation. Like all such bodies, it has great difficulty in arriving at viable compromises, and functions essentially in an advisory capacity. It is therefore not taken very seriously by the very groups who compose it, for it lacks that capacity for compromise and integration which makes parties and parliaments such crucial cogs in the machinery of parliamentary government. Even so, the very participation through membership produces numerous and continuing contacts between the interest groups and the ESC, divided as it is into three sections: the employers, the employees, and the "mixed" group (including agriculture). It is an estate-type setup, having its conceptual roots in the postfeudal early modern kind of government "by and with estates" (*Ständestaat*), with a considerable appeal to a conservative view, but also to a guild socialist and even a Fascist sort of outlook. In the Europeanization process (and hence also in the federalizing process) it occupies a marginal position.[30]

All of the foregoing goes to show that the activity and the role in the process of informal community formation of economic interest groups (for what has been said above about business groups applies *ceteris paribus* to farm groups, trade unions, and other professional groups) are closely related to the governmental structure of the European Community. Both an integrating and a differentiating potential find their reflection in such groups for the reason that such groups must adapt to the structure of the decision-making apparatus of the community they wish to influence. Hence the apparatus needs to be briefly reviewed here. All decisions must be seen within the context of political forces from which they emerge. Decision, policy, and institution—all partake of this dependence upon the political community. The hot arguments which have divided political scientists for years over which is more important have more recently been superseded by the recognition of their interdependence.[31] Institutions are progressively transformed as a result of decisions continually being made in the pursuit of policies recurrently adopted, such policies constituting in themselves major decisions. When, therefore, the Association for the Development of a European Political Science in November 1966 organized an international colloquium to discuss decision-making in the European organizations, a considerable number of papers straddled the issue and dealt with policies and institutions as well as decision-making as such.[32] Among these papers there was one entitled "Action by Pressure Groups" by Dusan Sidjanski, an English version of which has since appeared.[33] In this paper, the author, after sketching a schema of the pattern of decision-making in the EEC, which is rather formalistic in its approach, develops a rather illuminating diagram showing the activity of interest groups at the national and supranational level (see Figure 4–2). He does not claim, of course, that this diagram fits all conceivable situations, but as-

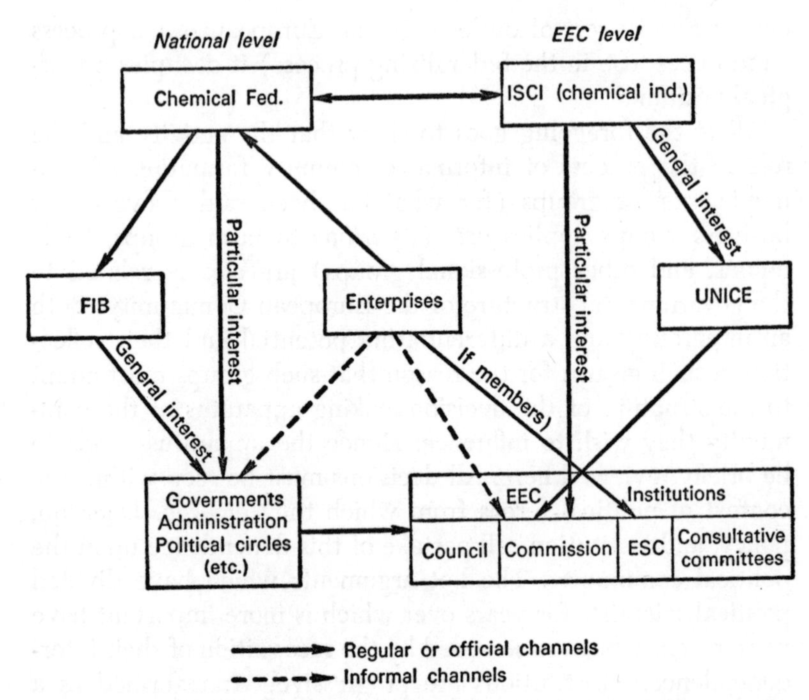

Figure 4–2. Diagram of Action–Groups of Socio-economic Interests in the EEC. (After D. Sidjanski, "Pressure Groups and the European Economic Community," *Government and Opposition,* Vol. II, No. 3 [April–July, 1967], pp. 397–416, at p. 412.)

serts that it is illustrative of a typical situation. Professor Sidjanski offers a number of discriminating comments to the effect that the situation will vary, depending upon whether the interest group is concerned with a special interest of its own membership or with more general interests, such as the antitrust legislation which led to concerted action. Obviously, in either case the interest and position of the chemical industry may coincide, conflict, or be indifferent to the wider concerns of UNICE. The ramifications of these possibilities will appear below (Chapter 5) in the discussion of the 1965/6 crisis. What interests us here is that the origin of a *European* decision may be found in the special concern of a national interest group (as such a decision may originate with an imaginative official on a relatively low level in the hierarchy[34]). As the Europeanization of the business community spreads, the political implications of informal community formation in this sector have a definite channel through which to effectuate any innovative and integrative initiative that may suggest itself to them.

Several years ago a thorough researcher came to the conclusion that "the representation of interest groups in the EEC has in large measure become institutionalized."[35] Besides the Economic and Social Committee, he is referring to the several committees which we have discussed and shall explore in succeeding chapters. Interest groups participate in the decision-making process on all levels and thus are legitimized as major factors in the process of European community formation, strengthening the democratic character of the procedures. At the same time, all these relationships contribute to the gradual extension of a European mentality to the ever-widening circles of the European businessmen.

It would be interesting at this point to illustrate all of the foregoing and to offer a prime example of the political implications of European community formation by analyzing the crisis of the summer of 1965. It was so severe as to mislead even responsible scholars into proclaiming it the end of the EEC. Due to the vigorous action of interest groups, business, agriculture, and workers all pulling in the same direction, the crisis was overcome. But since French agriculture along with German and French industry were the most determined in exploiting the opportunity offered by the presidential elections in France, and since we possess a special study on this aspect of the story, it seemed preferable to deal with the crisis in the next chapter.

5. The Agricultural Community[1]

Farmers, although from an economic viewpoint very much the same as other producers—divided into employers (owners) and employees—do, from a political and sociological standpoint, constitute a very distinct and separate group. The recognition of this fact is manifested in modern states by the existence of a separate government department or ministry and usually a parliamentary committee to deal with agricultural affairs. The EEC has followed suit by setting up a general directorate for agriculture, and the European parliament likewise boasts a committee on agriculture. Furthermore, and significantly, the field of agriculture is the first for which a Common-Market-wide European policy has been worked out, which is briefly sketched below.

In Europe (as well as in Asia, Africa, and Latin America) a large percentage of farmers are called peasants (*paysans, Bauern*), small-scale proprietors whose outlook and way of life are linked to preindustrial and precapitalist forms of economic life and activity. Their way of life has been romanticized, as well as decried. In the evolution of modern communism, the problem of how to assimilate the peasantry to the industrial proletariat has been of great importance and complexity. The soviets, or councils, set up after the 1917 Revolution were called councils of workers and peasants. After efforts at compromise, Russian communism has sought to liquidate the peasant as an independent proprietor; other Communist states, such as Yugoslavia and Poland, have re-established the independent peasant proprietor, and Mao's most distinctive contribution to evolving Communist doctrine has probably been on the subject of the role of the peasant.[2] It is not to be wondered at that the peasant should also have emerged as a major figure in the process of European unification, despite the steady and rapid decline of the agricultural population in all industrial countries. Some of the figures are given in Table 5–1.

TABLE 5–1. AGRICULTURAL EMPLOYMENT IN 1954 AND 1962

Country	1954	1962	Difference in Mill.	Difference in %	Agriculture in Comparison with Total Employment 1954	Agriculture in Comparison with Total Employment 1962
Belgium	322	240	−82	−25.5	9.7	6.9
Federal Republic	4,400	3,378	−1,022	−23.2	19.7	13.5
France	5,195	3,888	−1,307	−25.2	28.0	21.0
Italy	6,843	5,474	−1,369	−20.0	39.9	28.5
Netherlands	498	415	−83	−16.7	12.8	9.5

SOURCE: "Paysans," *Tableaux de l'agriculture Française,* No. 61, August–September (1966).

These figures clearly show a uniform decline in agricultural population, both absolutely and percentagewise. The trend is a world-wide one, and not confined to the Common Market, of course. It is to a quite substantial extent a matter of generations, as Table 5–2 documents.

These figures speak a persuasive language; the loss by death in the most advanced age group, those born before 1904, is not made up from the younger group which actually exhibits as large a loss, or even larger, due to departure from the farm. So rapid a decline in the agricultural population cannot but affect its political influence in an egalitarian mass society. Parties

TABLE 5–2. DECLINE IN AGRICULTURAL POPULATION

Year of Birth	Male in 1954	Male in 1962	Number Who Left	Percentage
1935–39	428,100	205,500	218,900	51
1930–34	385,600	237,600	142,800	37
1925–29	384,200	279,600	63,900	18
1915–24	500,000	431,100	58,800	12
1905–14	664,500	574,500	55,500	8
1890–1904	874,700	582,000	151,500	18
before	335,800	83,800	117,300	35

SOURCE: Michel Gervais, Claude Servolin, and Jean Weill, *Une France sans Paysans* (1965), p. 8.

based upon peasant support have declined with them, and the agricultural population is rapidly becoming an entrenched minority threatened with extinction and battling for survival.

It is only natural, too, that such a group should find a way of cooperating on the European level for the joint representation of its shared interests. At the same time, the clash of competitive market interests would make such cooperation difficult and create numerous conflict situations. There is also the traditional propensity of landowners toward a kind of defensive nationalism. This propensity has made the peasants inclined to support fascism and national socialism. Mussolini considered the peasants his staunchest friends, and Hitler created a kind of agricultural estate to effectuate his policy of blood and soil.[3] This inclination to support fascist movements has often been misinterpreted by making the peasant into a radical opponent of political and social change—against modernization and development. But actually the peasant has often been found on the side of revolutionary movements—in the peasant revolts of the fifteenth and sixteenth centuries this group was the very core of the upheaval. But peasants also supported the French Revolution vigorously, and many French peasants have remained in the Jacobin tradition; in both France and Italy they have even turned to Communism.[4] At the same time—and the Jacobins show it—peasants have shown a recurrent propensity to turn to emotional nationalism; indeed, they have been the main support of such mass nationalism, numerically speaking. Ever since the French Revolution the French farmer has been militant in his patriotism. Agriculturalists have "a more developed attitude of nationalism, in the sense of love of their own country or region, than the bulk of the urban population." This phenomenon has been explained by the fact that a rural population is more homogeneous, that it contains a smaller number of outsiders and foreigners, that it has much less contact with foreign countries and peoples, and finally, that its mobility is much more limited. Since the farmer's entire existence depends on the piece of soil upon which he is usually born and raised and upon which he toils to the end of his days, the "fatherland," or "patrie," becomes central in his thought. And this is still true of him to a much larger extent than of others.

Typically, the farmer has had to this day fewer direct contacts than others with the world outside his own community —a result of the above-described situation being reinforced particularly in France by the great number of small individual holdings and the lack of economic inducement to combine larger holdings. Unlike businessmen and workers, farmers do not encounter their fellows in other lands to any extent, except in the rather limited field of guest workers. As a consequence, the Europeanization has taken place very largely on the level of organized cooperation of interest groups. It is to this topic that we shall next turn before dealing with the crisis of 1965–66 and the farmers' role in it, and to the agricultural policy which in part precipitated it and in part arose from it.

The farmers' organization corresponding to the UNICE for industry is the Committee of Professional Agricultural Organizations of the six countries of the Community (*Commité des Organisations Professionelles Agricoles des Six Pays de la Communauté* [COPA]), which had as a looser frame and antecedent, the European Committee of Agriculturalists (CEA). COPA unites the top associations of the six countries: one each for the Federal Republic and Luxembourg; three each for Belgium,

France, Italy, and the Netherlands. These fourteen associations consider themselves the representatives of European agriculture; they are of course linked to, and in part subdivided into, a good many more specialized bodies.[5] Farmers were encouraged by the EEC itself to form themselves into an effective overall interest group, perhaps more so than any other group except consumers. The Commission has also encouraged the effective coordination of all agricultural interests by means of this organization, and looks toward COPA for presenting the views of the several special interests. Numerous special committees are at work under the aegis of COPA, concerned with the market regulations of agricultural products. Since COPA has thus become the effective voice of agriculture, specialized interests have become somewhat dependent upon its help.[6]

Besides COPA there exists a Committee for the agricultural cooperatives in the six countries (COGECA: *Comité Général de la Coopération Agricole*), which shares the secretariat of COPA. Both pursue related interests in shaping overall agricultural policy and cooperating in its execution. Their vigorous concern accounts at least in part for the fact that the Common Market has gone further in developing a general agricultural policy than in any other field. COPA and its associates are convinced that they have played a vital part in promoting this development by exercising pressure both at Brussels and in the several national capitals. In the process, COPA and its personnel have become more and more European in outlook and behavior. At the same time, on the Commission's side the general directorate of Agriculture under the able and determined leadership of Commissioner S. Mansholt (Netherlands) has had the satisfaction of seeing its CM concept adopted by COPA, COGECA, and a good many of the special interests, even though violent conflict breaks out from time to time. The development of joint committees of the directorate and agricultural interest group representatives might prove very effective in this connection, supported as they would be by both parliament and the Economic and Social Committee (ESC). Up until now there exist only advisory committees, composed of representatives of the appropriate agricultural associations, of which some authorities claim that they represent a "system of contacts *sui generis*."[7] COPA would like to see these committees merged with the administrative committees which unite officials of the several ministries of agriculture for specialized purposes. The student of government may well question the wisdom of such a commingling of private and public interests, and hence side with the Council of Ministers, which has resisted these efforts on the part of COPA and its partners.

What is the internal structure of the agricultural interest group setup? In keeping with its dispersed consistuency, COPA has a general assembly composed of representatives of participating associations, without fixed numbers assigned.[8] The average assembly numbers between 45 and 50 delegates. A presidium composed of one member for each country functions as the assembly executive committee, is responsible to the assembly and is presided over by one of its members chosen by itself. This presidium is gradually gaining predominance because of the heavy work confronting the organization. It meets quite regularly, often with Commissioner Mansholt, but relies upon the general assembly to dramatize major issues and carry their challenge to farm folk throughout the CM area. The elaboration of a European farm policy has provided ample opportunity for such undertakings; so did the crisis of 1965 described below (pp. 106–108).

COPA has, of course, also a substantial secretariat which is increasing gradually as EEC policy in the field of agriculture is becoming a joint one. After the settlement of many basic issues of agricultural policy during the last few years, a large number of administrative questions are arising from day to day, calling for effective participation. In 1965, COPA sponsored 176 meetings of various specialist groups—and even more in 1967. Considering this kind of activity as paradigmatic, one can only agree with Neunreither that the COPA secretariat, like that of UNICE, is understaffed, with the result that much of its work has to be done by the national associations which have much larger staffs. In the case of the Federal Republic, where one all-inclusive association, the German Peasants Union (*Deutscher Bauernbund* [DBV]), speaks for all farmers, such dependence may have hampering effects; but it also means that a much larger number of agricultural interest group functionaries is being Europeanized, i.e., informal community formation is affecting a much larger number of people. In view of the limited amount of direct contact between farmers of the several countries this is rather important. Such impact is reinforced by the financing of COPA; unlike UNICE its resources are contributed in equal shares by the national associations in the four components of the agricultural community, Benelux counting as one, and is estimated as running in the vicinity of $100,000. Since, therefore, the DBV has to vote $25,000, its functionaries will be motivated to familiarize themselves with the activities of COPA, and to watch its performance.

How is consensus achieved under these conditions? Essentially by unanimous decision of the representatives of the constituent groups. In view of the numerous conflicts of interest, the achievement of such consensus is a major task. It is therefore noteworthy that the statutes of COPA provide that "in case the Committee does not arrive at a unanimous agreement (*accord*), it makes public (*fait connaître*) the different positions and all relevant information concerning the different viewpoints." Thus even a majority opinion may in many technical matters become part of the record and influence the policy makers in the EEC.[9] It is this policy which probably helps to bring about unanimous decisions; we badly need further studies, adequately detailed in quantitative terms, to elucidate these processes. But even our general knowledge allows one to conclude that a European orientation and outlook is becoming more and more widespread in the constituent national associations. Neunreither asserts, out of his intimate working acquaintance with these processes, that what accounts for this spreading of a European outlook is that an ever greater number have a certain familiarity with European problems, and are personally acquainted with their opposite numbers from other national associations and all that is humanly involved in these encounters.[10] Just as in industry, the operators of national farmers' associations are learning that it pays to compromise and that the interests of the local group are better served by a timely concession than by stubborn insistence upon the particular interest. It was impressive to read that the responsible leadership of the French farmers informed General de Gaulle when his government pursued a very hard line on the price of wheat, presumably to please his farming constituency, that he was much mistaken if he believed that French farmers did not sympathize with the plight of German farmers, that a certain transition period ought to be conceded to them, and that French farmers under comparable circumstances would certainly make objections similar to those put forward by their German fellow farmers.[11]

We noted in the previous chapter that such an *ad hoc* consensus which has to be rebuilt continually constitutes a rather fragile basis compared to the solid base of national consensus. Even so, as time goes on, and as crisis after crisis is surmounted, recurrent precedents turn into habit and the underlying general consensus gains in strength. Thus in spite of the sharp conflict over special positions on agricultural policy between the French and German agricultural interest groups, the BDV and its three counterparts in France (see pp. 101 ff.), each side adopted or adapted itself to certain positions of the other, for example, arguments for raising the price of certain cereals to bring the French prices closer to the German ones. What is reported below in the discussion of the crisis of 1965–66 is also relevant and provides striking evidence.

It does not seem necessary to repeat here what has been said above (pp. 77 ff.) about the activity of interest groups in their dealings with the Commission, the Council of Ministers, and the parliament. What was described there for UNICE applies to COPA as well, except that, as already noted, there exists a rather especially close contact with Commissioner Mansholt, who is in charge of the agricultural directorate. Hence, the officials of this directorate have no hesitation in submitting to COPA drafts of ordinances, even before they have been submitted to parliament and the Economic and Social Committee. If one scrutinizes with care the detailed reports on what happened to these ordinances, he finds that the evidence points to the conclusion that the European interest group assists the Commission in its work with the Council of Ministers, even when important alterations are made by the latter in the proposals of the former. Thus we find that an ordinance on wine, in 1962, was concerned with precisely those matters demanded by the interest groups: the establishment of a register of viniculture, the reporting of annual crops by vineyardists, the determination of available amounts and the estimating of demand in the community, and a plan for a communitywide regulation of quality wines and their origin. The more far-reaching proposals of the parliament were not accepted, as is often the case;[12] presumably they represent pressures exerted in one of the national parliaments.

Within the context of this organizational structure, the effective cooperation of the Commission, the several national governments, and of COPA and its national constituent bodies has led to the evolution of a common agricultural policy for the EC, as previously mentioned. What is meant by this agricultural policy which today covers about 90 percent of all agricultural production?[13] The member countries of the EC have common problems in the field of agriculture: lack of capital, inadequate mobility of manpower, the problems of size of the production units, and so on. We are told officially that a common agricultural policy has three bases: free trade for agricultural products throughout the community; joint financing of interventions in the market, of modernization, and of export aids; and a common trade policy with outside countries.[14] For most agricultural products a uniform price has been in existence since July 1, 1967. Of these, the three most important plant products were cereals, 10.7 percent, vegetables 7.6 percent, and wine 5.9 percent; the three most important animal products were milk 19.1 percent, beef 14.6 percent, and pork 13 percent. It is expected that gradually these products will be distributed according to the optimal production costs, with France gaining and Germany losing due to soil and weather conditions. After a transition period, national governments will no longer be permitted to grant subsidies, except in accordance with the general rules of the EC concerning competition. How difficult it may at times be to hold this line was seen during the summer of 1968, when due to an exceptional fruit crop, German farmers were not granted subsidies by their government, while French, Dutch, and Italian farmers were able to destroy parts of their crop with the help of the agricultural fund. What is this fund?

The European Fund for Agriculture which spent almost $500 million in 1966–67, devoted about three-fourths of its funds to paying various kinds of subsidies and the rest for agricultural capital investments likely to improve the productivity and efficiency of farming operations. The Fund is expected to dispense $1.5 billion in 1968–69, in conjunction with the extension of a common agricultural policy. Where European prices involve heavy losses for particular members of the Community, the Fund makes payments to equalize these losses. Thus in cereals for which the Council of Ministers fixed prices on wheat, barley, corn, and rye, Germany received 560 million DM (Deutsche Mark) in 1967–68 and is scheduled to receive 374 million in 1968–69; Italy, 260 million in 1967–68 and 176 million in 1968–69; Luxembourg, 5 million and 3 million, respectively. In fixing these prices, the Council proceeded on the assumption that such prices, while being as high as possible for the producer, should avoid undue burdens for the consumer; the wheat price was therefore fixed between the high German and the low French price.

It is a common feature of many of these price-fixings that they constitute compromises for the countries that have varied interests. Thus France has a major interest in cereals, while

Italy and the Netherlands have one in fruits and vegetables. The continuous effort at finding compromises for these conflicts has steady implications for the informal community formation and its political consequences. Thus there is slowly growing among European farmers a sense of common concern for the well-being of agriculture in all the countries of the Common Market. A major test for this growing sense of an overall consensus was offered by the Kennedy Round. The Commission, after it was decided in 1964 to include agricultural products—a major American interest—in these negotiations, prepared "completely novel proposals for the regulation and liberalization of world trade in foodstuffs." With a mandate from the Council of Ministers, the Commission represented the six countries, basing its proposals on the assumption that "in all countries agricultural policy is directed toward the support of agriculture." We cannot here be concerned with the further elaboration of these bargains and their ramifications. What matters is that in this important international sphere the European Community spoke with one voice; unfortunately, the results left much to be desired and were greatly below expectations. A lowering of quite a few tariffs was achieved, but the more revolutionary proposals of the EC, especially the consolidation of various forms of subsidies, were not adopted. As a final point in this brief discussion of the common agricultural policy, mention might be made of the extent to which the European Community is self-supporting. This is largely true (between 85 and 100 percent) except for fats and oils (36.8 percent in 1965–66) and in citrus fruit (47 percent for the same year).[15] The figures show that the European Community is, in this respect, a much more nearly viable economy than was that of its component parts, except possibly France, which suffered, however, from surpluses, for example, in wheat. This self-sufficiency is likely to continue as a major concern of European agricultural policy, along with the protection of its farm population against unfair competition. Most Europeans of the Common Market, but more especially its farmers, are content with these achievements of integration and hence are ready to defend it against all comers. This was dramatically illustrated in the crisis of the summer of 1965 and its aftermath—a story to which we shall now turn.

French farmers played a decisive role both in the precipitation of the crisis and its eventual resolution. In order fully to understand these developments, we must go into greater detail about the French farmer and the European Community.[16] Generally speaking, the French farmer has been favorable to European unification, and increasingly so. But there have been and remain sharp differences between different groups of farmers, depending upon their position in the economy. France is a country of surpluses of production in many farm commodities, such as wheat, wine and chicken, fruits and vegetables. Production in most of these is rising steeply, as French agriculture is undergoing a veritable revolution in modernization. But there are groups that have been disturbed about foreign competition, such as the fruit growers, who worry about Italian farm production in many of their lines. Another major division has been between generations.[17] This generation conflict has found expression in the organizing of a major special interest group, the National Center of Young Farmers (CNJA), who have espoused a markedly more progressive course of development while sharing the general pro-European views and attitudes of the older generation as organized in the *Fédération Nationale des Syndicats d'Exploitants Agricoles* (FNSEA). The latter includes many associations, specialized either according to product line or regionally and locally. It is supported by the Chambers of Agriculture, semi-official bodies committed to a conventional approach to the problems of the farmer. The assembly of their presidents, along with FNSEA and the overall organization of the cooperatives (*Confédération Nationale de la Coopération, Mutualité et Crédit Agricole* [CNCMCA]), constitute the basis of the French participation in COPA.

FNSEA has been supporting the general idea of European unification since the beginning, but in the course of time a rather vague general support of the idea has been replaced by a detailed concern with specific policy issues.[18] Indeed, in response to the crisis of 1965, the FNSEA became militant, as will be documented below. Since the national government under de Gaulle has often been impervious to their pressure, they have found EEC and the Commission a welcome ally to their concerns. Their view that France's problems of agricultural surpluses can be solved only within the wider European market is sound, especially if agricultural methods and proprietary relations are to be maintained and the farm income is to be raised. A crucial factor in this setting is the relatively low price of French agricultural products, which the government of the Fifth Republic has been trying to hold in connection with its general policy of price stabilization. French farmers were bound to gain by an adaptation of the French to the German and other European price structure, especially in grains, sugar beets, and wine. Hence economic advantage has tended to reinforce ideological inclination. Also, the long-standing distrust of French farmers of a strong government became involved in farmers' attitudes on European unification. At first they feared that the Common Market might be a remote technocratic colossus, but experience taught them that the High Commission at Brussels was considerably more cooperative than the national government at Paris; the fact that Pisani, the French Minister of Agriculture in the first years of the Fifth Republic, was an ardent partisan of European integration helped to foster this change of outlook. The policy objectives of the more conservative elements of French agriculture were price increases in line with the harmonization of agricultural prices for the Community, protection against outside competition, and maintenance of traditional forms of agriculture. The agricultural policy developed by the EEC has actually been along these lines and has culminated in the marked emphasis upon price protection and income guarantees through the Fund described above (FEOGA). Hence, it is not surprising that the majority of French farmers, represented by FNSEA, has become highly favorable to the Common Market.

The younger farmers, originally quite dubious about European integration because of their belief in the need for a well-integrated, carefully planned policy of modernization for French agriculture, have gradually come around to a much more positive viewpoint since the EEC has been developing a common agricultural policy.[19] In keeping with their critical and progressive outlook, CNJA thought that the crisis of 1965 could be turned to good account, because it made it possible "to make policies more precise, and to revise the goals and the methods employed in building Europe."[20] A detailed examination of the evolution of their views leads one to the conclusion that their position has gradually come closer to that of the more traditional elements. They favor Europe because it constitutes an adequate market for French agriculture. Yet for the younger generation this implies a transformation of traditional French agriculture, unsuited as it was for an industrial society. Especially through FEOGA, radical changes can be effectuated, they believe, in agricultural methods and therefore in the entire structure of French agriculture. Without going into specifics, it is clear that such a policy will appeal especially in areas in which methods have lagged behind the revolutionary transformations achieved elsewhere, both in Europe and overseas.

A much smaller dissident group is organized in the movement for the defense of family farms (*Mouvement de Défense des Exploitations Familiales* [MODEF]). This conservative-sounding label is deceptive; for this movement is closely associated with the Communist party and hence hostile to the integration of Europe. Curiously enough, the MODEF proposes to defend the existing system of agriculture in France, with its small properties; it believes this can be achieved only by massive governmental intervention and support, and it expects such support only from a national government committed to these goals. Most recently, however, the MODEF has, like the Communist-led trade unions (see below, Chapter 7) taken a more positive line, and has commenced to interest itself in European institutions. How else could it hope to influence the common agricultural policy?[21]

It would lead too far afield to analyze the different positions even of the main lines of agricultural production. Tavernier and Delorme have given us a very convincing panorama of their several positions and policy lines. They are able to show that in spite of the sharp differences between, for example, wheat farmers and corn farmers—the latter being much more sceptical because of the lack of help they have received—and between cattle and chicken raisers, and so forth, the general trend has been toward increasing acceptance and cooperation. What logic would suggest is borne out by empirical inquiry, namely that those farm groups most in need of expanding markets outside France—the producers of wheat and other grains, sugar beets, wine, and milk—were the first to perceive the very considerable advantages Europe offered to the French farmers. But others followed, as they realized that it would be possible to influence European agricultural policy and thus to share in the benefits to be derived from such integration. Fruit and vegetable farmers came to understand that FEOGA and the agricultural policy underlying its operations would for the first time secure an overall policy to cope with the marketing problems in their fields.

Studies of the attitudes of French farmers[22] must be seen against this background of organizations and interests. They provide the centers of information and propaganda as well as the identification of the vital concerns of French farmers. The polls conducted by the French Institute of Public Opinion show that there has been a steady evolution of French farm opinion, with some ups and downs of course, but becoming more explicit in support of the Common Market. At the same time they also disclose a continuing lack of information and a consequent absence of opinion on the part of many farmers. Two polls taken in 1965 (unfortunately based on rather broad and vague queries) produced roughly similar results. The French Institute of Public Opinion (IFOP) found that 33 percent of French farmers were favorable to European federation, 27 percent were for preserving national sovereignty, and 40 percent had no opinion (see Figure 5–1). A better formulated in-

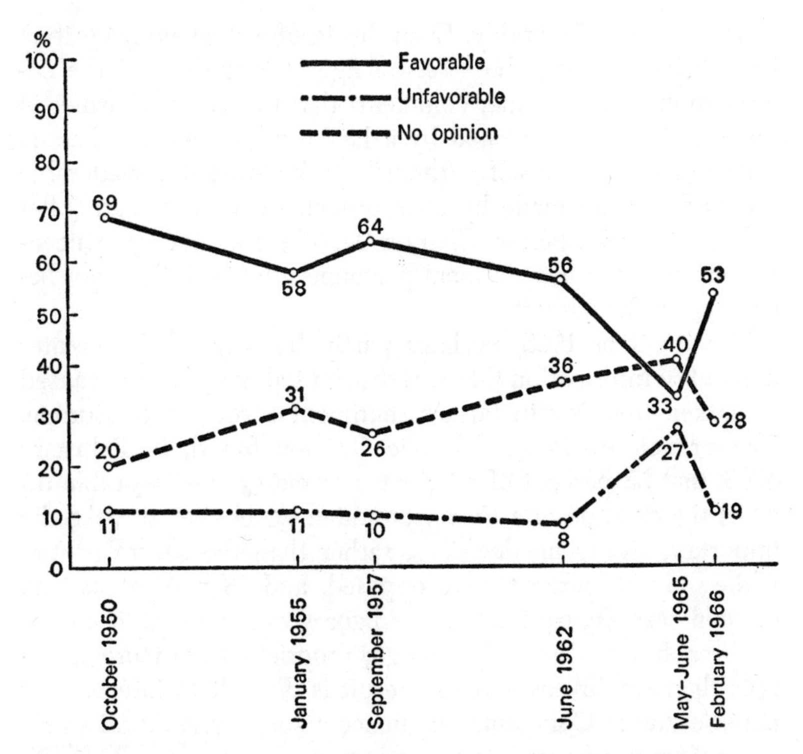

Figure 5–1. (Adapted from *Sondages*. Polls were conducted by the Institute of French Public Opinion [IFOP].)

quiry among young farmers[23] broke down the question into three alternatives of a more practical sort: questionnaires asked if the Common Market meant "an improvement, or an aggravation of the farmer's situation, or no change," and the answers in France were as follows: 37 percent thought the Common Market meant an improvement, 12.8 percent that it meant an aggravation, and 16.3 percent thought it meant no change; 33.1 percent had no opinion on the question. This shows that of those who had an opinion, 56.5 percent considered it favorably, and only 19.1 percent unfavorably. (The comparative figures for Germany are 36.1, 24.3, 9.2, and 30.4 percent, respectively; in other words, the major difference is that almost 35 percent considered it unfavorably. Even this is, of course, no majority.) The striking thing in both sets of figures is the size of the no-opinion group. Tavernier comments that the average farmer in his isolation and burdened by a heavy work schedule has no time to concern himself with such problems. Yet considerable efforts are being made by farm organizations to spread fuller information (see below, Chapter 9). These efforts are concentrated upon the associational personnel, but in crisis they become more far-flung.[24]

The crisis of 1965, perhaps partly because of the greater amount of information that was distributed in its course, caused a marked upswing in farmer sentiment favorable to Europe. The French Institute of Public Opinion found, in February 1966, that 53 percent of all French farmers were favorable toward the creation of a European union which would make the important European decisions, rather than the several states, while only 19 percent were opposed, and 28 percent had no opinion (see Figure 5–2). These figures were close to those for all Frenchmen. Curiously enough, proprietors are more favorable than employees, but this result is difficult to interpret. It may be due to Communist influence among agricultural workers; unfortunately, no attempt was made to determine the party affiliation of those questioned. SOFRES also made a poll in October 1965. It showed 46 percent of the farmers favorable and 27 percent unfavorable, while 27 percent had no clear opinion (among farm women more were favorable and fewer unfavorable, which may again be traceable to divergent political influences, including the church). In any case, the drop in no opinion is roughly the same as that found by IFOP.

After this brief attempt at highlighting the organizational and attitudinal situation of the French farmer, we now return to the specific test that was provided by the crisis of 1965.[25] This crisis broke out during the night, from June 30 to July 1, 1965, in the midst of one of those marathon sessions which have characterized EEC negotiations, especially in the agricultural policy field. The Council of Ministers was considering proposals

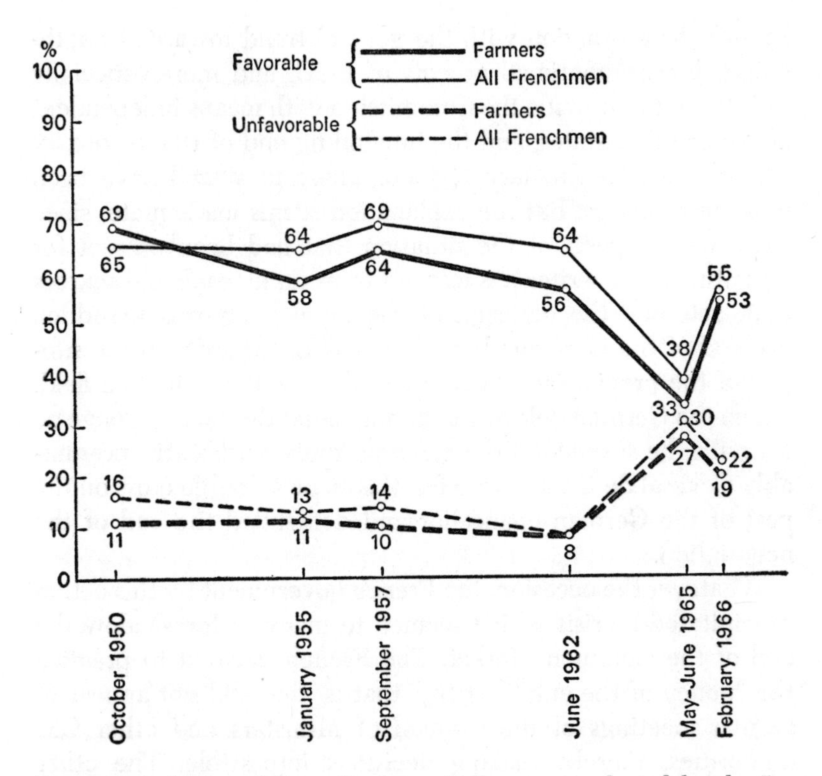

Figure 5–2. (Adapted from *Sondages*. Polls were conducted by the Institute of French Public Opinion [IFOP].)

of the Commission for the financing of agrarian subventions and credits to the end of 1969. The Commission had introduced the issue of what to do about the distribution of customs revenues after the Customs Union came into effect on July 1, 1968 (a still unsolved problem). It had suggested that the customs duties on farm commodities imported into the Common Market be placed at the disposal of the FEOGA. About midnight, the French foreign minister, Couve de Murville, broke off the meeting with the statement that the partners had shown a lack of readiness to reach agreement and there was no sense in continuing the discussion. It is generally believed that this action was due to

French dissatisfaction with the general trend toward strengthening the supranational aspects of EEC, and more especially the attempt to provide the Commission with means independent of the member-states, and the impending end of the unanimity rule planned for January 1, 1966. These may well have been important factors, but the explanation seems inadequate, since these were aspects of the situation that had been present for some time. The writer has learned from unimpeachable sources that, actually, the occasion of the breakdown was a sudden reversal of the German chancellor, Dr. L. Erhardt, on the subject of the previously agreed-upon plans in the industrial field. When the German delegate communicated this fact to Couve de Murville, he suspended the meeting, spoke with Paris, presumably General de Gaulle, who felt this to be a double cross on the part of the German chancellor and demanded the end of the negotiation.

Whatever the occasion, the French government by this action precipitated a crisis which seemed to many to foreshadow the end of the Common Market. The French decided to practice the "policy of the empty chair," that is, they did not appear at regular meetings of the Council of Ministers and other CM authorities, thereby making decisions impossible. The other governments thereupon adopted a policy of compromise, with the Commission submitting altered proposals as soon as July 22. But it is doubtful that these efforts could have succeeded, had there not immediately occurred a vigorous reaction and eventual campaign of the economic interest groups against this threat to the Common Market and against the French government. De Gaulle at first sought to escalate the conflict, through a press conference on September 9, 1965, and a speech by Couve de Murville before the National Assembly on October 20. Both of these actions were related to the impending French presidential elections, to be held in November (1965). The results showed that de Gaulle and his ministers had miscalculated French opinion, especially that of the farmers. The General failed to win re-election, and as a result a sharp change in policy was effectuated which brought the French government back into the EEC as a full participant. Eventually a partial resolution of the agricultural policy problem was found and further progress on other fronts, though considerably slowed down, has since been made.

What was the role of the interest groups and more especially French agriculture which, in this writer's view, played the decisive role? A first reaction of COPA was to the effect that European farmers consider themselves firmly committed to the Common Market and the Treaty of Rome. Early in September, COPA produced a lengthy memorandum in which it was argued that the crisis endangered the agricultural policy vital for European farmers. The memorandum was not, in Neunreither's opinion, a vigorous defense of the Commission's proposals, but that seems natural enough, since it would have meant weeping over spilled milk. Very similar reactions, and perhaps even more vigorous, came from UNICE which, in a meeting of its council of October 7, 1965, pointed out that European businessmen had proceeded and planned on the basis of the EEC and that any uncertainty about its continuance would endanger the transformations which international competition (Kennedy Round) made necessary. Similar positions were adopted by the Chambers of Commerce and Industry, and so on. Earlier, business, agriculture, and labor had even united to protest and to demand the continuance of the European Communities (July 16—Brussels).

But even more important than these positions adopted by the European federated interest groups were the actions adopted by their national constituents and more especially by French agriculture. Both businessmen and farmers in France turned to the public with vigorous statements, among which the most emphatic was one prepared by FNSEA. This powerful body had decided in September 1965 to "organize an information campaign to explain to their constituent bodies the reasons for the crisis."[26] The Federation, considering itself the representative of all French farmers in this matter, wanted to prove the responsibility of the French government for the abrupt (*brutal*) stop of the negotiations and to bring pressure to force a change of position.

In mid-October there appeared on the initiative of FNSEA and the other six leading French farm organizations, a "white paper" dealing with European agricultural policy and sharply critical of de Gaulle's policy.[27] Seventy-seven thousand copies were distributed and discussed all over the country in farmers' meetings, newspapers, and periodicals during the final weeks of the electoral campaign. An unconfirmed report had it that this pamphlet originally ended with an open appeal to the farmers of France not to vote for de Gaulle, and that Pompidou persuaded the farm leaders with the greatest difficulty to omit this conclusion. The language of the broadside was so explicit, however, that the conclusion was pretty obvious. It declared that the crisis precipitated by the French intransigeance is "*un ferment de dissociation et un germe de nationalisme.*" The farmers are radically opposed to such trends. They pronounce themselves unwilling to accept any weakening of the provisions of the Treaty of Rome and demand that it be maintained and implemented, including its provisions on voting by majority, on the role of the Commission, and on its other institutions. The "white paper" recites all the advantages which French agriculture had derived from the Common Market and refutes the notion that these could be secured by alternative means. It declares that French farmers, more clearly than others, face up to the political implications. This position is so central to our basic problem that the key passage must be cited here.

Ce qui est en cause dans la crise actuelle, ce n'est pas seulement l'Europe économique, mais aussi l'avenir de l'Europe politique. La réalisation du Marché Commun appelle à la création ultérieure d'une Europe politique unie, qui demeure l'aspiration des peuples européens. La France a apposé sa signature au Traité de Rome, elle ne peut la renier. Certes, elle a le droit de discuter des modalités d'une construction qui doit se réaliser dans un esprit communautaire, mais, pour discuter, il faut reprendre le dialogue sans préalable contraire au Traité de Rome. Les agriculteurs le demandent avec insistance.[28]

The political implications of the formation of a European community of farmers could not be put more straightforwardly. In the opinion of informed observers, "this document had probably a great echo among farmers." It is obvious that all the opponents of the President picked it up, stressed its importance in public meetings and broadcasts, and that as a result "in the smallest village, at least one farmer knew of the criticisms directed by farm groups against the European agricultural policy of the French government." Few would disagree with the judgment that French farmers, thus engaged in opposition to the government's policy, "contributed to the President's defeat," especially since FNSEA's regular publication *L'Information Agricole* published a special issue of 900,000 copies containing a summary of these criticisms. Perhaps the impact would not have been as great, had it not paralleled the position of industry and businessmen generally who, in their publications and manifestations, stressed that French exports to its community partners had risen even more dramatically between 1958 and 1964 than had industrial exports. To give the figures used: French industrial exports to the EC had risen 195 percent, while exports to other countries rose only 40 percent; similarly French agricultural exports to the EC countries rose 253 percent, to others only 53 percent. It was also felt in these quarters that merely a customs union, without an economic union, was a very dangerous prospect, especially since it made it virtually impossible for French business to decide what investments to make both in France and in other countries. The publication *L'Usine Nouvelle* is very interesting and detailed on this score (September 2, 1965).

French farm interests adopted a particularly impressive policy in an effort to force the hand of the French government, which they were enabled to do because a new five-year plan was being worked out at that time in the *Commissariat du Plan.*

They decided not to participate in the technical preparations of the new plan as long as the French government had not "clarified" its position on European policy.[29] In the *Journal Officiel* one finds a report about the deliberations of the French Economic and Social Council concerning the *Plan* in which the general reporter of the Council points out that the proposed plan rests upon the assumption that the Common Market is being realized and that therefore it cannot be accepted that its development remains blocked. More particularly, the agricultural section of the Council offered a highly critical analysis of the government's position and its effect upon the needed agricultural policy. The Council concluded that a plan could be formulated, analyzed, and adopted only when and after the uncertainties concerning the EEC had been eliminated.[30]

The voice of French farmers, reinforced by the position of industry throughout the Common Market, was sharply contradicted only by that of the German farmers, and more particularly of its vociferous president, E. Rehwinkel. Having been highly critical of the line of the EEC's agricultural policy that the German government had at last compromised on, the German farmers seized upon the crisis to proclaim loudly their general conviction that a revision of the Treaty of Rome was "both urgent and irremissible." They agreed with de Gaulle that the Commission's rights and competencies were far too great, that the Council of Ministers ought to be given the right of initiative, and that majority decisions would be premature. In short, in the name of German national interest, they adopted the French government's position. This paradoxical constellation is itself a striking indication of how far Europeanization of political attitudes has already progressed as a result of the impact of European policies and procedures. It is not surprising that German farmers at the same time reminded the French government that the crisis had been precipitated by its aggressive pursuit of a policy advantageous only to French agriculture, especially in the matter of grain prices (December, 1964). Feeling that their government had sold them down the river in the interests of European integration, they nonetheless paradoxically wanted to strengthen the role of the national government in the process of European integration.

In sum, the conclusion which follows pretty clearly from the data and developments described and analyzed in this chapter is that farmers and peasants have begun to shift their soil-bound allegiance from the national to the European land. For the German and Italian peasants this change is somewhat less of a strain than for the French or the Dutch, because the Germans and Italians had to undergo a similar shift of allegiance from a principality—such as Bavaria or Hanover, for example, and Tuscany or the Piedmont—to a unified Germany and a unified Italy. Indeed, the foreseeably much more federalistic structure of an integrated Europe is bound to leave much greater leeway for regional and national loyalties than did the earlier integrations. It is extraordinary that the French farmers were the ones who most clearly demonstrated the political implications of this transformed community. The rationale of the pocketbook made the French peasant leaders perceive that Europe has become the *patrie des patries*. At the same time, we should recognize that what Banfield has identified as amoral familism as the core of peasant behavior in Southern Italy[31] shapes to a considerable extent the attitudes of farmers throughout the Common Market; the ego- and family-centricity of the French and German peasant are proverbial in their lands. It is the very fact of concrete benefits to the individual landowner-farmer which the Common Market has been able to provide which has mobilized the European farmer in support of the emergent Europe, in spite of his traditional allegiance to the *patrie*.

6. The Labor Community in the Factory and the Guest Worker[1]

In a rapidly developing and urbanizing Europe, which the steadily declining farm population highlights, the industrial worker constitutes an ever larger part of the human community. This is not the place to go into the complex problem of why such migrations occur. It has been studied in various contexts. Nor can we deal with the general question of what happens to them after they reach their new habitat.[2] The migration overseas apart, during the years since World War II great numbers of Italian, Spanish, Portuguese, Greek, Yugoslav, Turkish, and North African (Arab) people have migrated to Switzerland, Germany, France, Belgium and elsewhere looking for work and finding it. It is not too much to say that they have contributed considerably to the development of a single, viable European labor market; they have also contributed markedly to the economic growth of Europe.[3] Relatively little is known about the political outlook of all these migrants, and more especially those moving within the Common Market.[4] That at least some of them would come to develop a sense of European community and would become interested in its growth and promotion stands to reason. How much, especially in view of Communist opposition, is inadequately known and hard to assess. Hence it is perhaps more important how workers feel about integration, especially since industrial labor is often very hard hit by the forward movement of industrialization. For the location of industry is increasingly affected by the Common Market as particular lines of production are concentrated where conditions are most favorable for the market as a whole.[5] A whole lot of activities have been initiated by the Common Market authorities to deal with these problems; they form a major part of the work of the general directorate of social relations. In its Annual Report for 1967, the Commission states that it "has not only fulfilled the task allotted to it by the Treaty as regards free movement of workers, the European Social Fund and vocational training, but has continued its researches into the multiple aspects of social conditions of the Community."[6] It is obvious that these undertakings, as well as the linkages between particular enterprises dealt with in Chapter 3, present the European worker with novel and challenging tasks. In this chapter the implications of the direct contact between workers of different European countries will be taken up, while the activities of their unions and associations will be the topic of the next chapter. In dealing with the direct contact between workers we shall first consider the problems of the "guest worker," as he is still called—though many of these mobile workers are no longer "guests" but have become reasonably permanent in their new places of work—and thereafter the kind of situation created when French and German business firms establish more or less close-knit cooperative relations, including the actual merger of two enterprises.

The free movement of workers and other professionals has been an important and, perhaps, in some ways a key feature of the Common Market. It is explicitly and firmly provided for in the Treaty, Article 59, which says: "Restrictions on the free supply of services within the Community shall be progressively abolished."[7] These provisions were implemented by a succession of regulations[8] and have profoundly affected the life of workers throughout the Common Market territory. The new regulations were made final on July 29, 1968, by decision of the Council. The principal innovations were as follows: (1) In employment, member states may no longer give their nationals preference over workers from other countries. The same conditions apply to all workers no matter where they come from. (2) Community workers, regardless of nationality, can vote for and be elected to bodies representing workers in an enterprise. (3) Work permits for workers from other member states are abolished. (4) The right of residence is recognized for workers of one country working in another. They must be granted residence permits. (5) The rights of workers who wish to bring members of their family to live with them have been extended. (6) The machinery for matching labor supply and demand has been improved. (7) Employment agencies will submit applications from foreign European Community workers to prospective employers, as they submit those of native workers. (8) A special procedure has been established for coping with regional or professional oversupply. It will be seen from these regulations that, at least in law, any worker within the European Community, no matter where he resides, has the right to work in any country of the Community, go there to look for work, and to work under the same conditions as workers who are nationals.[9]

Since the movement of workers from France to Germany and vice versa has been very limited, the Italian workers will be dealt with as well as the French workers in Germany; the two bodies of data and analysis give a reasonably adequate picture of this side of European community formation and some significant hints as to its political implications.[10] The most recent Regulation abolishes, as we just saw, "once and for all" any priority for native workers in access to employment. It is a tough proposition for labor to live with when unemployment begins to rise in a particular nation, as happened in the recent recession of 1966/67 in Germany. During that period a substantially larger number of "foreign" workers lost their jobs than natives, and it is difficult to see how any regulation can cope with such a propensity on the part of native employers—short of complete manpower control incompatible with a free market economy, even if qualified as "social." The provision of equality of treatment in the matter of social security benefits and taxes is easier to regulate than to enforce, as are the new provisions for a foreign worker's participation in representative factory councils and similar representative bodies.[11] In a special report (1967) on the free movement of workers and on labor markets in the Common Market area, the Commission noted that the trend toward increasing demand for foreign workers was declining. Whether this was a temporary or a permanent reversal remains to be seen.[12]

The migration of Italian workers into France and Germany (as well as Switzerland and other countries) antedates the establishment of the Common Market by many years. But migration subjected the guest worker to many iniquities, and these are now on the way out, as far as the Common Market is concerned. For example, the humanly crucial problem of the admission of a worker's family has been regulated so as to give him complete freedom in the matter, whereas formerly the regulation stipulated that he had to have adequate housing before his family could be admitted. (In Switzerland families have been barred even in the case of men who have been working in the country for a number of years.) It is evident that particularly in view of the large families of Italians such a regulation is bound to create very serious problems of schooling, sanitation and so forth in the communities to which such workers come in substantial numbers. Under modern conditions of industrial employment it is particularly important that social security provisions become harmonized within the Common Market and that, more particularly, workers from one country are entitled to the unemployment and old age protection in another in which they are employed and have been working for a reasonable period of time. As will be shown below, these matters constitute an important factor in the minds of workers when they decide to move (p. 144). Passigli, in the conclusions to his detailed study, has advanced the hypothesis that as a result of these rather different conditions one is entitled clearly to distinguish this "new European migration" from the traditional forms of migration, and that it manifests itself in a different attitude toward the host country and its citizens: the "new migrant" adopts a more positive attitude and is inclined toward adapting himself to the host society. Indeed, he goes so far as to apply to these migrants a number of generalizations that were first formulated concerning internal migration from rural to urban areas.[13] There is found increasingly among these migrants an anticipation that they will be accepted in the host society and that the "cultural distance" between the migrants and their fellow workers is diminishing. In this connection their political attitude and leaning toward communism, previously attributed to their migration abroad, is shown to be not at all the result of such migration, but due to the transfer from a rural to an industrial environment, to the greater organizational activity of the Communist party both in the native and the host country and so on.

In this connection, Passigli has analyzed a mass of electoral statistics comparing different regions with each other, which enabled him to show that the new European migration is probably not nearly as exclusively from the south of Italy as had previously been believed—and never was, except in the case of migration to the United States. (See Table 6–1.) And furthermore, he could show that the provinces with the greatest migration are not the provinces with the strongest Communist electorate.[14] Rather, where the Communist party is already strong, it manages to strengthen itself further with the help of the migrants.[15] Even so, where the Communist party is particularly strong, it has a greater vote in the districts with low rather than high emigration. All this does not seem surprising if both emigration and voting Communist are seen as expressions of a break with the native culture, as they provide alternative courses of escape and opposition. Negatively, then, one can conclude that migration does not reduce thoughts and feelings favorable to European integration, such as a Communist vote

TABLE 6–1

Average Expatriated 1961–63 ‰ resident population		Average Repatriated 1961–63 ‰ resident population		Average Settled 1961–63 ‰ resident population	
Lecce	47.8	Lecce	35.3	Avellino	18.5
Avellino	41.2	Belluno	32.3	Campobasso	15.2
Belluno	35.3	Sondrio	28.3	Benevento	14.8
Sondrio	33.0	Avellino	22.7	Lecce	12.5
Campobasso	32.6	Potenza	18.2	Cosenza	11.1
Benevento	31.1	Campobasso	17.4	Potenza	10.5
Potenza	28.7	Benevento	16.3	Chieti	10.1
Chieti	24.5	Chieti	14.4	Enna	9.6
Teramo	18.6	Udine	12.6	Agrigento	9.2
Cosenza	18.5	Pesaro Urbino	11.6	Matera	8.6
Catanzaro	18.2	Teramo	11.3	Frosinone	8.3
Foggia	17.7	Caserta	10.2	Catanzaro	8.1
Caserta	17.1	Catanzaro	10.1	Foggia	7.8
Matera	16.9	Foggia	9.9	Reggio Calabria	7.4
L'Aquila	15.5	Val d'Aosta	8.8	Teramo	7.3
Salerno	15.0	Salerno	8.7	L'Aquila	7.0
Udine	14.5	L'Aquila	8.5	Caserta	6.9
Enna	13.9	Matera	8.3	Salerno	6.3
Pesaro Urbino	13.1	Cosenza	7.4	Caltanissetta	6.3
Frosinone	13.1	Treviso	7.0	Latina	5.5
Agrigento	13.1	Bari	6.4	Pescara	5.2
Latina	11.5	Siracusa	6.2	Bari	4.7
Bari	11.1	Latina	6.0	Sondrio	4.7
Pescara	10.7	Trapani	5.6	Messina	4.4
Reggio Calabria	10.6	Pescara	5.5	Belluno	3.1
Caltanissetta	10.1	Frosinone	4.8	Siracusa	3.0
Val d'Aosta	9.6	Ragusa	4.5	*ITALIA*	2.2
Siracusa	9.2	*ITALIA*	*4.3*	Ragusa	2.2
Treviso	8.5	Enna	4.3	Udine	1.9
Messina	6.9	Agrigento	3.9	Pesaro Urbino	1.5
Trapani	6.8	Caltanissetta	3.8	Treviso	1.5
Ragusa	6.7	Messina	3.5	Trapani	1.2
ITALIA	*6.5*	Reggio Calabria	3.2	Val d'Aosta	0.8

SOURCE: Adapted from Stefano Passigli, *Emigrazione e comportamento politico* (1969), Tav. III, p. 101.

would to some extent betray. Rather, one could say that the Communists would be stronger yet, if there were not such massive migration which syphons off a good many of their potential recruits.

A further fact that stands out in these researches is the generally low level of participation in politics which has been characteristic of Italy and other Mediterranean countries for a long time. It is obvious, therefore, that the growth of a European mentality will be rather slow, and will not find strong expression in political activity for some time to come. Nonetheless it is there. The study we have already referred to in the chapter on farmers reported that of about 7,000 young farmers, many of them farm laborers, only about 3,000 said they followed the news (*information*) about the Common Market, while more than 4,000 said they did not. Interestingly enough, the percentage increases with age, the size of the farm, and the level of education. Such interest is markedly lower among girls. When countries are compared, it appears that only in Germany is the percentage of interested youth appreciably higher.[16] Passigli comments that "a low degree of participation is a common trait of all types of Italian migrants (*movimenti migratori*), but it seems to apply particularly to the new European migration." Contrasting it with the emigration to America, he further remarks that whatever the reasons, Italian workers do not seem to form separate cultural communities and seem little inclined to develop a strong associational life of their own.[17] He believes that it is due to the much greater mobility of Italian workers in the several European countries from one place of employment to another. These workers are also relatively young and without family attachments and at any time ready and able to return to their families in Italy for more or less extensive stays. Actually those with families are frequently able to provide, from the fairly high extra payments they receive under German law for such families, a relatively good life for wife and children in their home town where living costs are relatively low.

This absence of Italian groups as separate communities ("little Italies") would seem to favor their integration into the society of the host country, with consequent reinforcement of their Europeanization. But their ready access to an even temporary return to Italy counteracts their integration, especially since the process involves difficult adaptations and in some respects seems to lead to a complete abandonment of traditionally accepted values and beliefs. This, of course, raises the danger of anomie becoming widespread among such groups.[18]

Italian workers in Germany did not in the past participate to any significant degree in trade union and similar activity, though they are entitled to it, as we have seen above; in this respect they seem to contrast with the French workers analyzed later in this chapter. But such participation is increasing, and the German trade union leadership and membership have become more hospitable than they once were toward such participation. Besides this, there is, of course, the immediate contact with German comrades at the place of work. These contacts are much more close and significant in the small than in the large enterprises where the foreign workers form a special group which is separate and apart. Much of this contrast is related to the length of stay; for generally speaking, workers pass to the small firms from the larger enterprise which, having the necessary personnel for handling all that is involved in the way of contracts and the like, originally brought him. It should be borne in mind that the Italian worker is generally not very much inclined to participate in or feel very loyal toward his trade union. This is part of his rural background. A recent interpreter has put forward some very illuminating observations in this connection about the extent to which Italian workers are inclined to identify themselves with the lower-middle class (*petite bourgeoisie*), which may also be a factor in this situation. The formula which he uses to sum up his overall conclusion concerning the relation between communism and migration is suggestive: "Alors que le mouvement migratoire pousse au Nord, le communisme se *méridionalise;* alors que le pays s'urbanise, le communisme se *ruralise;* alors que l'Italie s'industrialise, le communisme *s'agrarise.*"[19] He also puts this into the formula that while the men go north, the ideology moves south. This, in turn, may be related to Edward Banfield's thesis about the "amoral familism" of Italian culture, with its stress on particular and local values and beliefs.[20] A recent inquiry into the mentality of even the organized Italian worker has disclosed a low level of political information among trade unionists in Italy. To eight questions concerning elementary political data, only 22 percent could give exact answers to more than half, 32 percent did not reply at all or did not answer a single question correctly, and 27 percent answered correctly only to one or two questions. About half of them belonged only nominally to a party. This investigation shows how wary one ought to be about figures concerning party and union membership in Italy.[21] Passigli seems, therefore, justified in stressing that "a low degree of participation is a common trait of all migratory labor, but it seems to apply particularly to the new European migration."[22] And it has had the result that there has been little group formation among the Italian migratory workers. This may facilitate their adaptation and integration into the host societies, but there are so many social-psychological crosscurrents that it is difficult to assess the eventual outcome.[23] Trends and countertrends have in the past been adding up to a rather small participation in German trade union and factory council activity. Whether the new regulations will bring a change remains to be seen. Some indication may be derived from the story of the French workers in Germany and German workers in France.

For the story is a rather different one. It may be a special case, but for the developing European labor community the French guest workers in Germany are probably paradigmatic. Although it may be objected that their small number, namely approximately 20,000,[24] forbids any significant generalization, it is nonetheless true, as the following discussion will show, that the data that have been secured throw significant light upon the problems of this labor community. Although it has not been possible to investigate the German guest workers in France with the same attention to detail, the general impression is that their experiences are similar. Naturally, a good many of these guest workers are working near the French border, which presents some very special problems connected with any border population. It is also important to bear in mind that the relatively high degree of integration of French guest workers in Germany and German guest workers in France, while possibly indicative of future trends among Italian guest workers, is dealt with here largely because of its intrinsic interest for the problems involved in informal Franco-German community formation and the political implications it might have. To some extent, this story also has implications for what happens when French or German workers find themselves joined as employees of a firm which has mixed or transnational management and/or ownership. But let us look first at some basic facts.

The French workers are primarily concentrated in steel and metal industries and in the building trades. Regionally they are primarily found in Rhineland-Palatinate, in the Saar, in Baden-Württemberg, and to some extent in North Rhine-Westphalia. Our study was for that reason primarily concerned with workers in these regions.[25] The data which follow are based upon a sample of 1,279 of these French workers, of which 75 are in mining and energy, 617 in iron and metal production and utilization, 470 in manufacturing industries generally, 27 in the building trades, 29 in commerce, banking and insurance, and 61 in the public service. Of these workers 604 are in the Rhineland-Palatinate and in the Saar, 560 in Baden-Württemberg, and 115 in North Rhine-Westphalia. The sample contains about one-fifth office workers and employees. Among the workers proper 34 percent were unskilled, 40 percent semiskilled, and 26 percent skilled. The average age was 30–31 years. Nearly 50 percent of the workers were employed more than 200 km. from their homes, and nearly 70 percent were employed more than two years in the Federal Republic. These figures relate to the permanently employed workers, whereas the border crossers contain over 70 percent of unskilled workers.

The question now presents itself: why did these French workers come to Germany? It is interesting to discover that no one motivation predominates. For many the chance of earning higher wages was of considerable importance, and nearly 40 percent also praised the German social security legislation. But besides these, quite a few professional and other motivations are found. Twenty-three percent thought that the Federal Republic offered a better chance for professional education. Over 30 percent also mentioned their desire to learn the German language. Not many, but in any case 12 percent, had gone to Germany because of structural or regional unemployment. Almost 10 percent were persons in the middle level of business administration who had been sent by their French concerns into branches and subsidiaries located in the Federal Republic.

Among the personal reasons a fairly large percentage, namely 23 percent, seemed to have resulted from encounters between French and Germans during the war and the French Occupation; and 20 percent had at that or some other time married a German. Better housing also is a factor. To an increasing extent touristic encounters play a role. The desire to avoid service in the Algerian war seems occasionally to have been a factor. This much can be said about the permanent workers. As to the border workers, better wages along with the preferred social security legislation are the primary motivation for 87 percent of those who replied. For the rest the syndrome of motivations seems to be similarly scattered and diversified.

There can be little doubt that the motivation pattern will change as the Common Market community becomes more fully established and social security legislation is adapted to the mobility of labor, as has now been done (see Chapter 5). For the European worker the social security protection and the other forms of equalization, especially for his family, will mean an increasing Europeanization. This need not express itself in making him more knowledgeable about European and other political affairs—though it is hard to believe that some spillover will not occur—but it does mean that these workers will, in their unions and parties, become supporters of European initiatives on the part of the leadership, especially in crisis situations which threaten their jobs.[26]

Clearly, in the labor community the desire to forward the European Community as such will for some time remain a minor factor. But with mobility increasing, the impact upon the mentality of the individual worker will become more diversified and presumably more widespread. Hence the next problem to be considered is that of the degree of integration. What are the factors which forward integration? What are those which prevent it or inhibit it? We have already mentioned the steps which have recently become final, implementing as they do Articles 48 and 49 of the Treaty concerning labor mobility.[27] They are the culmination of innovations which to date do not seem to have produced a marked impact on the workers' minds. The Council of Ministers in 1961 and 1964 decided upon certain specifics concerning this free labor market. In effect the ordinance of May 1, 1964, already adopted the following regulations: (1) Foreigners from other EEC countries have the full right of employment and they retain these rights even when for particular reasons and a limited time there are restrictions, provided they have worked for a certain length of time in the guest country. (2) Wives, children and other close relatives may be brought in and in turn may seek employment. (3) Foreigners within the EEC territory may, after belonging three years to a particular factory or enterprise, participate in workers' representation. These legal provisions did not, of course, create the social reality which might eventually correspond to them; but they provided a framework, as did the Treaty itself. The Treaty itself specified in Article 60 what is to be understood by professional services. It detailed them as (a) activities of an industrial character, (b) activities of a commercial character, (c) artist activities, and (d) activities of the liberal professions. We shall briefly summarize Schierwater's findings concerning Franco-German labor migration under ten different aspects, namely: (1) language; (2) education; (3) place of work; (4) relationship to co-workers; (5) food; (6) chances of advancement; (7) social security legislation; (8) participation; (9) housing; and (10) contacts outside the work.

(1) Turning first to language, it is significant that only 11 percent of the French workers were handicapped by a lack of knowledge of the German language, whereas the remainder thought that even rather rudimentary knowledge gave them adequate contact. This enabled the French workers to avoid many of the difficulties which Italian and other south European workers have encountered.[28]

(2) As far as education is concerned, French workers profit greatly from the relatively great similarity of French and German elementary and high school education. Fifty-three percent of those questioned thought that their education was helping their integration. Some divergencies there are, but these do not appear serious.

(3) The third point is particularly significant, for the integration of a worker is indicated by the way he feels about his place of work. Sixty-eight percent of the French workers found their place of work familiar, and the remaining 32 percent thought it was more the personal relations than the material conditions which appeared unfamiliar. The French workers liked the cleanliness, the high quality of materials and related matters; but they criticized the human atmosphere, more especially their lack of human contact. French workers felt that the relations not only with them, but among German workers themselves, lacked human warmth. It is difficult, however, to be certain of the significance of these observations. They differ between large and small enterprises, and it may often be the transfer from a smaller to a larger plant which actually is the factor involved. These problems present themselves in an aggravated form in the case of workers from south European countries who mostly come from villages and find the adaptation to life in a modern factory very difficult.

(4) Relationships with fellow workers is closely related to the preceding. It appears that the distribution of reactions here is quite normal. About one-fifth, when asked about their colleagues, felt that the relation was very good, while another fifth felt that it was entirely unsatisfactory, and the rest considered

it about average. It is, however, interesting that those who are critical are found largely in 2 among 24 firms. It must therefore be surmised that these are enterprises with unsatisfactory labor relations. One answer was given jointly by eight workers—one semiskilled, three skilled, and four employees—who stated: "Generally speaking, we feel that we are friends rather than mere colleagues. What this means is that our contacts outside our work are even better than inside. We invite each other to dinner and have discussion evenings." Incidentally, this is quite a young group—about 25 years of age. Sixty-five percent of the French workers, when asked whether the relation between German and French workers was particularly good, answered affirmatively and only 18 percent negatively. This is undoubtedly explainable in part by the fact that workers of other nationalities are predominantly unskilled and, as previously mentioned, many were formerly farmers for whom the problems of adaptation are very much greater. Indeed, while for the southern worker the modern factory is the greatest stumbling block, for French and German workers accustomed to industrial life the factory environment is the initial bond. Many German factories maintain a special function of *Sozialbetreuer*, or social worker, who concerns himself with the problem of adaptation of foreign workers; he is, by many who were asked, strongly approved of.[29]

(5) While the food is considered uncustomary by a majority of the French workers, they praise the quality of what is offered in dining halls in the factories, though they regret the lack of bread; but what French workers do not like is that the breaks for lunch are too short and that even these short meals are at times interrupted. Curiously enough, it appears that a good many of those who thus criticized the German luncheon breaks were also critical of their relations with German fellow workers.

(6) When we come to the sixth point—chances of advancement—it must be said that truly free mobility obviously would require that foreign workers have the same opportunities in this respect as the natives. It is interesting that two-thirds of the

French workers felt they had good chances for rising in a factory. The personnel departments did not quite agree. They thought that because of the linguistic handicap it was more nearly one-third who had such chances. On the other hand, nearly 20 percent of these foreign workers felt they were handicapped and indeed discriminated against. Objectively speaking, there seems to be very little discrimination against French workers, for the percentage of those who complain is no larger than that among German workers. It is interesting to recall in this connection that paragraph 9 of the above-mentioned ordinance of the Council of Ministers calls for such equalization of opportunities.

(7) Turning next to social security legislation, 58 percent of the French workers felt that German social security legislation was more advantageous than that prevailing in France. They thought that the German emphasis upon unemployment and old age insurance as against benefits for large families was distinctly to be preferred. Such comments are possible because to date there has been only a beginning of equalization of social security provisions in the countries of the Common Market.[30] It is recognized as a desirable eventual goal, but it was not made a precondition for the establishment of the mobility of labor; while an eventual economic union might necessitate it, a customs union does not. Nonetheless a series of ordinances have undertaken to protect the guest worker increasingly against being disadvantaged. More particularly they provide that what he has earned by way of seniority in one country will be recognized in the other.

(8) The eighth aspect (participation in the factory community) is also rather significant. Thirty-six percent of the French workers participate in union meetings and work. And those French workers who participate do so very vigorously and often more frankly than their German comrades. French workers often appear to their German colleagues as rather radical, but it does not appear that this seriously affects the relations between German and French workers.

(9) Housing constitutes a ninth important factor in the adaptation of a French worker to German life. So much of the well-being of the individual depends upon satisfaction on this point. Public authorities tried hard to assure adequate solution of this problem, *before* the foreign worker arrived; but in view of the housing shortage in Germany this requirement often remained unfulfilled.[31] The French workers in Germany constitute in this respect a favored group. Ninety percent stated that they were satisfied, though 35 percent only after repeated changes. Only a small percentage (11 percent) were (in 1965) living in communal facilities, often quite contentedly, since these provide contact with countrymen in an unfamiliar environment.

(10) Finally, contacts outside the place of work are an important feature. French workers were disappointed on this score. Over half of them reported a complete lack of such outside contacts, usually because of linguistic difficulties. Many of these "isolated" workers are unskilled; often they are those who also complained about the impersonal and cool relationships at the place of work. Everything points to a real divergence in cultural tradition and hence a factor of permanent difficulty. To some extent, this aspect may be aggravated by deep-seated prejudices which we discussed above (Chapter 2). Even so, 32 percent considered their outside contacts quite normal; generally these were the skilled or professionally trained foreign workers who had a common ground upon which to build that kind of relationship. It is clear that workers in this position are apt to develop a European outlook more rapidly. In the case of 13 percent these contacts were actually close to the point of intimacy. It is worth adding that Schierwater's and other studies have shown that the development of outside contacts is also helped by youth and the resulting adventurousness and open-mindedness.

It remains to add a few words concerning the contact between workers in factories that come under joint or foreign control. If a French firm acquires a German factory, or a

German firm a French one, or if two firms unite to control jointly French and German factories, the workers in such plants are bound to establish direct contacts for the purpose of cooperating effectively in dealing with the "common adversary," or as the Germans say, somewhat unctuously, the common "social partner." Such direct contacts are bound to lead to a considerable number of interesting confrontations which tend to have a Europeanizing effect. French workers are generally more inclined toward political action, especially if a large percentage of them are Communists, while German workers are more concerned with wages and working conditions. As a result of direct contacts, both sides show a tendency to "acclimatize" themselves. Unfortunately, the detailed empirical and quantitative studies which have been initiated are not completed at this writing.[32] They tend to confirm, however, a working hypothesis to the effect that the "communism" of French workers is made less doctrinaire, while their concern with wages and working conditions is intensified. We know a specific case where wages in a French plant have increased as much as 50 percent in the course of the last five years, after a plant was acquired by a German firm.[33] We also have had occasion to observe specific instances where the overall political alertness of German workers was increased through contact with their French comrades. The fact that many of the older German workers, having had occasion to observe working conditions in the Soviet Union, could give firsthand reports has had a sobering effect upon their French comrades, and so forth.

However, we need much more detailed exploration of specific cases, based upon interviewing *sur place* and recording of the findings on a comparative basis. Even then, it would remain an open question whether, on balance, the political implications are favorable to European integration or not. The general hostility of workers of Communist orientation toward European integration might be reduced, but these attitudes might also spill over and reduce the favorable disposition of German workers. It is a problem that we already touched upon in discussing the Italian guest workers, but the impact may be considerably stronger in the case of such fusions of actual businesses. Apart from this issue there exists also the possibility that certain antagonisms are hardened rather than softened by closer working contacts. Instances of both these alternatives have come to our attention and need further exploration.

One very interesting, and possibly pathfinding, case occurred in 1967 in the Europe-wide firm of N. V. Phillips' Gloeilampenfabrieken (electronics). On the initiative of the European Committee of the International Metals Federation, a meeting took place at Brussels on March 22, 1967, and another one at Eindhoven, the home office of the firm in the Netherlands, on September 14, 1967. A central concern of the union representatives in these meetings was the extent to which the closing down of factories or branches of production in connection with the European integration of the firm was displacing trained personnel or forcing them to move to other locations.[34] This is, to be sure, a problem which is by no means restricted to Europe. Already on May 23 and 24, 1966, the International Metals Federation (FIOM) had held a meeting in Washington in connection with the displacements of large numbers of French technicians and workers in the sequel of General Electric's having taken over a French firm, Bull Electric. Such radical alterations feed the opposition of the workers at large against international trusts and monopolies. Thus the very argument in favor of European integration on the part of business becomes the most forceful argument against it for organized labor. Only an effective cooperation of workers on the level of individual enterprises is likely to be able to cope with this danger (as is the case, of course, in the United States).

Another very interesting recent case was provided by the link established between Citroen and Fiat. Without going into the complicated problem of this Franco-Italian combine, a typical relationship developing between the workers in such an entrepreneurial complex can be gleaned. Delegates of the French and Italian unions, affiliated with the *Comité Métal* (*Comité des syndicaux métaux des pays du Marché Commun Européen*) and of the International Metals Federation, mentioned above, met at Geneva on November 13, 1968, to discuss the "social" consequences of this combine ("social" meaning here, as usually, "of interest to labor"). They thoroughly explored the particular problems of workers in the two firms, especially the protection of places of work against the effects of economic and technical rationalization. They went into the need for common union initiative for collective bargaining and the general standard of living (*conditions de vie*). Proposals were made for permanent coordination of union activity. A recommendation was agreed upon that the Comité Métal (see above) was to take the necessary steps for organizing an encounter between the affected unions and the management of the two enterprises. Since there are also other firms, notably the German NSU works, involved, FIOM will have to pay special attention to the financial situation, the production and working conditions of this powerful international combine.

In conclusion it seems possible to say that the worker in the factory is being affected by the informal community formation, and that there are noticeable political implications to be observed wherever the data have become available for analysis. These workers constitute, statistically, a minority of the total working force. But as we said at the outset, a common labor market with all its implications is in the process of formation. Not only the workers immediately involved in direct contacts, but many others are being "touched" by these implications. This "radiation" of the implications of community formation is in part due to the fact that many a worker commences to think about the problems of his comrades in other European countries because his own situation forces him to. There is also the radiation resulting from the contacts provided through overall trade union organizations. To this topic we shall next turn.

7. The Trade Union Labor Community[1]

While the links between the working force of particular plants and industries are sporadic and range all the way from close cooperation to only distant contacts, as described in the previous chapter, the bonds which unite the trade unions of the Common Market, and especially the unions of France and Germany, are structured, formally institutionalized, and of considerable operational importance. They are important not only to the unions and workers themselves, but also to the functioning of institutions of the Common Market, as exemplified by the Consultative Committee of the High Authority of the Coal and Steel Community and the Economic and Social Committee (ESC) of the EEC Commission, which has now become the Economic and Social Committee (ESC) of the merged European communities. Something more will be said about these institutions presently. But by way of an introductory summary, M. Levi-Sandri, vice-president of the EC Commission, may be cited; he said to the Board of the German Union of Trade Unions (DGB): "On the occasion of the tenth anniversary of the Treaty of Rome we can say, on looking back upon the road that we have travelled together and in looking forward to goals yet to be achieved, that many expectations and hopes of the workers gradually are becoming a reality: higher standards of living, better employment and greater mobility of labor. The activity and cooperation of the trade unions have proved fruitful, indeed decisive."[2]

Before we enter upon a more detailed discussion of these developments, it is necessary to remind ourselves that the Trade Union movement has always been internationally oriented. From the days when Karl Marx and Friedrich Engels penned the famous conclusion of the Communist Manifesto: "Workers of all the World, Unite! You have nothing to lose but your chains!" to the founding of the Third Internationale,[3] industrial and other workers, conscious of the similarity of their situation in all countries, have been inclined to band together for the representation of and agitation for their joint interests and beliefs. This broadly conceived international community has been badly split since the Revolution of 1917, but there can be little question that a European labor community is a subcommunity of the global community of labor, just as the national labor communities are and have been. This circumstance has produced an equivocal attitude on the part of organized labor toward the European projection of their national interest representation: on the one hand, their traditional internationalism induces them to welcome the weakening of the national state; on the other, the idea of a growing European community feeling has seemed to them at variance with their global outlook.[4] But as the development of the European Community has raised concrete and practical problems, this rather ideological paradox has slowly been yielding to a more pragmatic view of the situation, and to a corresponding commitment to the community that is actually developing.

The situation is further complicated in France and Italy because of the presence of powerful unions directed by Communists. These unions, the *Confédération Générale du Travail* (CGT) and the *Confederazione Generale Italiana del Lavoro* (CGIL), although having a larger membership than the free trade unions in those two countries, have been excluded, by decision of the Council of Ministers, from participation in the work of the Communities, more especially the Consultative Committee of Intersyndicale (CECA) and the Economic and Social Committee of the CEE. They continue to be so excluded from the Economic and Social Committee of the merged European Communities. The Communist-dominated organizations have, of course, been increasingly dissatisfied with this decision. As the beneficial economic effects of the Communities have become evident, the attitude, especially that of the Italian Communists, has changed and repeated demands have been made for their proper representation. It may be argued that since these unions belong to the national labor communities, they do in fact also constitute part of the European labor community. Pietro Nenni has described the task of labor leaders in arguing for a "critical adhesion" to the European community thus: to protect the Common Market against monopolistic groups; to prevent it from functioning for the benefit of the strongest economies and the most powerful interests; to unite Europe within the compass of a pacific policy.[5] The policy of exclusion dates from the time when the task of European unification was primarily seen as part of the struggle against the spread of communism. It may be questioned whether such exclusion is equally justified today, when the governments concerned seek actively to develop their relations with the Communist governments of Eastern Europe. Hence both the French and Italian governments have taken the initiative in breaking the deadlock. The latter nominated two representatives of CGIL for the Economic and Social Committee, and France nominated one representative of the CGT for the Committee on Free Circulation of Labor, and had commenced negotiations for additional representatives. Furthermore, these two Communist-dominated unions have opened a joint bureau at Brussels for the purpose of observing the developments in the Common Market.[6]

Since the trade union situation in the six countries of the Common Market is, as the foregoing suggests, by no means uniform, it may be well to sketch it briefly. In all countries confessional and socialist trade unions compete with each other; in several of them Communist trade unions play an important role. The balance of forces is different in each country. As just noted, in France the old and established General Confederation of Labor (CGT, or *Confédération Générale du Travail*) has since the Second World War been dominated by Communist elements and has led to the splitting off of another union, known as Workers' Force (or *Force Ouvrière*) and generally referred to as FO. Besides these two major unions the Christian trade unions and other elements play a minor role.

The CGT claims 1.3 million members; it is composed of many different kinds of unions and has in recent years been further weakened by the authoritarian trend in French government. The union is highly political in outlook; and though it engages in a certain amount of social and welfare work, it does not achieve anywhere near the practical results which American, English, and German trade unions consider essential for the maintenance of their membership. In consequence, the membership of the CGT is not particularly loyal to the organization and is very lackadaisical in paying its dues. The aforementioned *Force Ouvrière* is an even weaker organization, with a claimed membership of between 0.4 and 0.5 million. Another weak union is the Christian Trade Union, with a membership of about 0.65 million. These organizations also suffer from lack of loyalty of their membership, and consequently from weak finances.

In Germany, by contrast, the largest part of organized labor is united in one organization, the German Union of Trade Unions (*Deutscher Gewerkschaftsbund* [DGB]), which is by all odds the most powerful trade union organization in the Common Market. With the old Communist party outlawed under the constitution of the Federal Republic,[7] open Communist influence among German trade unions is restricted to the German Democratic Republic, which is firmly in the hands of the Communist party and remains outside the Common Market anyway. It remains to be seen how much influence the newly admitted

(1968) Communist party will be able to develop in the trade unions.

The German Union of Trade Unions (DGB) has a total of 6.3 million members and federally unites sixteen industrial unions comprising all the major industries and constituting the real master.[8] In conventional terms the DGB is a confederation rather than a federal union, since the component elements are clearly in control. Besides the DGB there is a Union of Office Workers (*Deutsche Angestelltengewerkschaft* [DAG]) and the Union of German Civil Servants (*Deutscher Beamtenbund* [DBB]). Each of these claims about 600,000 members. So, all told, German trade unions comprise about 7.5 million members. These members are firmly committed to their organization, pay regular and substantial dues, and participate in the democratic process of decision-making in a way very similar to that practiced in England.

The Italian situation is similar to the French in that the workers are split between Communist and Socialist trade unions; but the Italian organizations have a much larger membership, namely 3.5 and 2 million, respectively, and they are able to play a more significant role in the national life. Barnes, in his interesting and detailed study of the Italian Socialist Party (PSI), provides evidence for the continued cooperation between Communists and Socialists in local administration and the trade unions. "Feelings ran strong on these two questions," he reports, "with an extraordinary 91 percent of the leftists agreeing strongly that the PSI must maintain friendship with the Communists in the trade unions regardless of what happened" elsewhere, namely, on the national level.[9]

Without entering into the special situation of the Benelux unions, the overall situation of the trade unions within the Common Market may be summed up by pointing out that there are all told about 15 to 18 million organized workers, of whom about 13 million are members of non-Communist unions in the area of the Common Market. Since the CM contains a working population of about 48 million, they constitute about 25 percent. In view of a total population of 170 million, total union membership in Europe presents a situation roughly similar to that in the United States; but the more firmly entrenched organization of the AFL–CIO gives the unions in the United States a more powerful position than can be claimed by the European unions. Even so, and in spite of the sharply contrasting position and pattern of the national unions, a Europeanwide organization has been erected, joining all the non-Communist trade unions in the International Union of Trade Unions with about 13 million members, including the Christian trade unions with their 3 and 5 million members.

The attitude of the existing trade union organizations at the start of European integration was, in accordance with their different national setups, quite different. In France some of the unions closely associated with the governments of the Fourth Republic were outspokenly in favor of the proposed arrangements under the Treaty of Rome. The larger Communist-dominated CGT was, of course, decidedly opposed. Since the Communists adopted a nationalist posture, which they did particularly effectively in the fight against the European Defense Community,[10] not only the entire CGT, but also the competing FO were more nationalistically inclined in their attitudes than were unions in other European countries. There was a spillover also of the broadly felt apprehension in French industrial circles that foreign, and more particularly German, capital might take over French industries on a large scale, and thereby virtually make French workers dependent upon foreign capitalists. Indeed, in commenting upon the Coal and Steel Community, a publication of the CGT spoke of the High Authority as a "super-monopoly of capitalism." The position of the French unions was also influenced by the generally prevailing protectionist sentiment in French economic thought, which is indeed inclined now to transfer protectionism to the European level. One might mention in passing that in Italy the situation at the outset was quite similar to that in France, especially due to the strong anti-European line taken by the able Communist leader,

Togliatti; but as the favorable effects of European integration began to be felt throughout the Italian economy, all the Italian trade unions, even the Communist ones, shifted to a pro-European position. This will be analyzed in the sequel. In the Benelux countries there was from the beginning a strongly favorable attitude toward European integration.

As previously mentioned, the several national organizations proceeded to develop a Europeanwide organizational frame soon after the Coal and Steel unions founded a permanent committee, with headquarters at Luxembourg, consisting of 21 members. This was in fact initiated by the International Union of Free Trade Unions. Operating through an executive committee of 8 members and a secretariat, the Committee of 21 constituted the first European lobby of the free labor unions. However, here as among the businessmen, the national organizations retained an absolute veto on any action and thereby had the final decision on any position to be taken. This meant, of course, that the operational possibilities of the Committee of 21 as a pressure group were rather restricted.[11] The reason for this rule of unanimity was in part the fear among non-German labor representatives that the German union delegates, largely chosen by the DGB and constituting almost half of the members of the Committee, would dominate the decisions to an extent unacceptable to the French and other unions. But since this fear could have been mitigated by the provision of a qualified majority, it must be presumed that the strong sense of local autonomy in the constituent unions was the primary motivation. The political influence of the Committee of 21 has also not been very great, but it took some significant steps which are expressive of a growing labor community. In 1957 it issued an *aide-mémoire* looking toward the revision of the Schumann Plan. In 1958 it advanced the proposal of a European statute for mine workers. In 1960 it formulated an *aide-mémoire* for dealing with the coal crisis. It has continued since 1958 under the name of Intersyndicale–CECA.

However, by 1958 experience had shown that it would be

desirable to create a new overall European trade union organization with a general assembly and an executive committee. It is called the *Confédération Internationale des Syndicats Libres* (CISL), and has turned out to be a rather complex organization, as might be expected in view of the complexity of the national situations. The General Assembly is constituted by representatives of the six countries,* whereas the Executive Committee is based upon the participation of the chairmen of the national trade unions. This Executive Committee is of special interest. It holds five or six meetings a year, at which, just as in the meetings of the corresponding Committee of Presidents in the UNICE, the main task is the coordination of national trade union policy so that they can work together toward European integration. The process involved is essentially that of bargaining, as might be expected under the circumstances. On the operational level a Permanent Secretariat of this European Union of Trade Unions has been developed, the Secretary being the same man who also served the Committee of 21, Secretary General Harm G. Buiter. He is a key figure in European trade union politics. Of Dutch nationality, he is deeply committed to the building of an integrated Europe and profoundly convinced that the establishment of a Europeanwide labor community is a decisive factor in such a development. He has acted as the general lobbyist before many different bodies of the European Communities, but he has also given a good deal of time and energy to explaining the attitude and point of view of the High Authority and the Commission to the representatives of the national trade unions. He is reported to feel rather strongly that the trade unions must adapt themselves to the growing demands of the European economy; for unless they do so, they will lose their influence within the EC.

Besides the CISL (and the corresponding Federation of

* 16 each for France, Germany and Italy, 9 each from Belgium and the Netherlands, 4 from Luxembourg, and 3 each from ERO (the European regional organization of the International Union of Free Trade Unions), and from the Special Committee for ECSC and Euratom.

Christian Trade Unions [CISC]), an increasing amount of European trade union cooperation has developed in the several fields of industrial activity. A detailed exploration of these activities shows that marked differences exist in different industries.[12] Thus more effective cooperation is found in the metals and automobile industries, as the cases at the end of the previous chapter indicate. But joint action is rare; the cooperation is generally restricted to informing each other about the worker's position in the industry of the other countries. When such information discloses marked differences, this may of course have important results. Late in 1968 the workers of the Belgian Ford works, being less well paid than those in Germany and Britain, staged a successful strike and thereby secured substantial improvements in their wages and working conditions; they were supported in their strike action by workers in Germany and Britain.[13] It is a case which in part belongs to the plant cooperation discussed in the previous chapter.

At present Europeanwide organizations of the several separate unions are inclined, however, to utilize the international secretariat established by the free trade unions rather than to develop offices of their own. In this respect also, therefore, the situation of the trade unions closely resembles that of the business world.

Separate mention should be made of the fact that the Christian trade unions in 1955 created their own Federation of Christian Trade Unions (CISC), also based upon the principle of unanimity and largely dependent upon the national organizations which provide the real strength of the organization. Cooperation between the Christian trade unions and the Free Trade Union Organization has been worked out from time to time, but has not always proved feasible. The difficulties have been particularly great where, under the setup of the EEC, the unions had to agree on a common candidate. It is considered one of the most pressing tasks to strengthen such cooperation.[14]

Altogether, it must be said that the development of the European labor community on the trade union level is lagging behind that of business and industry. This is natural enough in view of the limited amount of community formation in plant and factory. Even so there is beginning to develop, on the basis of the experience of trade union members of the European organizations, a certain amount of spillover into the thinking and policy discussions of the national trade union bodies. Otto Brenner, a top leader of the German trade unions, has in fact called for a complete revamping of the European trade unions and the establishment of a common European trade union organization.[15] One swallow does not make a summer, but in this case there is every indication that this demand by one of the most responsible leaders of European labor is indicative of a growing trend. Quite recently E. Deschamps, the general secretary of the CFDT, said to his national committee (April 21, 1968):

> The cooperation between the European secretariat of CISL and of CISC is developing. Many positions are worked out in common.... But in spite of this positive evolution, economic Europe is being constructed "en dehors du syndicalisme." The necessary transformation of unionism with national preoccupations into a unionism of European proportions is slow.... It is urgent to make up the delay. ... We must now participate with realism in the search for a truly European union structure, European in spirit as well as extent, and we must explore the necessary transfer of a national union sovereignty to a European union structure.[16]

Some months before this, the CCN of the CGT-FO had resolved on December 16–17, 1967:

> The Committee believes that a positive communitarian social policy, essential token of the effective participation of the workers in the building of Europe, must be realized. For this purpose, the CCN emphasizes once again, how imperative it is for the free trade unions of the Six to harmonize their positions and to pursue their own integration in order to achieve a true and powerful European trade union confederation.[17]

As far as the relations of the trade unions to the European Communities' governmental authorities can be gauged, they have been rapidly evolving along lines similar to those of employers and farmers. (In a previous chapter we have had occasion to mention their joining with businessmen and farmers in protesting the action of the French government in the crisis of 1965—see above, pp. 106–110—and we shall deal with this issue in greater detail, below.) These relations started with the establishment of the Consultative Committee of ECSC,[18] but since these have been adequately dealt with, we shall do no more than summarily assert the effectiveness of the Committee of 21. It attended to what had been the key argument in securing organized labor's assent to the ECSC Treaty, namely that the establishment of a common market would enable the unions "to obtain almost automatically better living standards, better working conditions and better wages."[19] These results were, however, achieved more often by direct consultation between the High Authority and the unions than through the Consultative Committee.

The general pattern of relationships established by the ECSC persisted in the EEC and Euratom, and it presumably will be continuing now that the Communities have been merged. Already in 1965 the general European secretariat of the Union of Free Trade Unions could report: "A spirit of collaboration has gradually developed with the bodies of the Communities, particularly with those members of the European Commission who are ideologically close to the Free Trade Union Movement."[20] Such a development was anticipated by one leading American analyst when he wrote: "... patently a far greater degree of ideological cohesion has been achieved by labor than is true of trade associations." He speaks of a "far more striking espousal of supranationalism, facilitated by the possession ... of a frame of reference going beyond the national state."[21] This solid basis in thought for effective cooperative relationships facilitates the spread of political implications as the informal community formation among European labor progresses.

The Commission has from the very beginning, and following the precedent of the High Authority, taken the initiative in organizing an exchange of views through meetings, round tables, and discussions. They have been repeatedly reported; and while they served to inform the unions of the work and problems of the Commission, they at the same time enabled labor representatives to present a whole range of proposals for the harmonization of conditions of work, social mobility, wages, social security insurance, fringe benefits, and so forth.[22] Again we find, as in agriculture and business, that continuing contact is maintained with the officials of the European Commission and the general directorates; the contacts are, of course, especially close with the directorate on social affairs. But labor is also represented in all the technical committees, *ad hoc* working parties and similar institutionalized arrangements for the consultation of experts on a great variety of specific issues, although their influence is more limited than that of business and agriculture.

That labor's influence is more limited is in part due to a less urgent concern with the problems of European integration. But it also results from the fact that their more limited funds make it harder for labor organizations to secure the services of technical experts and hence prevent them from being as helpful to the Commission and its directorates as are the organizations of business and agriculture. Nevertheless, their role is important and growing. This is in part due to the fact that the several committees on which representatives of labor serve have gradually gained in stature and operational importance. Such gain was bound to occur with the growing activity of the European Communities themselves. It may be well to analyze the structure and work of some of these committees in greater detail insofar as they relate to trade union cooperation and provide bridges over which the political implications of such community formation can become felt. We turn first to the most important of these committees, the Economic and Social Committee (ESC).

The establishment of the Economic and Social Committee represents an effort to institutionalize the participation of trade unions and other interest groups in the policy-making process of the EEC. It was preceded by a similar body, the Advisory Committee of the CSC. As already mentioned, both have now been merged in the Economic and Social Committee of the European Community.[23] Contrary to the hopes and expectations of its promoters, it has shared the fate of other such bodies representing interest groups in various countries,[24] though perhaps not quite to the same extent, since the European parliament does not possess the same power national parliaments traditionally wield. This is not the place to explore the reasons for the relative weakness of such bodies, except to note that the constituencies of such economic and social councils, namely the economic interest groups, are readily accessible for consultations and cooperation to administrators and parliamentarians, and in turn find it often to their interests to bring influence to bear through such more direct channels. For direct contacts correspond more effectively to political needs and hence to the "laws of power." If A has the power of making a vital policy decision for IG–1 and IG–2, and if the interests of IG–1 and IG–2 are sharply in conflict, it will usually seem more natural to IG–1, and in turn to IG–2, to seek to influence A without the knowledge of its competitor than to try to arrive at a compromise with IG–2 and then try to influence A by joint action. There are, of course, situations in which the latter procedure may be preferable, but these are typically exemplified by the federated interest group, such as UNICE, COPA, and the labor groups analyzed above, in which overarching joint interests mitigate the conflict between particular interests.

Even so, the ESC has had a certain role to play, because it supplements the inadequate supervisory power of the European parliament. This was put in the foreground by the then president of ESC, M. Emile Roche, who said in 1962 (May 4): "Upon our shoulders rests a heavy responsibility as long as the political institutions . . . have not been created which are needed in order to secure the indispensable democratic control of the . . . executive. We are called upon to participate in this control."[25] It would, however, not be correct to base upon this justified position a claim that the ESC is more important than the European parliament. This opinion was explicitly and sharply rejected by the then president of the EEC, Walter Hallstein, who called it a "complete misjudgment regarding the position of the two bodies in the real European constitutional order."[26] At the same time, Hallstein emphasized that the ESC had made very valuable contributions to European integration. One aspect crucial in our perspective is that the members of the Committee are being continually confronted with the most diverse problems of economic groups in countries other than their own and thus come to understand these problems as part of the overall task of building a European order. The constant contact and discussion of these formerly unknown issues gradually bring about a profound change in mental outlook and viewpoint among all the participants. "One can say that some who came as 'nationalist' into the ESC have, through this concern with the needs and worries of others, been changed into 'Europeans'."[27] This has significant political implications, because the changed outlook is carried over into the work of such persons in their national associations and groupings.

For no one is this more true than the trade unionists participating in the ESC and other committees of the EC. The sharp conflict which caused unionists often to adopt a narrowly national interest viewpoint regarding concrete questions while rendering lip service to international rhetoric[28] is here resolved in favor of a supranational European conduct. And although unionists at times still do engage in such fights, there is a marked shift to be noted among those who have had occasion to face their problems of the Common Market and its labor force together with unionists from other countries. The markedly insular position taken by British unionists is, in this connection, a source of considerable concern, but it too may change after British entry. Let us see then how the ESC is composed.

The ESC consists of 101 members, proposed by the member

states and appointed for four years by the Council of Ministers.[29] They are to represent the various groupings of economic and social life of the Community (not necessarily of its members). An effort has been made to equilibrate skillfully this representation among the different groupings and organizations. Such equilibration presents serious practical difficulties which can be resolved only by negotiation and compromise. According to the annual report of the ESC there were in 1962, 33 representatives of labor, 27 of the employers, and 14 of agriculture; the remainder represent consumers and the general public. There has been no significant change since 1962. As far as their national origin is concerned, there are 24 members each for France, Germany, and Italy; 12 each for Belgium and the Netherlands; and 5 for Luxembourg;[30] the considerable overrepresentation of the smaller countries is explained by the need to get some balance of interest groups, and can be justified by the "purely advisory" nature of the ESC's functions. (Jurists "explain," with typical formalism, that the ESC is not an "organ" of the EC—surely a highly artificial view which "explains" nothing.) The fact is that in terms of political function the need of establishing an effective working relationship with the interest groups in each country cannot be fulfilled unless a certain minimum membership is made available. It would, of course, have been possible to enlarge the committee, but this was deemed undesirable if an operationally satisfactory body was to be had. Labor was actually dissatisfied with the tripartite division adopted for the committee, fearing that a considerable number of members in the third group would tend to side with the employers. The extended efforts of its representatives to have a bipartite grouping, with employers and employees confronting each other, although supported by the Commission, have so far failed.[31] The decision of what group to belong to in the ESC is a voluntary matter, each member being able to choose for himself; but for labor this is, of course, purely illusory. Obviously, a member who has been proposed by his government upon the initiative of his union will have no alternative but to join the labor group in the ESC.[32] But the same is not true of members in the third group, and even to some extent of the employers' group. In the composition of subcommittees and their chairmen these groups are nonetheless basic, though national balance is also sought.[33]

So much, then, on the composition and functioning of the ESC. Among the other committees which are of particular concern to labor and in which their participation is institutionalized are the Committee for the Social Fund and the Committee for implementing the mobility of labor. These committees are, like the ESC, composed of an equal number of representatives of business, labor, and the public (consumers), and work in close cooperation with the general directorate of social relations.[34] The first-named has as its function the improvement of the "social substructure" of the community. This task involves the relocation and retraining of unemployed workers under programs the national governments initiate and then are reimbursed up to 50 percent by the EEC. The most recent report of the Commission contains a hint of how this institutionalization can affect the work: "Because of the delay in renewing the powers of the members of the European Social Fund Committee which expired on 14 October, 1966, the Commission was unable to make any decisions granting aid from the Fund during the fourth quarter of the year."[35] It shows that the lives of the workers in the six countries are severely affected by the weak or ill functioning of these committees. Thus, another such committee with comparably direct impact—for example, the Committee for the free movement of workers—very actively participated in the Commission's work, based upon a Council decision of May 10 and 11, 1966. This decision contained a regulation and a directive to establish complete freedom of movement and settlement of workers within the Community, following upon the coming into effect of the Customs Union on July 1, 1968. In connection with such free movement, the harmonization of social security provisions—coordinating the social security systems—is a vital task; for this undertaking another

Committee is in existence.[36] Such harmonization is one of the most vital tasks in connection with the Europeanization of labor in the Common Market, facilitating its mobility while at the same time reducing the propensity of labor to move just for the sake of securing differential advantages. Member governments have shown a rather surprising lack of interest in pushing such harmonization. M. Schwamm believes that this is due to a variety of factors. Among them he stresses (a) the intrinsic difficulties of the task; (b) the cost, if such harmonization takes the form of increasing social security benefits in the less generous countries; (c) even the mere "meaning" of terms, such as "illness," or "invalid." All these present major obstacles. In addition, social security legislation is so central a part of the policy of the welfare state that governments are reluctant, to say the least, to give up their control over it. There is also the problem of effectuating the participation of the "social partners" which the Treaty does not mention (Article 118 provides that collaboration of the governments should be promoted in the field of social security, as in a number of fields of social policy with which the Treaty in its Title III is concerned, such as employment, etc.). Social security is a field in which the lack of adequate financial resources of the Common Market organization is felt strongly. The contrast with the supranationally financed High Authority for Coal and Steel is striking; the latter could contribute to the financing of over 100,000 workers' homes, while the EC could only recommend action to the government. It is obvious that in such a situation the trade unions must continue to exert pressure primarily on the national level, and do in fact do so. Brussels may be interesting as a supplementary platform for pushing demands, but it cannot meet workers' needs in the decisive field. The result is disharmony, rather than harmonization, with the consequent stresses and strains.

Even so, the several committees, including that on social security, are important, and organized labor has every reason to be represented. In these committees labor has a third of the representatives. But contrary to the wishes of labor, it is not represented in the administrative committees; its position parallels that of business and agriculture and, like them, labor has to try to influence the work of the administrative committees through national ministries of labor and their officialdom.

Generally speaking, Schierwater concludes that the possibility for influencing the decisions of the EC authorities varies, but is considerable. One reads that "The trade unions possess an adequate number of possibilities for influencing and representing the interests of labor."[37] But since the social aspects of integration were seen as a natural sequence to economic integration as such, and since the national governments have retained much of the ultimate decision, it is difficult to distinguish between what the trade unions are able to do by way of influencing European authorities, and what by way of their powerful impact upon national policy. The trade unions are fully aware of this need to work through the national unions; unfortunately the fact that the most powerful unions in France and Italy are Communist-directed proves a considerable handicap, both because of their own attitudes and viewpoints and because of their lack of effective contact with the respective governments. This situation is very much in contrast to that in Germany and the Benelux countries, where socialist parties have been in and out of governments and are closely tied into the officialdom of their countries.

8. A Community of Communities: Grass-roots Integration

The violent upheavals of our time have revived interest in the local community.[1] Its importance for the functioning of constitutional government is common knowledge. The local community has proved surprisingly resistant to the pressures of totalitarian government. When the Nazi armies conquered France and the central government of the Third Republic was swept away, the tradition of French life found refuge in the villages and small towns, where intimacy of personal contacts enabled people to know friend and foe. Again, when the conquering armies of the West had completely destroyed the government and party of Hitler, an older and better German tradition re-emerged in the local communities. Local government turned out to be more disaster-proof than the broader, more far-flung structures of state and nation.

During the turmoil of the last great depression, a phrase became popular which was meant to express this foundational aspect of local government and the local community: grass-roots democracy. It was often used with conservative implications; as contrasted with the swiftly changing scene of national politics and the popular majorities which were presumably supporting these policies, "democracy at the grass roots" was supposed to represent the steady and persistent outlook of Americans in the local community, especially in the rural community with its settled ways.[2]

Any thorough analysis of the way in which the "common man" participates in the common concerns of the community will disclose that he hesitates to assent to what he does not understand; hence his inclination to vote for persons, rather than policies, when it comes to national and international affairs. There are recurrent important exceptions, but as a general propensity it holds true in all Western countries. It is also true in local elections, though perhaps less so. As a matter of fact, a certain amount of genuine local autonomy makes for diversity: one community stresses public parks and other kinds of landscape beauty, another stresses schools, still another public safety. All these objectives have to be given some attention in every modern community, but there is considerable leeway as to emphasis. Whether to extend the town water line down in a certain direction and gain the added fire protection will be of vital concern to all citizens, for it will affect the future growth of the town. These statements hold true primarily for the small community where the electorate is reasonably familiar with the practical tasks in hand; in communities over 100,000 it proves impractical, and has led to many breakdowns. Districting has modified these difficulties, but on the whole only the small town is able to make good use of the right to govern itself. (It is often forgotten that the notion of local self-government was developed at a time when few cities had over 500,000 inhabitants.) The small town therefore can be, though often it is not, the "school for democracy."[3] To some extent, the decision the people make may seem unwise from the standpoint of the expert town planner, the architect, the engineer—but if so, the citizens will discover it in time and they may learn a vital lesson in self-government. Popular government includes the right of the people, and that means their majority, to make mistakes.

It seemed well to recall this background for a better understanding of the present movement. It goes a long way to explain the vigorous stand taken by a significant number of European communities in developing grass-roots support for the unification of Europe. That movement has come a long way in the last decade. In May 1961 a conference was held to assess this program. It devoted several days to the discussion of the "local communities and the construction of European Unity."[4] A clear image emerged of the vital role which the communes are bound to play in a united Europe and are playing in its unification. One paper, being especially germane to the problems of this analysis, established five "groups of requirements" involving such matters as constitutionally guaranteed local autonomy and self-government, popular elections, delegated administration and central supervision, strictly limited by law. Within this framework, the author noted that Europe's problems in this field were complicated by the contrast between the "Anglo-German group," whose local government organization is characterized by the survival of historical institutions, and the "French group," which has adopted uniform local institutions based on general principles of a "rational" nature. Nonetheless he concluded that "the improvement and development of the organization and functions of the minor territorial bodies far from being a hindrance to the process of European unification would be an indispensable promise of it."[5] What is the background of this movement? Who initiated it?

A group of forward-looking men founded the Conseil des Communes d'Europe in 1951. Edouart Herriot, the long-time mayor of Lyon, put the viewpoint of these founders as follows:

> Whenever there have been organized societies, there have been (local) communities beneath and the State on top. States oppose each other.... Between states, conflicts continually arise. But when I step down from the national order, from the state to the local community, I come close to human beings. If I talk with an English mayor, or a German or Russian one, I discover that we have the same preoccupations; it is important to watch children, to educate them under like conditions, to protect the citizen against illness by opening hospitals for them, by providing asylums and other institutions for aid,

whether it is a matter of education of the citizen, of help for the aged, of protection for the child, it is always the same, for all human beings, wherever they are, wherever they work, to whatever nation they belong. That is why I believe that the bringing together of the local communities is the best condition for the bringing together of men: it is the limited and precise ground where men naturally encounter each other.[6]

Herriot had met in Switzerland in the summer of 1950 with Adolf Gasser, a Swiss professor and author of a book on the importance of communal freedom and autonomy,[7] to discuss the problem of how to defend the autonomy of local communities. As a result, seven leading Frenchmen, Germans, and Swiss met on October 1, 1950, in Seelisberg on the Ruetli (Switzerland) and founded, under the chairmanship of Professor Gasser, the initiating committee which brought the council into being. Local self-government was the central topic at this meeting. The discussion was based on the premise that the local communities provided an essential contribution to European reconstruction.[8] It is significant that the founders believed that "the increase in the power of the state constitutes a growing totalitarian threat to the local communities, even in the democratic countries. . . . Through the guarding and strengthening of their autonomy, the local communities are the last bulwark of democracy and human rights."

The Italians soon joined the group, especially some men, like Umberto Serafini, closely associated with the movement of reform, founded by Adriano Olivetti and highlighting *Communità.* (Communità, in Olivetti's understanding, is not simply community, let alone commune, but is dynamically defined in terms of the concrete, living context, larger than a village at times, smaller than a large city.[9] These communities, when formed, were, as the constituent bodies, expected to be united in a federal state, to be called the Federal State of the Italian Communities.) Although little has come of this beautiful dream, it is evident that it provides a measure of intellectual support for the outlook that the Council of Communes (i.e. of local communities) was fostering: an emphasis on the local community and on the federal uniting of such communities.[10]

The founding meeting of this Council took place on January 28 to 30, 1951, at Geneva, with participation of sixty mayors and town councillors from eight countries: Belgium, Denmark, France, Germany, Italy, Luxembourg, Netherlands, and Switzerland. They reaffirmed the original ideas by stating that communal self-government is the bulwark of personal freedom. They also said that this communal freedom is threatened by the interference of the state (central government) and that the federation of Europe is being delayed by the recurring opposition between the states in spite of the will of the peoples. They insisted that the mayors and elected representatives of the local communities and their organizations who are in direct contact with political reality and the people, through their functions as administrators facing problems which transcend all frontiers, are co-workers in the building of a free and united Europe which respects national differences.

These principles became the basis of the Council structured as a typical cooperative association, with an assembly of delegates, an international secretariat, and a presidium.[11] Biennial gatherings have been held, the first at Versailles in 1953 with 400 delegates participating, and a second one at Venice the following year. Three supporting institutes have been founded: one for communal credit, at Turin; another for comparative studies of communal problems and institutions, at Rome; and a third, a union of French and German mayors specially concerned with the question of Franco-German relations. For the purposes of this chapter, it is not important to explore the organizational details except to add that the members included England and Austria besides those mentioned, the work of the Council thus going beyond the limited Community of the Six.

In response to these activities the Council of Europe formed, in 1957, a Permanent Committee of its Consultative Assembly and, in 1955, an official Conference of the Communes of Europe (CCE).[12] More recently a charter has been put forward for the

Conference which embodies the basic principles the previous initiatives were based upon. In line with these actions a special representation of the local communities in a future European Assembly has been advocated. Called by the Permanent Committee (in recent years Dr. Henri Cravatte of Luxembourg has been the chairman, as well as president of the CCE), this Conference meets annually and addresses itself to those problems which are of special concern to the local communities in connection with the activities of European authorities, more particularly the Common Market. While there is a good deal of ritualistic resolutionizing and repetitive speechmaking, there is also evidence of a steady increase in mutual understanding and the growth of a European consciousness such as would provide the effective underpinning of European democratic politics.[13]

In this connection, a special activity fostered by the Council of Communes itself has played a considerable role, and that is the establishment of so-called *jumelages*—a pairing or partnership of particular communes with each other. In German such affiliations are called *Verschwisterungen* or sisterhoods—a term which is more expressive of the emotional aspects of these linkings of two or more towns with each other.[14] While many other activities are part of these partnerships, the opening ceremony culminates in an oath by the mayors, called the "serment du jumelage," which in its essential part reads:

> En ce jour, nous prenons l'engagement solennel de maintenir les liens permanents entre les municipalités de nos Villes, de favoriser en tous domaines les échanges entre leurs inhabitants pour développer, par une meilleur compréhension mutuelle, le sentiment vivant de la fraternité européenne; de conjuguer nos efforts afin d'aider dans la pleine mesure de nos moyens aux succès de cette nécessaire entreprise de paix et de prosperité: l'union des peuples européens.

A partnership may occur between two very large cities, such as that between Lyon and Frankfurt, or it may unite two or more very small towns. They are often initiated by some individual having had an experience which prepared him for such an undertaking. For example two businessmen from Aubenas (France) saw a motion picture about the Napoleonic wars; and as a result of their stirred imagination the towns of Aubenas, Sirre (Switzerland), Zelzate (Belgium), and Schwarzenbach (Germany)—all small communes—became affiliated with each other. Again, a teacher of French or German may have studied in the other country and established friendships. In other instances the affiliation resulted from the encounter and mutual respect of two or more mayors in one of the meetings that have been mentioned earlier. But whatever the initial spark, a considerable amount of work of the self-governing kind has to be put into preparing the ground.

The eventual meeting for the formal establishment of the affiliation is preceded by extended negotiations and explorations. Indeed, the CCE warns against starting a partnership without adequate groundwork. In this preparatory work, the CCE, through their Paris office, provides a certain amount of guidance if it is asked for, but the initiative is invariably local and has to be. It has been found that it is important to have communities with roughly similar resources linked with each other. It has proved easier to link towns resembling each other in social and industrial structure—mining towns with mining towns, trading cities with trading cities and so forth—though at times sharp differences have provided interesting possibilities.

The primary activity after the establishment of a partnership is, of course, exchange. Such exchanges are of many kinds. Exchanges of teachers and students, of municipal officials and workers, and of books and industrial products are some of the more usual kinds. Thus the French city of Troyes sent 54 difficult children to Darmstadt as a prize for good behavior—the exchange being the outgrowth of extended consultations between the teaching personnel in both cities concerned with such problems. Juvenile delinquency has, as a matter of fact, been one of the recurrent themes of such consultations.

If it is clear why communes affiliate, it may be interesting to consider the process by which such affiliation is established.[15]

The Council insists that a partnership be clearly distinguished from temporary or limited links, such as those of industrial enterprises, universities and the like; they are good and useful, but should not be confused with true general affiliation. Whether the original bond is economic, cultural, or functional, the partnership is given general scope. If a particular town has decided to seek affiliation, it takes up the question with the national office of the Council which explores the possibilities on the basis of a detailed questionnaire; visits and countervisits follow, consultations with the central office of the CCE in Paris, as well as the enlisting of the host of organizations which characterize a pluralistic community: churches, trade unions, schools, professional societies, and the rest. It would be tedious to go over such a long list in detail. The reports indicate clearly that the activity is complex and involves every element of the local community.[16]

There are, of course, problems and difficulties. The financial cost, especially the outlay for travel, is a considerable one—notably for the small communes. There is the language problem. The stimulus to foreign-language study is one of the significant results of the movement. Public relations are another important aspect, because deep-seated prejudices must be overcome or at least attenuated. To the student of administration, it is significant that a partnership, if well organized, is apt to permeate the entire local body; it provides a profound challenge to which a whole range of novel responses must be made which serve to enliven the local community. Often potentialities which lay dormant are stimulated into active growth by the encounter with a corresponding activity elsewhere, when brought into vivid focus by such an encounter. Most significantly, perhaps, the French and Italian communes have discovered that local autonomy is more deeply entrenched and more fully enjoyed in Switzerland, Austria, and Germany; a consequent determination to strengthen local government is engendered, and may have considerable importance in view of the decline of parliamentary institutions in France, and their weakness in Italy.

The active participation of local communities and governments appears to provide a significant ingredient in the formation of a European community. To test the range of issues, it appeared desirable, however, to study a significant number of such pairings, twinnings, or partnerships (*jumelages*) in greater detail.[17] There were, according to the Council of European Communities, on February 29, 1964, 158 such partnerships or pairings between French and German towns. (These had increased by September 1, 1968, to 350, with 156 more in the process of being formed.[18]) These towns were asked to answer a questionnaire: 105 German and 64 French towns replied; in 43 cases both the French and German partner replied; 11 towns replied that no such pairing existed, among them Bonn and Paris. It seemed also desirable to investigate the cases of pairings which had not succeeded; a certain number of towns, 77 in all, had been included in earlier lists of the Council, but had since disappeared; 47 of these towns also replied to the questionnaire.[19] These partnerships are, as mentioned, part of a wider movement including many countries besides France and Germany.[20]

The results of these inquiries carry some clear implications for the development of a European community spirit on the basis of local communal partnerships. It is quite evident from the results of our inquiry that wherever they have occurred, they have made the confrontation and encounter between French and Germans a matter of course, something familiar and generally accepted. Old prejudices and resentments have usually been reduced or eliminated, though there are cases where these encounters have rather confirmed the former sentiments of antagonism. Much depends upon the skill with which the partnerships are initiated and carried through. It is natural that some persons who have suffered personally by official actions and policies of the former enemy will remain reserved or even hostile, in spite of the atmosphere of good fellowship created by the *jumelage*, its festivities and undertakings. Even so, a partnership may change the psychic *mise-en-scène* so that such feelings, formerly considered representative, are now seen as personal deviations, to be respected, surely, but no longer to be treated as symptomatic of the attitude of the two peoples toward each other. Often, the persons themselves shift their outlook significantly; they may refuse to have any share in the confrontation, but accept the partnership *comme un fait accompli.* Frenchmen who were deported to Germany by Hitler's agents at times refuse to have any contact with Germans, but may nonetheless allow their children to go on a students' exchange to Germany.

These, in any case, are the statistically marginal cases. The elimination of prejudices is much more a matter of the large majority of Frenchmen and Germans who have never had any close personal contact with each other—that is to say, to whom the human reality of the other people is largely unknown, and may indeed constitute a cause of anxiety, an enigma. It is a peculiarity of these partnerships that they reach, especially through the exchanges, groups of the population who never had an opportunity to get acquainted with persons of a different nationality. This is equally true of the lower classes throughout France and Germany, especially the women, as it is of the inhabitants of the more remote regions of the two countries. To be sure, the military operations had brought quite a few Germans to France, and the occupation Frenchmen to Germany, but the contacts under these conditions were at best of a tenuous and distant kind. It is also true that to an increasing extent international tourism (as indeed the other phases of community formation, which we have dealt with in Chapters 3–6 and 9) and transnational mass communications, such as the ever closer cooperation of French and German radio and television broadcasters,[21] are rapidly reducing this sort of social and territorial seclusion. Even so, the close human togetherness of the communal partnerships adds a vital dimension to these more casual contacts, and provides a setting for the particular and professional links, such as the partnerships of business and universities (see Chapters 3 and 9).

The importance of pairing communities which are far removed from each other, rural in character and often quite small, is in these perspectives especially great. Such *jumelages* meet considerable difficulties, financial and other; but the impact is startling and often surprising. The human relationship replaces an abstract image of the "other"; it was put very well by a Frenchman who reported: "En montant la voiture, nous étions deux Français et deux Allemands; en descendant, il n'y avait plus que quatre amis." (Report from Le Cheylard.) The man who had been "de l'autre côté de l'eau" has become "de ce côté" and is accepted. This process is particularly striking in cases where a measure of abstract competition persists: throughout Burgundy the traveler is nowadays greeted at the entrance to the villages bearing the names of celebrated wines by a sign, stating that "cette ville est jumelée avec . . ." and then follows the name of a well-known German vineyard town in the Rhine Valley or the Palatinate. If one were to express the political process in psychological terms, relating it to the individuals involved, he might say that a consciousness develops of a wider "inside" which includes the fellow townsmen of another nation in a common community.

In evaluating all this, it is necessary to bear in mind that the great celebrations which accompany the initiation of such a pairing of two towns generate a festival spirit. In other words, the element of play and fun enters the picture. The *exchanges* are also *excursions*. Both on the official and personal level there is much good eating and drinking—activities which have always had much appeal to both French and Germans. The splendor, pomp and circumstance of communal ritual, so highly developed in Europe over the ages, is brought into play for the celebrating of intercommunal encounters. Since they are free of the usual problematic character of international political encounters, the participants can enjoy the occasion without mental reservation. The factor of mere play,[22] which also helps in the initiating of a partnership, has a function to perform in all such pairings. The personal relations which are being established in the course of a developing partnership are at the start molded by the festive air of ceremonial receptions. The joy and gayness of such an atmosphere serve to overcome much initial hesitation and difficulty; but of course it is an exceptional situation. Relations may soon cool as the routine of workaday existence returns, or they may develop into deeper and emotionally secure situations, and indeed may lead some to the marriage altar. Intermarriage is an accompaniment of the *jumelage* of communes, as it is of businesses, associations, unions, and universities.[23] At times, the emotional factor is curiously nonrational; Dr. Grauhan cites one report which stated that "they did not understand each other, but on parting they wept." Even so, there is widespread feeling among those participating that the durability of these relations ought not to be taken for granted.

An advance stage of genuine intimacy is at times reached through very frequent exchanges and visits. Then it may happen that the participants feel that they can criticize each other. "Our relations are now so intimate," states the report from Montier-en-Der in Haute Marne, "that we can make remarks to each other about certain details which leave something to be desired without our giving offense."[24] The same source hinted at the remaining uncertainties, when it pointed out that "even if the *jumelage* does not succeed, if the hopes built on it prove vain, we can nonetheless be sure to have done something positive and good, and in any case no one could criticize us by saying that we had acted badly."

This element of doubt and anxiety about the possible long-range effects is to some extent engendered by excessive political expectations. It appears that those partnerships which were started with an especially high degree of political enthusiasm have at times been failures. "To provide a great outburst of Franco-German reconciliation" means to anticipate too much at the outset. If the building of personal relations between students and the establishment of collegial bonds between similar fraternal bodies are from the beginning burdened with much political purpose, such relations are deprived of the spontaneity which is needed for their flowering—or even their proper start. Perhaps one could say, as Dr. Grauhan does, that the all too great public attention generated doubts and hesitations which the *jumelage* was meant to overcome. Elaborate self-consciousness often has the effect, as everyone knows, of spoiling a human relationship.

This aspect of the partnerships shows how much difficulty is created for these pairings by the fact that they are neither truly public nor fully private. What they are intended to do is to stimulate private initiatives by public demonstrations and to influence public opinion by manipulating private experience. The only basis on which such an undertaking can have a chance of success is a clear and specific separation of the two spheres; both the public and the private activities must be allowed to function in their own particular way. If private contacts and relationships are at the outset seen in the political perspective, any malfunctioning, any breakdown or misunderstanding becomes a "political" issue, and is dramatized as a public conflict. This means that personal experience then seems to confirm the traditional national prejudices. The festival spirit which is to encompass a feeling of brotherhood is, as the term suggests, rooted in the private sphere. In such festive atmosphere private feelings become merged with public sentiments—the credenda and miranda of politics[25]—and the reaction becomes possible which makes out of two Frenchmen and two Germans four friends. It requires a good deal of delicacy and tact to allow the private feelings to influence and mold the new relationships by not overdoing public declamations and official oratory. If they are seen and understood as ritual formulas for enhancing the festive character of the occasion, they can help to intensify the festival spirit, as they do in the ceremonial of family feasts. There can be little doubt that cultural differences in the way such festivities are structured also create problems which only a keen awareness of the problems such differences create can solve. Intelligent management must accompany the felt desire to fraternize. Considering these experiences and the reflections just outlined, one is led to the rather paradoxical conclusion that *jumelages* are more likely to promote the political implications of a sense of community among the people involved if there is little talk about the political aspects; such *jumelages* serve European unification more if they are not understood and treated as instruments for it.

An interesting by-product of such partnerships is the change in attitude toward one's own community. A town, by presenting itself to its foreign guests also presents itself to its citizens. One mayor spoke of the greater contact with his own population as a consequence of the festivities (Darmstadt). The report from the city of Solingen (Ruhr) contained the following interesting comment:

> Quite different from contacts with tourists and vacationists the exchanges within the framework of the partnership provide genuine human relationships and an insight into the life and ways of the partner city. Every participating family, the administrations of the two cities, as well as the press, combine the personal encounters with inspections which provide a view of the history, the economic structure and the administration of the sister city. Even if the stay is limited to just a few days, it provides for more understanding than a vacation of many weeks, since the personal interests are hardly ever transcended. This may be illustrated by the remark of one of our citizens who for several days participated in taking care of our guests from France. He said: "Although I was born and raised in Solingen, I have during these days seen and heard much that I did not know about my own paternal city."

In other words, the aspect of self-presentation which the pairings contain has a favorable effect upon the relation of the citizens to their own community; it raises their self-respect. Such civic pride is distinguished from the usual exclusive feelings associated with it by the desire to lay oneself open to the foreigner rather than to seclude oneself. Thus new initiatives in local efforts are engendered by the partnership. This does not mean that one partner takes over the achievements of the other; no report speaks of that. Rather the comparison leads to a fuller appreciation of the differences, but at the same time causes awareness of one's own deficiencies and a desire to remedy them.

Since the pairings thus influence the citizenry in the direction of increasing self-esteem as well as understanding for the partner, some novel dangers appear. Jean Bareth, in a speech to the first Congress of paired cities in 1964, pointed out that "the pairing of two towns leads to a reciprocal glorifying of the two interested nations."[26] For the two nations are indeed involved; the effects of the partnership affect the human beings thus paired not only as members of their local community, but also as citizens of their national state which, as the number of such pairings increases, begins to exert an ever wider general political influence.

This circumstance raises, of course, the question as to how the effects of such partnerships are related to the policies of their respective national governments toward Europe and European unification. The answers that were received from the many towns who replied to our inquiries are bewilderingly complex. If there is a general line it is that of stressing the difference between such pairing and the national foreign policy. Frequently, the influence of such policies is denied altogether. As one report has it, "the ups and downs of the relations between France and Germany have had no effect upon the exchanges between the affiliated towns." (Walheim.) Again, such an influence is explicitly called undesirable; the partnership should be independent of the political relations of the moment (Fontenay-le-Fleury). On the other hand, quite a few reports stressed the influence of the partnerships upon the national policies. Thus it was asserted that the Franco-German Treaty of Friendship was only made possible by the degree of reconciliation achieved by the *jumelages;* also the Franco-German Office for Youth Exchanges could be organized only because within the framework of pairings many such exchanges had been started which the state could now promote (Chatillon-sur-Seine in the Côte-d'Or; Amiens in the Somme).

There is a widespread fear that the official national policies and relations could have a negative reaction upon a partnership, a fear which is real in spite of the fact that no such negative effects have as yet been observed. In a number of reports, it was stressed that the partnership should be kept free of any such unfortunate side effects of a temporary strain. In this perspective, many communities consider themselves, in keeping with the original thrust toward their union, as the true promoters of European union in contrast with the states which are delaying it. A French town wrote: "The Union of Europe will only come into being if the states yield to the will of the peoples to make a (united) Europe, and if it is realized, one will have to avoid having the reluctant states find reasons for returning to the former state." (Meursault.)

It is, of course, obvious that such desire to stress the distance between oneself and national policies often is an expression of political and party differences. In France, municipal politics is often dominated by the parties of the opposition; hence an influence of the state is denied because the policies of the (former) president, de Gaulle, were disapproved of. Thus the motto of the Council of European Communities: "For the Europe of the Peoples (Pour l'Europe des Peuples)" sharply contrasts with the allegedly Gaullist "For the Europe of the Fatherlands (Pour l'Europe des Patries)." A socialist-dominated municipality may be particularly eager to develop not only a partnership with a German town, but to extend such a partnership to include a British municipality in order thus to demonstrate against de Gaulle's exclusion of the British from the Common Market. On the other hand, a town in which the Gaullists are in control may argue that the failure of a partnership with a British town proves the rightness of the General's view and therefore may more insistently pursue the pairing with a German city. Occasionally, French reports have suggested that de Gaulle's views have furthered the pairings with German towns (Valenciennes, Nord).

A special aspect of the French situation is due to the powerful (and under de Gaulle reinforced) position of the French Prefects and Sub-Prefects. The reports concerning the attitude of these heads of the departments who represent the central government and govern in its name[27] are not uniform. A community ruled by the Independents and another led by Socialists, both said that the prefecture never had taken a position either for or against the partnership, but had remained indifferent. The mayor of a town in the Côte-d'Or belonging to the MRP (Catholic Party), on the other hand, insisted that the prefect had vigorously supported the partnerships under the Fourth Republic, and only after de Gaulle's take-over had the prefecture adopted an attitude of strict reserve. A Gaullist city in the département, contrariwise, claimed that the prefect supported the partnerships in every possible way.

There is no comparable situation in Germany. In spite of the fact that many municipal administrations, especially in the larger cities, are dominated by Social Democrats, the differences between the two parties in the field of foreign policy are not sufficiently marked. Hence German towns report no comparable inclination to draw a hard-and-fast line between themselves and national foreign policies. Rather, they incline to see the work done in connection with the partnerships as a "contribution to the national policy." (This view was taken by the director of the city of Braunschweig.) Party political differences apart, the greater integration of the local governments into the political structure of their several states, precisely because such self-government is constitutionally recognized and accepted, would seem to provide another reason for this contrast between the two countries.[28]

But often the reports expressed the view that the partnerships had nothing whatever to do with the unification of Europe (Schleswig) or that "partnerships between cities and political efforts at unifications are not on the same level"—a rather obvious observation. In this connection, pairings are seen as having a meaning that is more human than political (Montivilliers). If such remarks are supposed to imply that partnerships are beyond the realm of politics, they are of course untenable, and express a prejudice against politics in general which is widespread in both France and Germany. But often such remarks may rather be meant to suggest that the partnerships are not involved in the controversies about the future form of European unification, and more particularly the question of the degree of unity in a future federal order. There is also involved an old argument between the Council of European Communities and the World Council of (Paired) Municipalities (*Fédération Mondiale des Villes Jumelées*)—whether the partnerships should be directed toward promoting the unification of Europe. The Council, as can be seen from the oath we cited above, demands of its partner cities that they acknowledge the obligation of working for the political unification of Europe, while the World Federation describes its mission as "perfectly clear," namely "to place such *jumelages* in a non-political and multinational context." Of this strategy it asserts that "it alone excludes every mental reservation."[29] This claim seems rather farfetched, in view of the partnerships with cities in Communist countries such as the World Federation promotes. They would seem to be full of mental reservations.

The situation is particularly perplexing in face of the two Germanies. Thus the general secretary of the World Council has asserted that in the hands of the Federal Republic this peaceful means of reconciliation is on the way to becoming a formidable tool of propaganda and psychological activities. These activities, he thinks, are directed toward committing the French people by a mass integration to the German demand for reunification.[30] As might be expected, the German Section of the Council of Europe Communities has thereupon issued a warning against the World Council as a pro-Communist organization. This is surely an exaggeration, considering the fact that its secretary general is a Christian Unionist, and the board contains four Gaullists, including General Bilotte. It would be more precise to consider the organization as an instrument of the propagandists of the Eastern European Communist regimes, including the German Democratic Republic, which maintains a section, as was claimed at the World Congress at Strasbourg in 1964 by a German municipal official.[31] It is characteristic that this organization maintains no office in the Federal Republic, and by 1965 no community in Western Germany belonged to a *jumelage* promoted by the World Council. In France, by contrast, it has considerable importance, which the present trend toward cooperation with the Soviet Union is likely to increase, and towns may freely pass from one of these councils to the other. It may well be asked whether in view of the changing overall outlook of German foreign policy the German towns should not follow the French example, even though considerable difficulties have to be faced in belonging to the same World Council as the German Democratic Republic. Whether this would aid the growth of European community sentiment is another question. But it is noteworthy that a number of French towns which have paired with West German communities also work with the World Council and have thereunder entered into partnerships with an African (Avignon in the Vaucluse), an East European (Dijon in the Côte-d'Or), an East German (St. Etienne in the Loire), an Italian (Colombes), or a British (Dôle in the Jura) community. All of these have no connection with the Council of European Communities.

How will these partnerships develop? Those who deny any connection with the unification of Europe may do so in the interest of a lasting bond with their French sister. But others are inclined to believe that "as soon as the unification of Europe is achieved, the partnerships will have fulfilled their purpose": (Neckarsulm; Corbie, Somme; Digne, B. Alpes). Others emphasize the strictly human and unpolitical nature of the partnership in order to vindicate the permanence of the relationship; some also insist that even after a political unification, these partnerships will retain their political value; for as Saint-Cloud put it, "each European state will preserve its particularities and its way of life which give it its particular charm." It would seem that apart from this consideration, partnerships will be even more urgently needed because the coming into being of a political framework will by no means obliterate the need for European consensus formation which, in view of the deep roots of European national cultures, will be slow in coming. As was pointed out before, the formation of a European patriotism will follow and not antedate the establishment of a Union, as it did in the United States and other federal systems.[32]

It is not easy to predict the further development of these Franco-German partnerships on the basis of the present data. Both stagnating and expanding partnerships turned up in our sample. Some were not expanding because the maintenance of the existing relations absorbed all available energies. Others quite consciously wished to restrict themselves to the one partnership with a German city (Oullins; Cavaillon in the Vaucluse; Kornwestheim). They looked upon the existing relationship as something permanent. The truly stagnating ones were approaching the point of failure. Such failures or the cessation of a partnership are quite frequently the result of a change in leading personnel; if a mayor with a deep commitment to Europe is replaced by one without it, the result may be failure or at least stagnation. At other times it may not be the mayor, but a dedicated individual, such as a high school principal.[33]

This raises once again the question of failures in such pairings. Our inquiry revealed that it is not always easy to determine what is a failure: in two specific cases the partner cities gave contradictory answers, one saying that the partnership was operating, the other that it had failed or had not been consummated; in one case the failure was noted on the French side, in the other on the German. Often the partnerships are concluded after several tries that were unsuccessful, contact having been established by the overall organizations, the Council, and/or the Mayors' Union. Twenty-seven cases were found of partnerships that were attempted, but did not come to fruition. Besides the change in governmental personnel, structural differences between the partners are often the reason for a failure. Such differences may be those between an industrial and agricultural center, or they may be related to major transformations in a city that is undergoing rapid development. In one case involving Berlin, the tensions of the summer of 1961 were the reason for the failure. It is noteworthy, however, that in no case was a relationship dissolved because either the European or the Franco-German communal relations as such were deteriorating. But the memories of an evil past do at times intrude themselves most painfully. Thus a French community cancelled a sports meeting that had been planned, because within the same week a meeting of former concentration camp inmates had been scheduled in that city.

The groups of old veterans and deportees are most frequently the source of trouble. The Anciens Déportés naturally cannot be expected to entertain especially friendly feelings toward Germans, or any close link with Germans. Even older antipathies and hatreds are voiced by the Anciens Combattants 1914–1918. But that does not mean that all of these organizations, let alone their members, are committed to hostility or indifference. Rather some of the most determined advocates of partnerships also are from these organizations. Thus the mayor of a small town in the southwest of France (Oullins in the Rhône) whose father had been deported and died in a concentration camp, expressed such sentiments forcefully when he wrote: "We have chosen a German city—for a partner—in order that our children, German and French, do no more know such a war which murders the people—war and its atrocities." In this particular case, the German delegations always pay their special respect to the memorial erected to the murdered mayor. Naturally, if the pairing is initiated by a man who has thus suffered, it greatly strengthens the enterprise in the eyes of his compatriots. Curiously enough, there are also the cases of men who had had good experiences as prisoners of war; but these are marginal. On the whole it is fair to conclude that these organizations, as well as not infrequently the members of the Résistance, object and at times defeat the effort (in the case of the Résistance, the problems merge with those of the Communist opposition).

Apart from the possibility of failure due to Communist opposition, there is also the possibility, now not infrequently advocated by the Communist element in a municipal council, that they develop at the same time a partnership with a West and an East German city. There is, however, considerable objection from the other French parties to such a link. The nonrecognition of the German Democratic Republic forbids linkages with the East German towns, except on an unofficial basis. Incidentally, it is worth noting that the failures resulting from Communists' taking over a French municipal administration are due more to the Germans' refusal to have anything to do with Communists than the reverse.[34]

From the standpoint of an inquiry into the formation of European community sentiment—a European consensus—it is noteworthy that the objections and resistance to a partnership are most pronounced at the time it is entered upon. At that moment there have been isolated acts of violence, protest letters to the press, and similar acts; once a local band refused to play at a reception. But these protests are on the decline, whether permanently it is too early to tell.

Our inquiry disclosed that many of the people engaged in pairing French with German cities had been handicapped by popular indifference. Often the reports speak of an initial flare-up of enthusiasm, followed by apathy. This difficulty can be, and is often overcome by making the partnership expand, that is to say, to affect ever new and different fields of municipal activity (internally) or to extend to other European cities and form a ring of partnerships. There is no definite pattern; all seems to depend upon the particular local situation. Thus in addition to visits and student exchanges, there may be extended exchanges of artisans, workers, teachers, librarians, and so on. (For the additional impetus provided by an existing partnership of two universities like Montpelier and Heidelberg, see Chapter 9.) Eventually, of course, the whole range of professional and industrial activities could be involved, and ever new initiatives are needed and serve to lend vitality to the partnership. Such expansion may, on the other hand, multiply the difficulties, as industrial managers may object to being confronted with demands stimulated by observations in the paired city. (See for this Chapters 3 and 4.)

The expansion "outward" occurred mostly in cases where the partnership had achieved a certain measure of success and the relationship had become stable—very much in keeping with the general laws of politics. Additional cities may be added: in the case of Nancy, Trier and Berlin were paired with it in addition to the original partnership with Karlsruhe. Karlsruhe itself had been active in promoting this expansion. Similarly, a successful partnership may spread to the surrounding neighbors of a city. This possibility is significant where a larger city may involve a number of smaller rural communities in a network of pairings.

Besides these expansions within the framework of the Franco-German relationship, there exists the fairly widespread tendency to expand beyond the Franco-German link—a tendency which the overall organizations, such as the Council of European Communities, vigorously support. Thus the Franco-German *jumelages,* which at present are by far the most numerous, may in the future be somewhat reduced in their relative importance; "rings" of partnership may develop which dissipate the particular Franco-German community formation. But even this development may be interfered with if partnerships are sought with Eastern regimes, or even with those in other continents, although here again links with cities in that part of Africa which is associated with the Common Market may be seen as elements in a broader development.[35] The psychological attraction of novelty may indeed cause the *jumelage* with an East European or African partner to seem more exciting, but of course the difficulties are correspondingly greater, and indeed often insurmountable.

It is impossible to say at the present time whether the partnerships between local communities will become an integral part of the network communitarian relationships in the emergent Europe, or whether they will eventually disappear. It seems rather unlikely, in view of the impact they have upon municipal self-esteem. They feed upon a root deeply imbedded in the life of local communities; as such they do provide some of the genuine grass-roots support of an eventual European government, by providing community.

9. The Academic Community

The political role and significance of the academic community have not been recognized until recent years. One of the pathfinding explorations in the field of the connection between education and politics was Charles E. Merriam's *The Making of Citizens.*[1] Yet it contained very little in the way of a searching discussion of the universities. His basic theme is that "the political society constantly seeks to develop and maintain its solidarity through the impression of its traditions upon young and old alike," and that "the fund of common memories is an important possession of the tribe or nation; its cohesive value is very large, and is never neglected in any system."[2] These and related positions involve, of course, the universities, nowhere more so than in Continental Europe. It is apparent, then, or ought to be that any community formation will presuppose a Europeanization of the academic community. The linkages which have in recent years been forged, especially between French and German universities, constitute therefore an important part of our general inquiry. They have been analyzed and the results of these researches will be presented in this chapter. But some introductory remarks about the setting of these partnerships deserve to be made before we do so.[3]

Universities were developed in the early Middle Ages; they constitute in many ways a distinctive feature of Western culture and have spread with its expansion. They can trace their ancestry to the Greek and Hellenistic academies, but received their distinctive form since the twelfth century. Fostered by the ecclesiastic authorities, they were at the outset not subject to the political authorities, but operated under papal charter. As such they were European in outlook; both professors and students came from different countries and conceived of themselves as citizens of the *civitas Christiana,* though the students organized themselves into broad groupings which were called *nationes* and are considered one of the roots of the later national sentiment and consciousness which was to divide Europe into warring camps.

The political authorities, however, soon seized the chance of establishing universities. The first such efforts were made by the emperor Frederick II, when he founded the University of Naples in 1224 to train men for his government service, and by Count Raymond VII of Toulouse, in connection with the Albigensian troubles. Although not at first successful, these attempts were followed by other princes after the decline of the secular position of the papacy: in the fourteenth century Prague, Cracow, Vienna, and Heidelberg were organized, as well as Copenhagen, Uppsala, St. Andrews, Glasgow, and Aberdeen. But these universities became truly instruments of the state only with the coming of the Reformation and the subsequent emergence of the national state. When that happened, their autonomy and academic freedom became controversial; eventually the professors were made public servants, and the university became primarily a "school of public administration" for state and church. The notion of the university as a self-reliant corporate entity was replaced by that of its being a public institution and part and parcel of the governmental apparatus. This they have remained in Europe down to the twentieth century; and the totalitarian regimes in exaggerating this function have converted the university into a training center, removing the research function largely to separate academies.

These familiar facts are recalled here only in order to remind ourselves that the universities were European first and national afterwards and that therefore the present trend points to a return to a former state of affairs.[4] Such a return is now in full swing between the universities of France and Germany, and to a lesser extent between those of the other Common Market countries. But the European university community goes beyond that in some areas. Close ties have always existed between French universities and those of French-speaking Switzerland; and likewise between Germany and those of German-speaking Switzerland; German and Austrian universities have always been linked; and the connections between English and Scandinavian centers of higher learning, while not as intimate as the ones just mentioned, still have been significant.

Indeed, even at the height of cultural nationalism in the nineteenth and early twentieth centuries, there have of course always been extensive contacts. Mostly these were, however, of a highly esoteric, scholarly, and scientific kind; their political implications were strictly limited by the national framework and the official functions it imposed upon the university community. Only the rise of a new international, and more particularly a European, order has enabled the universities, professors, and students to rebuild a genuine European university community. This rebuilding has taken three forms: (1) overall European-wide organizations; (2) direct personal contacts and relationships; and (3) the establishment of partnerships by which two universities are paired, much as communes are paired, for mutual cooperation and exchange. We shall, in the following pages, first deal in a somewhat summary fashion with the first and second of these aspects, and then concentrate in greater detail upon the third because it provides a relatively stable and yet strictly academic setting for the development of a European outlook and behavior, political and educational.

First, however, a word concerning the Europe-wide student unrest. In a sense, it is a manifestation of a growing European academic community. But its political momentum would seem to be a result of the fact that progress toward a united Europe has been too slow to satisfy the ardent idealism of youth in France, Germany, and Italy rather than a response to the European idea. Because the connection is, at present, rather difficult to disentangle, we shall leave this movement, as well as the issues of university reform, aside in this chapter. Leaders like Dutschke and Cohn-Bendit are, in their call for revolutionary transformation of constitutional democracy and its underlying economic structure, adversaries rather than protagonists of a united Europe. Even if their activities are not Communist-inspired, as some would have them, their utterances are so clearly built upon Communist slogans that they sound anti-European; they certainly are anti-American. The choirs which shout "Ho, Ho, Ho" by the hour could instead fill the air with "Europe, Europe, Europe." For it is certainly a revolutionary undertaking. But they do not, as French and German students were inclined to do in the early fifties, make bonfires of the boundary posts. Let us turn then to the more humdrum organizational activity. The organizational collaboration is carried forward partly on an official and governmental and partly on a university level. In connection with the first level, OECE and OCDE, as well as the Council of Europe and the three Communities (ECSC, EEC, and Euratom), have played a significant role; while on the second level, certain overall organizations, such as that of the Rectors of European Universities, have been pathfinders of new approaches. In all this something that might be called the "Europeanization" of university instruction is playing an increasing role. It leads into a discussion of the somewhat diffuse development of personal relationships.[5]

National governments themselves have, of course, in recent years promoted bilateral exchanges of students and professors; this is particularly true between France and Germany, especially since the conclusion of the mutual Friendship Treaty (1963) and the establishment of the Franco-German Youth Office (*Office Franco-Allemand de la Jeunesse*). The latter has promoted youth exchanges on a very considerable scale, not limiting itself to students, but including workers, artisans, and many other categories.[6] These activities are, to be sure, part of a worldwide movement of student and youth exchanges, promoted especially by the United States, but they have achieved a considerably higher degree of intensity between France and Germany than between other countries. The negotiations for a mutual recognition of study periods and degrees within the Common Market—and especially between France and Germany, which have been going forward and are near completion between these two countries—will remove one of the main barriers to such exchanges as far as students are concerned.[7]

OECE and its successor have taken the initiative in promoting student exchanges, including management courses for business administrators. Their primary interest has been the preparation of engineers and administrators for underdeveloped areas, such as Greece and Turkey. They have not been a significant factor in the field of main interest for us here, but there can be little doubt that the graduates of these courses develop a European outlook in the course of their studies.

The Council of Europe, after engaging in a number of activities such as setting up the *Fonds culturel,* in 1962 organized the Council for Cultural Cooperation (CCC) as an overall organization coordinating a variety of activities. Its approach is very broad and covers the humanities and social sciences as well as the natural sciences; it also concerns itself with developing a European civic education, that is to say, the problems involved in creating a European loyalty. Under a Cultural Convention, an overall organization has been established. It consists of delegations appointed by national member governments, three members of the Consultative Assembly, and the chairmen and vice-chairmen of three Standing Committees: Higher Education and Research, General and Technical Education, and Extracurricular Education (Sport, Adult Education, etc.). These Committees provide the recommendations for action. The section (*Direction*) of the Council of Europe dealing with instruction and cultural and scientific affairs serves as a secretariat to the CCC; it serves as the initiator of the various activities undertaken. Considerable means are at the disposal of the CCC (1,500,000 Fr. in 1964) for the financing of its various programs. It has tackled fairly complex issues, such as the cooperation of universities throughout Europe. But although the CCC contributes its share to the development of a European university community, its action remains marginal due to the dispersion of its interests among too many nations and too many projects.[8]

The three European Communities, now merged in one organization, have engaged in considerable activities directed toward furthering the European academic community. Their activity is framed within the setting provided by bilateral agreements between the states composing the Community,[9] many of which antedate the formation of these communities; they contain the usual provisions about exchanges of students, language instruction, recognition of degrees, and so forth; they have recently been enlarged to promote explicitly "European culture and the unification of Europe."

The most important of such bilateral agreements is, to be sure, the Treaty on Franco-German Cooperation (January 22, 1963), which has been most fruitful in the field of cultural, and more especially, university collaboration.[10] It has provided a reasonably firm institutional framework for the whole range of academic relationships through organizing an office called Franco-German Youth Work (Deutsche-Franzosisches Jugendwerk). Presided over and directed by heads of government and foreign ministers, it has brought about monthly meetings of the key administrators of both sides for effectuating an ever-widening set of activities, especially of course exchanges, but also language instruction, adaptation of study programs and degrees, and so on. In this latter field, the *Conference of French and German Rectors* (see below) has been particularly effective in implementing the governmental policies, not only in carrying out governmental directives, but also in suggesting new approaches.

The Press and Information Service of the three Communities, now consolidated, has naturally been active in the field of cultural cooperation. It is the same world of youth and student exchanges, of adult education, press and radio that has been stimulated by this Service, often in cooperation with one or another of the many organizations that have become active in the field, notably the European Association of Teachers (*Association Européenne des Enseignants* [*AEDE*]); round tables, discussion groups, and more or less extended visits to Brussels and the other centers of European activity constitute a large part of this work. Direct cooperation with particular universities and their institutes of European studies have of course also figured among its activities.[11] Of the 15,000 visitors to the Community's institutions, it is reported that nearly 4,000 were teachers and students. In 1964, of 12,676 such visitors, a considerably larger percentage, namely 5,233, were of the academic world.

Among these visitors, many are of an advanced academic standing; seminars and similar groups remain in Brussels or Luxembourg for several days, receive detailed instruction from specialists in the various offices, and return with a greatly strengthened understanding of the European community.[12] The presentations are permeated by the sense of an emerging community; they are frank and calculated to appeal to the professional standards of academic and critical inquiry. As Dr. Sidjanski has concluded: "The students, chosen among the best and the most knowledgeable, establish a real contact with European realities and gain from such visits a fuller documentation, and verify their impressions in some special field or start new researches."[13] Naturally, Euratom, acting as an intermediary in many fields relating to its work, also contributes a good deal to the mounting sense of effective academic cooperation throughout Europe, but more especially within the Community of the Six.

A perplexing special issue is presented by the proposal that a European university be organized. This project was believed to have been authorized by Article 9.2 of the Euratom Treaty, which provides that "there shall be created an institution of university level. . . ." Indeed it seems to be definitely required.

Nonetheless, much controversy developed; experts were consulted and heard, committees of the CEE and of the CE were formed, and the eventual upshot of all the to-do was the virtual abandonment of these plans; at any rate, no positive decision has been taken. The many criticisms have led to the conclusion that "if the European university should be created, it should be an Institute, primarily for teaching and research in the social sciences and the humanities (*sciences humaines*) and not a vast multilingual establishment leading to the bachelor's and doctor's degree."[14] Open to all Europeans and not restricted to the Six, it is hoped that such an institute would not duplicate the instruction in existing universities and established centers of European studies, but would limit itself to special types of European studies and research, preferably of an interdisciplinary nature. The declared willingness of the Italian government to take the lead in establishing a European university (at Florence) has, however, not been implemented by any effective action, even though the Council of Ministers of Euratom welcomed such an initiative (July 18, 1961). Six departments were then envisaged: (1) Law, (2) Economics, (3) Political Science and Sociology, (4) History, (5) Mathematics, (6) Physics, to be implemented by a department of Comparative Languages and Literatures, and one for Art History. But nothing has happened since, and it does not seem likely that anything will very soon, unless outside (American) initiative enters the field. Nor does it seem necessary. The very pattern of interuniversity cooperation which has been developing suggests that in due course all universities and other academic institutions of higher learning will become European in outlook and methods of operation. To these methods of cooperation, other than actual partnerships, we now turn.[15]

There is a great deal of spontaneous private activity in the field of academic cooperation between European universities and their personnel. We can of course offer only some selected aspects of all these activities, but they are symptomatic for the development of a European university community. They may be divided into three major sectors or levels: (1) general cultural relations, (2) European academic associations, and (3) the Europeanization of higher education in the institutions of the Common Market. These three implement each other, and an intensification in one sector is apt to be paralleled by comparable intensification in the others.

General cultural relations are being cultivated by a number of organizations and institutions, notably the Center for European Culture (CEC), the Committee for Civic Education, the European schools,[16] the European Bureau for Popular (Adult) Education, the European Association of Teachers (AEDE), the International Center for European Education (CIFE), the International Federation of Europe Houses, and others.[17] They address themselves to distinct and different phases of education and culture and thus supplement each other, the Center for European Culture having a sort of coordinating function. Some go well beyond the Common Market area, or even Europe. Their work is much influenced by an ideological commitment to the unification of Europe, and in most cases is handicapped by the lack of adequate funds.

There is no particular reason for reviewing the activities of these several cultural organizations here.[18] They are part of the broad movement for European cooperation and eventual unification. Many of them are directed by deeply committed men and women who find in these organizational activities an outlet for their determination to see a united Europe come into being. There are, of course, among them many shades of opinion as to how such unification is to be achieved and about all the questions that go with the perplexing issue of the best way to federalize the European order. They have their ramifications in the academic world in many different ways: university teachers participate in their boards and administrative setups; students frequently do the same or utilize the programs in connection with their studies. All told, many thousands of the European intelligentsia are sharing in these enterprises and substantial sums are being expended in their multifarious activities. It is a highly pluralistic world, not free of some bitter personal rivalries and petty jealousies, but in their entirety constituting the avant garde of the wide sweep of advance toward a free and federal Europe.

It is within this context that the efforts of a more strictly academic type must be seen and evaluated. Unless that is done, a misleading impression of academic primacy would be created. As a matter of fact, the universities and university-like institutions of higher learning have been rather slow in responding. They have been, certain specialists excepted, conservatively reserved in their interest. Only since the coming into being of the Common Market have they become more active.

The discussion of the academic dimension of European community formation falls into three parts: (1) overall organizations, (2) special institutes, and (3) *jumelages* or partnerships. Our discussion will be primarily concerned with these last undertakings, but the other two deserve at least brief sketching of their range of activity.

Among the overall organizations, a prominent place must be accorded the quinquennial *Conference of European Rectors and Vicechancellors.* It grew out of an effort to implement the Brussels Pact (1948) which called for cultural exchanges; and its growth parallels the progressive enlargement of European unity: the creation of the Western European Union (WEU) in 1954 precipitated the establishment of the Conference after repeated conferences and colloquia held in England, France, the Benelux countries, and Italy in the early fifties. The search was for a common policy for European universities, stressing the autonomy, if not the independence, of the universities, as it had been traditional in England. From the first Assembly (Cambridge, 1955) to the most recent one (Göttingen, 1964), these assemblies, reinforced by meetings of a continuing committee of the WEU, the Committee of West European Universities and its secretariat, have dealt with very general problems in a consultative way. Since 1962, a Standing Committee of the Council of Europe, the CESR (*Comité de l'Enseignment*

Superieur et de la Recherche) has collaborated closely with the Conference. At Göttingen they set up a permanent organization with its own statutes; these stressed in their preamble the ancient tradition of the free university throughout Europe and its importance for the moral, social, and economic future of Europe. Its permanent seat is Geneva; the rector of the University of Geneva was elected president. The organization of the Conference is typically federal and based on the equality of the universities, not of the nations to which they belong, with the majority being constituted by the 102 rectors of the universities of the Common Market countries: 6 Belgian, 25 French, 35 German, 27 Italian, and 9 Dutch; to these should be added the 2 Greek and 7 Turkish universities, since the two countries are associated with the Common Market, making a grand total of 111. EFTA countries (and their associate, Finland) provide 60 rectors: Austria 7; Denmark 4; Finland 3; Great Britain 30; Norway 4; Portugal 3; Sweden 2; and Switzerland 7. There are also included 2 Icelandic, 4 Irish, and 11 Spanish universities. It is evident that an Assembly, meeting only every five years and producing very general directives, which are then "applied" or "implemented" by a permanent committee in which each country is represented and which also contains seven members elected at large as well as the president and the prospective host rector—that is, in all, more than 25 members—cannot hope to come to grips with concrete problems of university cooperation.[19]

For this reason and because of the need of closer Franco-German cooperation within the Common Market, a special *Conference of French and German Rectors* has come into being which since 1958 has taken the lead in intensifying interuniversity cooperation. It is, like the larger body, somewhat handicapped by the brief tenure of a good many of the rectors, notably the German ones who traditionally serve for only one year, though this is in process of being changed under new university laws.[20] Nonetheless, good work has been accomplished, especially in the fields of exchanges of professors, students, and the assimilation of programs of study and degrees as mentioned above. They, more particularly, recommended the establishment of *jumelages* between the French and German universities, in light of the initial successes, and adopted a charter for such partnerships in 1962. There can be little question that in spite of the great difficulties in assimilating higher education in the countries of the Common Market, real progress has been achieved.

The other overall organization on a university level, the *Association of Institutes of European Studies* (AIEE), had perhaps best be treated in terms of some of these institutes themselves.[21] They have undertaken a good deal of research as well as instruction, and have addressed themselves to the training of personnel for the various European offices and organizations as well as of diplomatic and business cadres.[22] They offer graduate and postgraduate instruction, mostly in economics, political science, and law. A large part of them are integral parts of a university or other institution of higher learning. Wherever they exist, they naturally become centers from which European community sentiment spreads into other parts of the university. Some of them, like that at Nancy, stress the broad historical and cultural givens and refuse to concern themselves with the immediate tasks of European unification; others—the majority—are frankly committed to these tasks, though usually stressing their neutrality vis-à-vis the rival programs of "federalists," "functionalists," and others. Challenges like those presented by the policies of General de Gaulle have caused sharp controversies at times, but have on the whole been stimulants rather than deterrents of research and writing on the problems of Europe.

In 1951 and at the instigation of the Center for European Culture, these institutes organized and have in the years since developed, as just mentioned, the Association of Institutes (AIEE), which now counts about thirty members, about half of which are French and German. The Association serves as a clearing house, seeks to coordinate activities—with rather limited success—and more recently has sought to foster some joint research. The presidency has rotated among directors of these institutes and has been serviced by a general secretariat located at Geneva (at the Center for European Culture). It publishes an annual volume which gives a fairly good idea of the overall activities of the institutes and the problems which concern them.[23] To the extent that the AIEE and the institutes which it comprises succeed in developing joint research themes (at present the reaction of pressure groups to the crisis of 1958 is being studied), it may contribute considerably to the development of the European academic community.

Besides these organizations on the professorial level (and there are others, such as the *Association for the Development of European Political Science,*[24] founded in 1964), we find a proliferation of student organizations. In 1965 the six student unions of the Community organized themselves into the *Unions d'Etudiants de l'Europe des Six.* Like the Conference of the Rectors, this body is actively concerned with the harmonization of degree and admission requirements as well as the problems of university reform. Besides this semiofficial body, numerous discussion groups have come into being, often university-wide, and are engaged in all the usual and typical student activities, from working groups to social evenings. Where dormitories have been built—and such housing facilities are becoming more numerous all the time—study groups are likely to spring up, especially where the students themselves are in control, and such study groups are intermittently focused upon the problems of European integration. This in turn leads to trips and excursions to the main centers of European activity; the EC alone received over 5,000 students. The writer himself conducted such an excursion in 1965 within the scope of his seminar and was greatly impressed with the readiness of the authorities at Brussels to meet with and explain to the students the work of the EC and related activities; the same happened in 1964 and 1966 at Strasbourg when such an excursion led us to the Council of Europe. Student and faculty initiative implement each other in these encounters. Another broadly based student association is the *Union des Associations Européennes d'Etudiants,* brought into being on German student initiative in 1961, and having strong roots in Belgium and Italy as well.

As a final point to this survey, mention may be made of the steady increase in both courses and seminars, as well as in dissertations dealing with problems of Europe.[25]

Turning now to the more particular problems of and observations on the partnerships (*jumelages*) of pairs of European and more especially French and German universities, it needs to be said at the outset that it has proved very difficult to assess them in terms of their political implications. Even the elementary data are difficult to ascertain.[26] These data show that of 25 such partnerships existing in 1965, 14 were Franco-German ones, while only 4 were with British universities, 4 with non-European ones, and 1 with a Yugoslav university. In addition to formal partnerships, 14 officially sanctioned relationships (*rapports*) existed of which some were with American (1) and Spanish (3) and British (1) universities: these relationships may, of course, come to resemble partnerships rather closely. Partnerships (*jumelages*) are formally organized and institutionalized systems of cooperation through professorial and student exchanges, within the framework of official receptions and other kinds of ceremonial acts; they resemble the partnerships (*jumelages*) of cities and towns (*communes*) described in the previous chapter; as there noted, they often parallel them, as in the case of Montpellier and Heidelberg. The list of such *jumelages* or Franco-German university partnerships includes the following: Aix-Tübingen; Bordeaux-Hamburg; Clermont-Ferrand–Cologne; Caen-Würzburg; Dijon-Mainz; Grenoble-Freiburg; Lille Münster; Lyon-Frankfurt; Lyon-Karlsruhe; Montpellier-Heidelberg; Poitiers-Marburg; Rennes-Keil; Rennes-Erlangen; Toulouse-Bonn; there exist also five doubtful ones, which can be left aside here.

It is curious that the Italian universities have been so uncooperative, as have been the Belgian ones; for this indifference contrasts sharply with the attitude of the general public in these countries, as well as their associational and political activity. In both respects Belgium and Italy have been in the forefront of European integration. The situation calls for more detailed investigation. There are some indications that it may in part be related to the same causes which explain the weakness of political science until very recently; but it may also be caused by cumbersome and antiquated university organization, as highlighted by recent strike and protest movements among the students who are very active in France and Germany where university cooperation and community formation have been flourishing. It is more likely that the lack of funds, repeatedly mentioned by Sidjanski in reporting his interviews, has a great deal to do with it. Certainly the Franco-German Youth Office has helped a good deal by assisting professors and students interested in forwarding university cooperation between the two countries.[27]

Turning now to some of the effective Franco-German *jumelages*—the doubtful ones are discussed by Sidjanski with great candor[28]—we find that they present a fairly uniform pattern. In a number of cases, such as Dijon-Mainz, Lyon-Frankfurt, Montpellier-Heidelberg, the *jumelage* between the universities parallels one between the two cities, and in all these cases they clearly reinforce each other. The author can confirm the interview and questionnaire data reported by Sidjanski from personal experience as a "participant observer" at Heidelberg. Obviously, the resources of a municipal administration available for representative functions significantly reinforce what the universities can do. At the same time, the prestigious position of the academic world lends a certain glamour to the partnership of two communes (see preceding chapter).

It is very difficult to assess the political implications of these undertakings. The multiplication of professorial and student exchanges, of longer or shorter duration, and the holding of joint conferences and extended discussions undoubtedly contribute toward reducing the national egocentricity in the academic establishment of both countries. This is not without value, since both French and German universities have been veritable fortresses of national sentiment, and if there ever is to emerge a European nation, its spirit will have to conquer these strongholds of past preoccupations with national culture, values, and beliefs.

Any realistic appraisal of the present situation suggests, however, that progress has been very slow. Is this "cultural lag" really to be wondered at? Long after the more venturesome spirits had abandoned scholasticism, it still held sway in the universities; during the English Revolution, both Oxford and Cambridge strongly inclined toward the royal cause; the unification of Germany found its most vocal advocates outside the universities, the majority of which remained faithful to the established order of the princely states. These cases are symptomatic; it would be easy to multiply them. In the process of forming new communities, the academic establishment tends to be rather conservative. It certainly is proving itself to be so in contemporary Europe. Even so, Sidjanski is probably right when he concludes his study with the assertion that the characteristic features of the academic and cultural relations which the *jumelages* have fostered "justify, in our view, at least to a considerable extent, the employment of the term 'European university community' (*Communauté universitaire européenne*)." He adds the caution that this is an emergent community (*communauté naissante*).

The *jumelages* are based upon a formal act, as mentioned before. The text of agreement between Cologne and Clermont-Ferrand may serve as an illustration. It was adopted by the Council of the University of Clermont-Ferrand on July 3, 1962.

A. The two universities will sponsor such *conventions de jumelage*, already concluded or to be concluded between its institutes and faculties.

B. They agree on the following procedures for their *jumelage:*

   1. For the duration of the *jumelage* (partnership) each university will:

a. designate a delegate of its council (senate) who is to watch over the relations of the two universities;
b. make efforts to provide in their budgets the sums necessary for putting the agreements into effect.

2. Each university will communicate to the other all useful information concerning changes in their teaching personnel.
3. They will make an effort to assure the professors of the sister university decent lodging, while they are on visit.
4. They will reserve, in student dormitories, suitable lodgings for assistants sent by the institutes, faculties, or universities so twinned.
5. They will reserve, at appropriate times, in such dormitories a suitably calculated number of rooms for the lodging of students of the twinned university.
6. They look forward to establishing fellowships for this *jumelage.*
7. They will encourage encounters of athletic groups.
8. They will exchange annually reports of the rectors . . . especially such as evaluate the concrete results of this collaboration.
9. During the *jumelage,* delegations of the Council and Senate of the two universities shall meet, at mutually agreed upon dates, in common assembly in order to exchange opinions on the progress and possible extension of the *jumelage.*
10. Each university shall address once a year to the deans of the faculties of the twinned universities, and in both languages, a summary report about the outstanding facts of its development during the preceding year.
11. The two universities will organize together university weeks prepared by a harmonization of both teaching and research involved.
12. The adoption of this agreement of partnership shall be made the subject of a notification to the governments concerned.
13. A solemn meeting is to be organized at the start of the *jumelage* which will permit informing the public.[29]

Signed by the two rectors, this and other like agreements show how the *jumelages* are conceived. Let us now see how they have in general worked out.

The overall record is not as impressive as it might be. Sidjanski found that only four of the *jumelages* listed above are really developed to any large extent, and among these only Frankfurt–Lyon actually is being carried forward without any formal agreement of the kind just reported. The reason given by the administration at Lyon, when interviewed, was that it seemed unnecessary to formalize such a relationship, that this did not appeal to the informality of the French—surely an astonishing argument to an American or even a Britisher. Certainly the French propensity to carry all manner of contracts, including international treaties, into the most minute detail would suggest that the kind of general language in which the typical *jumelage* agreement is cast would seem rather to run counter to this French propensity than to any dislike for formalism!

The three most active *jumelages* are, besides the one just mentioned, Heidelberg-Montpellier, Freiburg-Grenoble, and Aix-Tübingen. In all four of these we find regular exchanges of professors and students, more informal visits of groups of students, exchanges of information, and so on. We also find that all of them are somewhat handicapped by the French professors' lack of knowledge of German and a recurrent reference to the obstacles created by the differences in educational program and preparation of the students. But in spite of these obstacles there is also a general sense of satisfaction and a belief in the value of these enterprises, at least for the time being. One cannot help but wonder, however, if in course of time, and in case of the stabilization of good Franco-German relations, these *jumelages* will not be superseded by a more broadly dispersed mode of exchanges. Academic life and scientific specialization being what it is, there seems to be no particular reason why teachers and students in different fields should necessarily complement each other in two universities, nor would it seem that the political implications of such interuniversity relations would be reinforced by that kind of dual localization. At the same time, a certain measure of institutionalization is undoubtedly proving helpful in the beginning phase; that would appear to be the reason for the Conference of Rectors taking such a vigorous stand in support of the establishment of *jumelages*.

There are a few specific experiences and observations, which I believe germane to our overall concern in this analysis, to be drawn from the more detailed report of Sidjanski.[30] Taking first the problem of who took the initiative for it, one notes especially that the *jumelage* between Heidelberg and Montpellier had its origin and is receiving its continuing drive from student interest, curiously enough centered in the faculty of medicine. Montpellier claims to be the earliest medical school; more important, it remains one of the best in France. Whether that had anything to do with the fact that the oldest German university sought a close lien with it is hard to make certain of. It has become the "founders' myth" of this relationship. By contrast, the *jumelage* between Frankfurt and Lyon owes its existence to the devotion and enthusiasm of particularly interested professors in the respective linguistic fields. In the case of Aix-Tübingen, the *jumelage* between the universities appears, to all intents and purposes, to be a consequence of the *jumelage* between the two cities and has grown up as an implementation of it—precisely the opposite of Heidelberg-Montpellier, where the partnership of the universities has brought one between the cities in its train. It is clear from these four cases that the origin of such partnerships is neither uniform nor particularly revealing: they seem to occur in the sequel and as part of the generally favorable atmosphere created by the Common Market. These *jumelages* are clearly not the pathfinders of integration, but the result of it.

Even so, and more particularly in view of the unique position of the university in German intellectual life, the development of these *jumelages* ought not to be underestimated. That only a few are at present very active is natural enough; in this respect the university community does not differ from the other realms of community life we have been examining. Innovations are the work of the few in the very nature of things.[31] Nowhere is the freedom of man at once so irrepressible and so elitist. Our detailed inquiries have shown and support with adequate evidence that in the words of some interviewees, "colleagues have become friends." Whereas in the past, invitations to lecture and participate in conferences were rare between French and German universities, they are now the order of the day. Similarly, encounters between students of the two neighboring nations have become part of the routine of a considerable number of universities, and the establishment of lasting friendships, and indeed marriages, are becoming habitual. The latter is, according to accepted sociological findings, one of the most important indicators of community formation, assimilation, and the lessening of social distance associated therewith.[32]

It is in turn rather significant that *jumelages* are most frequent in the European Community, and within this Community between French and German universities. Indeed, as Sidjanski discovered, they constitute two-fifths of the total. And as he observes, this quantitative result is reinforced by a more detailed inspection of the intensity and the quality of the contacts. Observers have, often in a spirit of mockery, spoken of a love affair between France and Germany. This expression is very misleading and unconfirmed by detailed inquiries into the mutual attitudes.[33] It is particularly inept in the university field; for the detailed interview data presented by Sidjanski show that these contacts were approached by both sides with a great deal of reserve, sophistication, and indeed scepticism. In the course of them, however, many surprising discoveries were made, often of a strictly scholarly and scientific kind, and these discoveries extended to the personal and family life of both faculty and students. Hence instead of a love affair, the relationship institutionalized in these *jumelages* or partnerships has many of the characteristics, psychologically speaking, of a conversion rather than a love affair. It more particularly was and is no romantic *coup de foudre,* but the men involved in it exhibit some of the convictional rigidities of the convert.

If Sidjanski rightly insists, at the conclusion of his study, that the institutionalized and stabilized relationship, which the *jumelages* represent, enables us to speak of the beginnings of a European university community, one should add that his investigations do not permit any conclusion as to their political implications. Some French and German professors, too numerous to list here, have played leading roles in the movement for integration, as have professors of other European universities; others have, on the contrary, been among the most vociferous critics and sceptics, such as the late Pieter Geyl. Similarly, student groups have been in the forefront of the forces pushing toward European integration, but they have always remained a minority; and a large majority have remained indifferent, if not hostile. In France, the vociferous presence of a strong Communist contingent has combined with a substantial following of de Gaulle to strengthen these voices of doubt and even opposition; in Germany, the widespread desire for the reunification of the country has not only taken precedence, but has worried many, lest European integration prove an insurmountable obstacle to German reintegration. Partnership among the universities more than, but along with, the creation of a European University Center may prove a decisive factor in coping with these deep-seated reluctances of the academic community to abandon the familiar haven of national culture and community in which they have for so long played the central role.

10. Trends and Prospects

It is part of being clever nowadays to talk about the "end" of European integration, about "dead alleys," "crises," and impending collapse. The realities described in the preceding chapters tell a different tale. To be sure, the rosy optimism and enthusiasm of the early years are gone. In all the sectors of society we have examined there is sober and hardheaded work being done; we found limited and often rather humdrum issues engaging the daily attention of men who do not expect to realize utopia, but rather to moderate some of the more patent weaknesses of the traditional national state. A good part of the mood of resignation on the part of the wider public has been greatly fostered by the political positions taken by General de Gaulle and his government; more particularly his refusal to admit the British into the Common Market, even though strongly desired and repeatedly urged by the other five members—some more, some less—has strained the relationship to the point where a mood of rebelliousness came to the fore. And yet the economic bonds have continued to grow; and every year has brought more effective integration in business and labor as well as in agriculture, in communes and universities as well as in mass communications. It is when the other five try to open a way for

British participation, whether through the German trade plan of September 1968 or the Belgian proposal for foreign policy consultation and defense cooperation under WEU in October of that year (Harmel Plan), that the setbacks occur. Thus the vision becomes blurred and the failure to attain the larger objective obscures the steady progress in more limited fields.[1]

The monetary crisis which threatened the French franc in November 1968 brought to light how dangerous the failure to push forward in fact is. A New York banker was quoted recently as saying, "When you remove barriers to let Europeans trade freely, it is absolutely impossible to maintain an equilibrium in balances of payments without a common currency."[2] This statement is inaccurate in two important respects, although its general thrust is right. The Common Market does not only let Europeans trade freely, but it has removed the barriers to capital movement, and as a result funds can shift from place to place in the CM; it is obvious, or ought to be, that such an arrangement is incompatible with fixed exchange rates between the countries of the Common Market. At the same time, there need not be a common currency, desirable though such a development would be, if flexible exchange rates existed between the countries of the Common Market and a common fixed rate vis-à-vis the outside world. But even though this would help, a common currency would be a far sounder solution, and those may well be right who, like the above-quoted banker, maintain that "the biggest lesson to be drawn from the current crisis would be for the six members of the European Common Market to sit down and work out a common currency."[3] Unfortunately, the massive economic controls which de Gaulle proposed to deal with the crisis are likely to weaken rather than to strengthen such a prospect. That it will eventually be worked out seems quite certain, however. Such a prospect raises some of the most challenging problems of contemporary politics. That currency is one of the most important instruments of modern politics is too often forgotten over its economics. Since currency is at the heart of all economic policy and planning, the old liberal notion of making it simply "independent" no longer works.[4] Even so, a setup roughly similar to that of the Federal Reserve Board would seem rather well adapted to CM needs, with the several national central banks occupying a position comparable to that of banks like the Federal Reserve Bank of New York.[5] In any case, the increasingly close cooperation between banks in the several countries of the CM now being studied will presumably be able to show that in this sector of the economy too a process of informal community formation is going forward, and sentiment is crystallizing in favor of such a system.[6]

Such a development would seem to constitute an integral part of the development of an economic union, as contrasted with a mere customs union. We have seen earlier that a demand for it was voiced in connection with the establishment of the customs union in the summer of 1968. For an economic union means, according to the authoritative voice of the EC Commission, "all the measures required to create on the territory of the Community conditions similar to those obtaining on a domestic market." Spelling out what this means, they added that "these are (a) Free movement of goods; (b) Free movement of persons, services, and capital; (c) Implementation of the common transport policy; (d) Arrangements to protect competition from distortion; (e) Provisions to guarantee that the economic policies of the Community and the Member States share the elements needed to secure conditions similar to those obtaining on a domestic market."[7] Among these probably the most important (though not spelled out here) is a common currency. The common market of the United States, for example, could never function if some of the capital-distributing states, such as New York, had to be concerned about their balance of payments vis-à-vis the capital-consuming states.

We have shown in the preceding chapters how many informal human contacts are developing in the several fields in which individuals are taking initiatives and persuading groups to do likewise. There are others in which the same is happening, which we shall hope to deal with at a later date. Some brief indications will be given below concerning the fields of mass communications and the European civil service, as well as intermarriage, which is occurring at an ever-accelerating rate. Before we discuss these, a more strictly "political" field of emergent contacts might be mentioned, namely that of regional policy. For it has long been recognized that national boundaries often obscure and even efface the natural regions into which the European national states are divided (see map, preceding page 1, above). Such regions do in fact at times lie across national boundaries—a fact which has led an insightful student of these matters to speak of Europe as a *Europe des Ethnies.*[8] But one need not go as far as that in order to recognize that CM Europe needs a "regional policy." The Treaty of Rome does not offer explicit directions for such a policy, although regions are mentioned in the preamble and elsewhere and the intention is proclaimed of "harmonizing" Europe by insuring a "harmonious growth," "a harmonious development" and of "evaluating regional situations."[9] President Hallstein at one point said that "every action of economic policy involves an element of regional policy," and other members of the Commission have spoken in the same vein. But thus far "there are no proposals for concrete action."[10] But there are official working groups seeking to develop lines of policy which were embodied in a preliminary report in 1964.[11] In May 1965 proposals were presented by the Commission to the Council of Ministers. These proposals involve administrative decentralization. They are consequently eyed with suspicion by many. Nonetheless, as the "First Communication" put it,

> a regional policy, without tending towards a leveling of national incomes, nor artificially slowing down the progress of the more developed zones, must contribute to remedying the excessive disparities in income which exist between the various regions . . . and, although it is necessary to put development policies into practice in all the regions, the priorities of community activity should be re-

served for those areas which have the lowest standards of living or particular difficulties of adjustment.[12]

It is hardly surprising that such a policy, directed toward assisting underdeveloped parts of the CM, should have been slow in getting under way, when one considers how many have been the obstacles in the way of such a development within the national states composing the CM. It is in line with what we have had occasion to note repeatedly in the course of our analysis: namely that the European authorities become the target of advocates of emergent and innovating policies who have been able to convince national authorities of the justice of their cause or, perhaps more often, of the feasibility of their projects. In this particular field, the case is strong for seeking the help of the industrially stronger northern members of the Community in developing Southern Italy—a *Sorgenkind* of the Italian government for many years.

But there are regions which call for Community effort in all the Common Market countries. At times the particular regional difficulties may even be related to specific CM policies. Breton peasants and Walloon miners are as much involved as the regions of Germany affected by the division of that country. The Commission has increasingly recognized, and the European parliament has in fact urged and insisted upon it, that more effective action is called for in forwarding economic transformation and development according to regional needs.[13] As President Rey put it in May 1968, "three types of regions seem to merit absolute priority: the main outlying regions of the Community, which are often heavily dependent on agriculture, the older industrial regions now in decline, and the internal frontier regions common to one or more Member States. Nor, of course, must we forget the regions specifically affected by the division of Germany; the Treaty mentions these specifically."[14] These interior frontier regions are an especially interesting case; for obviously as the customs and economic unions mature, numerous activities in these areas bordering the former national frontiers are profoundly affected. But, of course, the modernization of the underdeveloped and now declining regions of marginal agriculture, more especially Southern Italy, presents the most pressing issues. Apart from the very substantial work done in facilitating the mobility of workers discussed above (Chapter 6), aid to the industrialization of Southern Italy has been promoted very actively under Article 56 of the Rome Treaty—the European Investment Bank has played an important role here—and the political implications of these activities are far-reaching as the daily lives of more and more human beings are being affected by Community policies and activities.

The growth of regional development policies suggests a word about the CM's relation to potential members not now forming a part of it. This is not the place to elaborate upon this complicated and much discussed subject.[15] But a few words are perhaps in order. For in a sense, regionalism knows no borders.[16]

The issue is much more pressing in some of the associated states of the European Community, notably, Greece, Turkey, and the former African colonies now united in an *ad hoc* association for the purpose of cooperating with the Common Market. In fact, these are underdeveloped countries, *Entwicklungslaender* as the Europeans more politely call them, whose association with the European Community is primarily intended to assist them in their more rapid development. This is not the place to elaborate upon the problems they pose, although their association has very considerable political implications arising from the numerous personal bonds which their association is multiplying all the time.[17] Great Britain and the Scandinavian countries have refused to consider a similar relationship, though it was suggested by the French. Political considerations outweighed economic advantage in this decision which blocked one possible road toward eventual merger. It is in a way curious that the British, who readily accepted such an association in the case of the Coal and Steel Community, should have been so certain that an association would not provide them with a sufficiently effective leverage; but all is speculation, and the contingencies are so numerous that "it is anybody's guess" how such an association might develop. As a new form of federalizing[18] it may have more of a future than conventional politics, in terms of power and prestige, is willing to acknowledge. In any case, it seems natural that the Common Market should have negotiated association for relatively weak states who receive more than they contribute, and been unsuccessful in arriving at similar arrangements with states that might constitute equal members in the course of time.

The issue is to some extent tied in with the development of a European civil service. The states so far associated with the CM are not very highly bureaucratized, and full membership would present real difficulties on that score. On the other hand, Great Britain and the Scandinavian countries can claim to possess highly developed services—indeed superior to those of the CM countries. The infusion of members of these services might create very serious problems, quite apart from the "crowding." Anyone familiar with the growth of the modern state knows the decisive role which the development of a central bureaucracy has played in the process.[19] And considering the close link between the growth of the state and the building of the nation,[20] it is very germane to our inquiry to ask: What is happening to the human beings that form the administrative services of the European communities—the European bureaucrats, or "Eurocrats," as they have been dubbed. A growing literature is concerned with their behavior and their problems.[21] These problems are basically threefold, and concern (a) relations between the Eurocrats and the national bureaucracies, (b) relations between the Eurocrats *inter se*, involving the clash of distinctive national traditions, (c) relations between the Eurocrats and the public, more especially the European interest groups discussed in earlier chapters. In a future study we hope to deal primarily with the first and second of these problems, and such indications as there may be about the changing attitude of Frenchmen, Germans, and Italians serving in these organizations: Are they becoming Europeans or not, or to what extent and in what way?

One would assume that the answer to this latter question is going to be a qualified affirmative. For in general, only men and women with a strong European motivation are likely to seek service in European organizations in preference to established careers in their national services. Years of work in these organizations will further strengthen their inclination to think in European terms. These positive motivations will be counteracted to some extent by the disillusionment and disappointments caused by the supposed slowing down of European integration. The same happens of course to all public servants as they confront the realities of politics.

Both the first and the second of these problem areas are comprehended in what has been aptly called "bureaucratic interpenetration."[22] Basically it is the intermingling of national and international bureaucrats in various working groups and committees. Such an intermingling may occur at the policy-making level, or it may be on an administrative and managerial level, though it should be remembered that this distinction is quite relative.[23] In any case, it might make a vital difference whether such intermingling occurs within the framework of a strictly international organization, such as UNO or NATO, or whether the framework is supranational, at least to some extent.[24] The international civil servant who is a Eurocrat, presumably is committed to more than mere *co*operation. To put it in sloganized form, he is committed to *operation*. Certain definite policies, laid down in the Rome treaties, are to be operationally implemented. Of course, the same might be claimed for certain policies circumscribed in the UN Charter; and a measure of commitment to an emergent world community is unquestionably part of the attitudinal equipment of the United Nations bureaucracy. Nor is it important for our present purpose to assert, let alone prove, that the attitudinal equipment of the Eurocrat is unique. It is sufficient if it can be shown that he is, in a very specific sense, the instrument and mouthpiece of an emergent European community. In any case, the Treaty itself provides that "Members of the Commission fulfill their function quite independently." And to make doubly sure, it adds: "They shall neither ask for nor accept instructions from any government or outside organ."[25] These norms would seem to hold *a fortiori* for the Eurocrats, properly speaking. But they do not, of course, exclude their being inclined to "anticipate the reactions" of their national governments.[26] Moreover, since the governments are often recalling an official and then putting forward (nominating) a replacement, the independence of the administrators is endangered. A certain amount of exchange is, of course, desirable; but if the career of officials is usually to be sought in the national service, their Europeanization is bound to be impeded.[27] There is a good deal of complaint also about the "dosage principle," which means that official positions are distributed according to national origin, in proportion to the amount paid by the partners to the common budget: one quarter each go to France, Germany, and Italy, and the rest to the Benelux countries. Since the population of the three Benelux countries is only a fraction of the others, it means that an interested Belgian or Dutchman, let alone a Luxembourger, has a hundred or more percent better chance to serve the European Commission than one of the other three. The principle of such proportional distribution is familiar in federal systems; both in the United States and Switzerland it is an important factor in the federal service.

This service has by now achieved a considerable size; a total of about 4,500 persons were employed by the three communities prior to the merging of their executives, which is expected to result in some streamlining and consequent reductions (or more adequate staffing). To the extent that a common economic policy is being developed in connection with the emergent economic union (see above), larger numbers of officials are obviously going to be needed: in agriculture, where a common policy has been adopted, a sharp increase is already in evidence, and complaints are heard about its being too limited. It is not easy to find candidates adequately prepared; they are supposed to know at least one other language besides their own, and with French having become the unacknowledged *lingua franca* of the Commission (all languages are supposed to be on an even footing), this second language is apt to be French. According to one view of an experienced leader in the field, former president of Euratom, Etienne Hirsch, the following is required as adequate preparation: familiarity with the legislation, practices, and problems of all the member states and, one presumes, that of the EC. Besides, he would urge that a European civil servant "should also have some understanding of differences in attitude, outlook and tradition and be able to adapt himself to them." Hirsch believes that such an official "must give unquestioning loyalty to Europe." "The recruitment of such highly qualified officials has been facilitated by the existence of a strong current of European idealism," Hirsch thinks, but he hastens to add that this idealism has been reinforced by good salaries, at least at the start superior to national salaries.[28] There is now a good deal of complaint about the relative decline and about the influx of "auxiliaries," personnel less qualified and less well paid. Yet the morale is rather higher than in national services, and as one observer notes, "the best Eurocrats feel themselves to be, not stateless technocrats, but charter members of Europe." To the extent to which this is true they also contribute significantly to the informal community formation and the development of a European mentality. Spinelli has said that the Commission is a "gigantic European pressure group," but this surely is an exaggeration. "Influence is not government," he has reminded us, but he has overlooked that much government is influence and that many genuine administrative decisions are made by the Commission, even though national administrations are brought into the process at every stage.[29]

If the Eurocrat may be said to be at the very center of informal community formation, mass communications media are at the opposite extreme. Catering to the individual Frenchman, German, or Italian, even if in the mass, they would seem to be far removed from the Europeanization process, and its political implications. Yet, in fact, highly significant changes have been taking place, especially in the field of broadcasting. It has happened more or less informally. The press used to be spoken of as the "fourth estate." But radiobroadcasting and more particularly television have not become a close rival of the press; rather, they have probably outdistanced the press as a molder of political attitudes. In full recognition of this fact, the French government has established and maintained full control of radiobroadcasting through ORFT (Office de Radiodiffusion et Television Française)[30]—a control which was sharply challenged by its own personnel during the unrest of May 1968. This close control, dubious from a democratic standpoint to say the least, has been of some advantage in furthering Franco-German community formation. For the policy of the French government, and more particularly that of de Gaulle, equivocal on political and economic unification, has been favorable to cultural and economic cooperation. This is generally true of French policy: while de Gaulle made very critical remarks about American foreign policy, cultural friendship and cooperation were emphasized and furthered in every way.

It is therefore quite normal for ORTF to seek to develop effective working relationships with German broadcasting stations. These are pluralistic and linked to German federalism. The setup is unique and resulted from a compromise between American Occupation authorities advocating American practice and the older German (and generally European) policy of having all radiobroadcasting facilities centralized and controlled by the government[31]—a monopoly which is bearable when firmly controlled by a parliament, as in Britain, but totalitarian when at the beck and call of the executive, as it was under Hitler and Goebbels. It consists today of nine rather independent regional radiobroadcasting and two television units. The attempt of the federal government to secure a third television facility for itself foundered upon the opposition of the states (*Laender*), and was eventually held incompatible with the Basic Law by the Constitutional Court.[32] These units are highly competitive and their top-staff positions, especially that of the

Intendant or president, are subject to intense party rivalry, especially at the time of recruitment; but due to the differing constellations, competition at the lower-staff echelons is also intense. The situation in Italy resembles that in France, except that the parliament maintains a much stronger control. One wonders whether making the former ambassador to Bonn the general director of the Italian broadcasting system does not have political significance; there were stories to the effect that he was to change the mass attitude in Italy towards Germany.[33]

The cooperation between ORTF and the German *Rundfunk-* and *Fernseh* stations has taken the form of continuous efforts at cooperation in shaping program content, especially where "hot" divisive issues are involved. Thus the fiftieth anniversary of the outbreak of the First World War presented such a challenge; for French and German conventional history was sharply divided on the issues. French and German directing personnel thereupon decided to invite several French and German historians of good repute to meet for a conference and discuss these issues in the hope of arriving at a common denominator which could guide broadcasters in dealing with the matter. The author was told in an interview with one of the directors of ORTF that the effort was successful.[34] A similar issue presented itself when the anniversary of the battle of Verdun occurred. In this instance, it was decided to invite veterans of the great encounter, both French and German, to revisit the battlefields and exchange views. As a human interest story this televised encounter must have had a profound appeal.

One wonders whether this cooperation did not also have its ramifications at the time of the student and worker rebellion in Paris. Since ORTF inclined to sympathize, its personnel went into strike (and thereby prevented de Gaulle from addressing the nation at a crucial moment, May 30, 1968). ORTF has since been purged and reorganized.[35] Since ORTF is now going to do all its own producing, which the Germans did anyhow, cooperation could become even more closely coordinated. At the same time, the closer control by the government, which always tended to manipulate the news, may persuade more Frenchmen to listen to Radio Luxemburg—an independent commercial station with a natural penchant toward Europe and indeed in fact a European institution with considerable political implications in so far as its listeners tend to form opinions and attitudes on the basis of these broadcasts.[36]

The world of the press presents a rather different picture. Here competition is the order of the day. The clamor about "monopoly," especially concerning the Springer press in Germany, is highly inaccurate in phrasing its criticism of the great power which such large combines wield. For all such power can be exercised only within the restricting confines of the competition that other newspapers, radiobroadcasting, and book publishing provide. Only in totalitarian regimes is anything approaching a "monopoly of mass communications" achieved. It is for that reason alone that it is misleading to speak of de Gaulle's Fifth Republic as a "fascist" regime. Newspapers and magazines of every conceivable hue, including the red and black of the extremes of the political palette, are published in the six countries of the Common Market. They present to their readers many contrasting views of Europe and European integration. It is impossible to pick out some of them as "elite"[37] and highly misleading to argue from the degree of enthusiasm displayed in some of them about the relative strength of European sentiment. What we have often had occasion to remark upon in earlier pages of this study is, of course, also neglected in the press: an increasingly pragmatic, matter-of-fact acceptance of the ongoing process of Europeanization without much fanfare, or indeed pleading.

The old and long-established system of correspondents apart, there is very little active "cooperation" between even those press organs which strongly favor European integration. *Jumelages* or partnerships do not seem to exist. Some conferences, especially under CIFE, have provided individual contacts; and in the younger group of journalists we find many who have studied abroad, but more often in the United States than in other European countries. Journalists have formed a certain number of organizations with headquarters in Brussels, but none of these appear to be either very active or influential.[38]

In the field of books—which do not constitute mass communication in the basic meaning of the term but are rapidly evolving in that direction through the expansion of the paperback—cooperation is still limited. Even so, translations are becoming more numerous and, more especially, between France and Germany joint ventures are multiplying. There has, of course, always been a significant amount of such cultural exchange; for example, on the anniversary of Goethe's death the distinguished literary monthly *La Nouvelle Revue Française* published a special issue devoted entirely to French and German essays on Goethe. But somehow the attitude was different. It was permeated by a degree of self-consciousness about the separate national identities, which has now yielded to ready acceptance.[39]

Such an attitude of ready acceptance, unmistakable sign of a certain measure of community formation, has come to be reinforced by a great increase in intermarriage. The basic figures are shown in Table 10–1; none are available for earlier

TABLE 10–1. NUMBERS OF MARRIAGES BETWEEN FRENCHMEN AND GERMANS

Year	No. of Marriages (In thousands)
1962	966
1963	1,064
1964	1,200
1965	1,348
1966	1,527

SOURCE: *Statistisches Jahrbuch für die Bundesrepublik Deutschland* (Bevoelkerungsbewegung), 1964–1968, resp.

years. The absence of intermarriage has been, at least under Western Christian traditions of monogamy, an indicator of social distance, not only between nations but also within nations—between classes, races, religions, nationalities, and other such groupings. Hence the accelerated pace at which intermarriage occurs today is not without significance.[40] But the mere brute fact could be satisfactorily explained by the rapid increase in contacts, especially within those contexts we have been dealing with: in education, in business, in labor, French and Germans and other Common Market nationals are encountering each other, forming friendships. But a novel and as yet quite inadequately explored *mise-en-scène* has added greatly to the political implications of such personal reinforcements of informal community formation. Formerly, when a Frenchman married a German, or vice versa, the event remained strictly personal and had no ramifications into the respective families. Usually, either partner was assimilated into the other nation, became French or German, as the case might be, and there it ended. Now it is much more typical for both families to be much involved, parents and siblings to exchange visits and "discover" the "other world," and to achieve a degree of human association formerly very rare between such families. The reason is, of course, that these unions now occur within the framework of the Common Market, and hence the human beings involved have convictions on the subject of European integration, and so forth. If they are keen about integration, it will add zest to their explorations; if they are sceptical, it may greatly affect their outlook.

Interesting testimony has recently been offered for the psychological setting of this "Europe of couples."[41] Jean-Pierre and Renate had encountered each other in one of these European student centers, and there was first friendship and then love; but as Renate puts it: "What surprise for my parents when I presented Jean-Pierre to them who did not correspond to their stereotyped image of a Frenchman: black hair and moustache. . . ." The gradual elimination of these stereotypes is probably one of the most important political implications of informal community formation. It is also taking place through the massive increase of travel. Tourism, once merely a trickle between France and Germany, has now assumed massive proportions.

(See Table 10–2.) In 1966 France had the largest number of tourists in Germany after the United States and the Netherlands, and in fact more than half as many as the United States.

From the traveling *hoi polloi* we return to the main concern of our study. In their significant research on European (French and German) leaders, Daniel Lerner and Morton Gordon came

TABLE 10–2. NUMBER OF NIGHTS FRENCH TRAVELERS SPENT IN WEST GERMANY AS REGISTERED BY HOTELS

Year	In Thousands
1960	985
1961	1.035
1962	1.110
1963	1.263
1964	1.420
1965	1.427
1966	1.439

SOURCE: *Statistisches Jahrbuch für die Bundersrepublik Deutschland* (Internationale Ubersichten-Fremdenverkehr), 1962–1968, resp.

to the conclusion that over a ten-year period there has been developing a genuine consensus in Europe to the effect that national answers to many pressing problems are no longer viable, and that hence only supranational (they say transnational) choices will do. A study such as ours confirms this position, as do the documents—more especially the Annual General Reports of the EC. The two authors in this connection state that they "have witnessed the passing of nationalism in the form which was familiar to previous generations and even to the early years of the generation now in charge."[42] In contrast to such a conclusion, it is claimed by Karl Deutsch and his associates that "the movement toward structural European unification since 1957 has been largely halted or very much slowed down," and on that basis it is predicted that "the next decade of European politics . . . is likely to be dominated by the politics of nation-states, and not by any supranational European institutions."[43]

Our data would suggest that neither the one nor the other of these affirmations is correct; moreover, the latter, while sounding very pessimistic, is actually compatible with substantial progress toward integration; for who would want to assert that European politics would be "dominated" by "supranational" institutions? Does this necessarily mean that it will be "dominated" by the politics of the nation-state? Or would it not be more nearly correct to say that decisions will be oscillating between the two poles of national capitals and Brussels? Did not the crisis of 1965 and its aftermath, the French President's election troubles, show that to be the situation? Are we not face to face with a highly fluid and complex pattern of interaction, where power and influence are so greatly fractionalized that none can be sure who rules?

This state of affairs also makes it impossible to apply the rigid and mechanistic model of a system which David Easton has developed to the European complex, as Leon Lindberg has attempted to do.[44] The unfortunate authoritarian formulation introduced by Easton when he defines a political system as concerned with "authoritative allocation of values" cannot be discussed here.[45] Political, like other organic, systems are primarily and basically characterized by creativity and growth, including reproduction. None of these vital phenomena is reflected in a model that talks mostly in terms of "input" and "output." Now it may be answered that Easton's insistence that "self-regulation by the members of a political system, even to the point of self-transformation in structure and goals, represents critical capabilities of all social systems," constitutes a recognition of this capacity for growth (as well as death). But actually the model does not serve to highlight these phenomena. Lindberg rightly observes that "for the European Community system this is an especially important point."[46] And indeed, Lindberg has provided a valuable survey of the various aspects of European integration and suggested some rough approximation to their quantification. It would seem in the light of our data, however, that these supposed "quantities" are deceptive[47] and pretend a degree of precision such as the data do not in fact permit. The most questionable aspect of this approach is, however, the tendency to overestimate quantifiable data as indicators of community growth.

The data we have been analyzing do not allow us to identify a political system that could be separated (either in theory or practice) from the economic and social sphere. Writers who have attempted such a separation are invariably found to treat them together when they become concrete in their analysis. What is happening in the economies and societies of the countries belonging to the European Community cannot be understood today without taking the European Community into account. But these economies and societies are not realistically describable as "subsystems" of the European system; rather the European system constitutes a subsystem for each of them. But evidently by putting it thus, we once again make manifest how much of a dead alley the mechanistic system concept really is for the analysis of what is happening in Europe by way of integration and indeed unification. The trends are forward; the prospects are that these trends will continue. But the trends are also slow, and the prospects are that there will be a great deal of up and down. There will be continuous talk of crisis, and at each turn the prophets of gloom will insist that the end of European integration is around the corner. But in the face of such challenges, and in part stirred and stimulated by them, the integration process will continue as long as the Europeans who are engaged in specific efforts in business and labor, in the universities and the communes, in agriculture, in communications and transportation, and in nuclear energy are determined to solve concrete problems which require European solutions.

Does all this mean that Europe is an emergent nation? In a way it all depends upon how a nation is defined. If by a nation we are designating that close-knit political and cultural entity which produced the modern European nation-state—Britain, France, Spain, Italy, Germany—then Europe is not and will not become an emergent nation. If, on the other hand, a complex and vast entity, such as India, is seen as a nation, then Europe may well be described as an emergent nation. What are the characteristics of such a nation? To state it once more, as was done at the outset of this study, a nation in this perspective appears, empirically speaking, to be "any cohesive group possessing independence within the international order as provided by the United Nations, which constitutes a constituency for a government effectively ruling such a group and receiving from that group the acclamation which legitimizes the government as part of the world order."[48] It is evident that Europe is not yet such an entity, except in a marginal sense; it is equally evident that Europe is more nearly such an entity today than she was in 1958, as even a casual inspection of the First General Report of the European Community will show.[49] It is quite contrary to fact to declare, as is so often done by writers of the day, that *en bref, le Marché Commun tend à devenir une unité commerciale*—"the Common Market tends to become a commercial unity, not an economic and even less a technical one. And the political failure, one knows, is complete."[50] Such judgments are basically due to the failure to appreciate the true nature of federal politics—to assume that unless there is centralized political power, indeed sovereignty, a political order is necessarily less than adequate. The process of achieving results in a federal context is admittedly slow, but it may be more lasting than the rush of precipitate decisions in a highly centralized system.

The basic insight, now increasingly accepted, is that federations of states and the federal state must be seen as particular applications of a recurrent form of effective organized cooperation between groups. A federal order is a union of group selves, united by one or more common objectives, a community of communities which retain their distinctive group being. It unites without destroying the selves that are uniting, and is meant to strengthen them in their group and communal relations. Thus, it is the particular relation which exists in fact that should shape the federal relationship. This relationship needs to be shaped, and is in fact so shaped in successful federalizing in such a way that it can be reshaped and transformed in an ongoing process. That process may lead to greater unity or to greater diversity, and the federal bond will become weaker or stronger in response to it. In any case, it is clear that the small state and the small political community can hope to survive only in a world of ever-widening contacts and interests[51] if federalism is recognized not as a panacea but as a useful instrumentality for good government. It remains to suggest once more that federalism also holds out the prospect of organizing the world at large, lest it be accomplished by imperial conquest and domination. Let us therefore conclude with a statement by John Stuart Mill: "When the conditions exist for the formation of efficient and durable federal unions, the multiplication of them is always a benefit to the world."[52] Thus the author of *Representative Government* foresaw, more than a hundred years ago, what has since been proved by political experience.

Notes

Since the notes which follow here contain references to all the more important works utilized, it does not seem necessary to cite them separately in a bibliography. Instead, the notes are cited here, by chapter, for ready reference.

1. The Background of European Community

1. See *Philosophy, Religion, and the Coming World Civilization—Essays in Honor of William Ernest Hocking*, ed. Leroy S. Rouner, The Hague, Martinus Nijhoff, 1966, esp. pt. III, pp. 320–353; and Hocking's own *The Coming World Civilization*, 1956; also Reinhold Niebuhr, *The Structure of Nations and Empires*, 1959. For an empirical and quantitative approach to these problems, cf. Bruce M. Russett, *International Regions and the International System: A Study in Political Ecology*, 1967, esp. chs. 1, 2, 6, 11, 12, and 14.
2. Salvador de Madariaga, *Portrait of Europe*, 1950, writes in these terms. He, of course, includes Spain and, I believe, rightly. A broad historical approach, informed by a clear vision of the unity of Europe, has been offered by Denis de Rougemont, *Vingt-Huit Siècles d'Europe—La Conscience Européenne à travers les Textes de Hesiode à nos jours*, 1961; while the impact of the idea of Europe has been skillfully traced by Jean Baptiste Duroselle, *L'Idée d'Europe dans l'Histoire*, 1965. Cf. for contrast, the masterly review by Ludwig Dehio, *The Precarious Balance*, 1962.
3. Charles Homer Haskins, *The Rise of the Universities*, first published in 1923; Hastings Rashdall, *The Universities of Europe in the Middle Ages*, 1895, as revised by F. M. Powicke and Emden, 1936; Henry O. Taylor, *The Medieval Mind*, 4th ed., 1925.
4. Alois Dempf, *Sacrum Imperium*, 1929; Heinz Gollwitzer, *Europabild und Europagedanke—Beiträge . . .*, 1951. The book contains a prefatory section dealing with the Middle Ages down to the eighteenth century.
5. On conciliarism cf. Dempf, *op. cit.* (note 4 above), pt. III, ch. 5.

6. Karl W. Deutsch and William Foltz (eds.), *Nation-Building,* 1963, esp. pp. 1–33.
7. See my *Inevitable Peace,* 1948, esp. ch. I and pp. 164–168.
8. Immanuel Kant, *Idee zu einer allgemeinen Geschichte in weltbürgerlicher Absicht, Werke,* ed. Cassirer, vol. IV, p. 159.
9. Crane Brinton, *The Jacobins–An Essay in the New History,* 1930, hardly deals with this missionary zeal of the Jacobins when he treats of their faith, in ch. VII; thus he misses entirely their world-revolutionary, all-European thrust as fully developed by Eugen Rosenstock-Huessy in his *Die Europäischen Revolutionen,* 1931, and restated in *Out of Revolution–Autobiography of Western Man,* 1938 and 1964, ch. V, esp. pp. 229 ff., "The New Messianism."
10. Cf. the essay in the appendix to my *The Philosophy of Kant,* 1954, p. 444.
11. *The Code Napoléon and the Common Law World,* Schwartz (ed.), 1956, esp. my "The Ideological and Philosophical Background," which has been reprinted in a German translation in *Verfassungstheorie und Verfassungspolitik,* 1963.
12. H. Gollwitzer, *op. cit.* (note 4 above), *passim.*
13. Henry Kissinger, *A World Peace Restored: Metternich, Castlereagh, and the Problem of Peace, 1812–1822,* 1957.
14. Walter Schücking, *The International Union of the Hague Conferences,* Oxford, 1918. The "system" created by these conferences was based on a permanent court of arbitration and codification of international law, ineffectually guided by an administrative commission of diplomatic representatives.
15. Arnold Wolfers, *Britain and France Between Two Wars,* 1940.
16. Richard N. Coudenhove-Kalergi, *Pan-Europa,* 1924.
17. Coudenhove-Kalergi, *op. cit.,* p. ix.
18. Cf. Hans Kohn, *Revolutions and Dictatorships,* 1939, ch. 11; the same, *Panslavism–Its History and Ideology,* 1953; the same, *The Mind of Modern Russia,* 1955, esp. ch. 10.
19. Cf. my *Trends of Federalism in Theory and Practice,* 1968, esp. ch. 3; cf. also Bruce M. Russett, *op. cit.* (note 1 above).
20. Talcott Parsons, *The Social System,* 1951, pp. 167 ff.; also, Carl J. Friedrich, *Man and His Government,* 1963, pp. 513 ff. and Claus Schöndube, *Grundsatzfragen der europäischen Integration,* 1968, p. 112.
21. Friedrich, *Man and His Government,* 1963, chs. 12 and 13.
22. Cf. Talcott Parsons and Edward A. Shils (eds.), *Toward a General Theory of Social Action,* 1952. In their own contribution, pp. 202 ff., they define integration similarly when they write: "The institutionalization of value-orientation patterns thus constitutes, in the most general sense, the mechanism of integration for social systems." (p. 203)
23. James Fitzroy Fraser, *Centrifugalism in the Caribbean,* forthcoming;

and a rather different view is taken by G. H. Flanz in his contribution, "West Indian Federation," *Why Federations Fail—An Inquiry into the Requisites for Successful Federalism,* Thomas M. Franck (ed.), 1968, pp. 91 ff. (with a good bibliography). He concludes that "it is unlikely that a new political design of federalism will be attractive to the West Indies."

24. Cf. my paper at Expo '67, "Man and His Government," in *Man and His World—The Noranda Lectures,* University of Toronto Press, 1969.
25. Daniel Bell, *The End of Ideology,* rev. ed., 1965, but the position is more forcefully stated in the original work, which in turn was based upon Raymond Aron, *L'Opium des Intellectuels,* 1955. Cf. also Adam Schaff, who sharply rejects the notion of an "end," rightly I believe, in "La definition fonctionelle de l'idéologie et le problème de la 'fin du siècle de l'idéologie,'" *L'Homme et la Société, Revue Internationale des recherches et de synthèses sociologiques,* No. 4, 1967, a paper which was first read at a meeting of the Institut International de la Philosophie Politique at Val d'Aosta in July 1967, to which the author contributed "The Function and Process of Political Ideology—The Revival of Ideology in the United States"; these and other contributions to the problem will be published in the *Annales de la Philosophie Politique.*
26. Clyde Kluckhohn, *Mirror for Man,* 1949; A. L. Kroeber, *Anthropology Today,* 1953, esp. "Problems of the Historical Approach."
27. The line is from Emanuel Geibel, *Werke,* Stuttgart, 1883, Vol. III, p. 214. In the original it reads "Am Deutschen Wesen wird einmal die Welt genesen."
28. Richard Pipes (ed.), *Revolutionary Russia,* 1968, esp. the papers by Pipes himself on Lenin, Marc Ferro, and Rubel. Cf. also Maurice Hindus, *Mother Russia,* 1942.
29. See my "Totalitarianism: Recent Trends," in *Problems of Communism,* Vol. XVII (May–June 1968), pp. 32 ff.
30. Andrei D. Sakharov, as reported in *The New York Times,* July 22, 1968, pp. 14C–16C; this essay, entitled "Thoughts on Progress, Peaceful Co-existence and Intellectual Freedom," has in the meantime been published as a separate pamphlet. Its importance should not be exaggerated as it is by certain circles who do not wish to face the implications of the intervention in Czechoslovakia.
31. See for this, Richard Löwenthal, *World Communism—The Disintegration of a Secular Faith,* 1964; and, though somewhat dated still penetrating, Donald S. Zagoria, *The Sino-Soviet Conflict, 1956–1961,* 1962.
32. Zbigniew Brzezinski and Samuel P. Huntington, *Political Power: USA/USSR,* 1963, have elaborately, and on the whole rather successfully, refuted these arguments. Cf. also my article cited previously (note 29 above).

33. Walter Lipgens, "Das Konzept regionaler Friedensorganisation–Resistance und europäische Einigungsbewegung," *Vierteljahrshefte für Zeitgeschichte,* Vol. XVI (1968), pp. 150 ff., gives an interesting analysis. Cf. also Altiero Spinelli, "European Union in the Resistance," *Government and Opposition,* Vol. II (1967), pp. 321 ff.; it is based on personal experience.
34. This fact is stressed by J.-J. Servan-Schreiber, *Le Défi Américain,* 1967, esp. pp. 299 ff.
35. V. O. Key, *The Responsible Electorate,* 1966; C. J. Friedrich, *The New Belief in the Common Man,* 1942. See also my *Man and His Government,* 1963, chs. 2 and 10.
36. Since the literature on decision-making is very large, I refer to the selection offered in Friedrich, *Man and His Government,* ch. 3. See also the papers referred to below (Chapter 4, note 32).
37. Coudenhove-Kalergi, *op. cit.* (note 16 above), pp. 120–124.
38. See for this *Gustav Stresemann's Vermächtnis–Der Nachlass in drei Bänden,* H. Bernhard (ed.), 3 vols., 1932; vol. II, esp. pt. I, chs. IV and V.
39. Stresemann, *op. cit. supra,* vol. II, pt. II, ch. III; and pt. III, ch. I. Sceptical voices were of course heard almost immediately, e.g. Alfred Fabre-Luce, *Locarno–The Reality,* 1928; (*Locarno sans Rèves,* 1927).
40. Cf. the work cited in note 33 above, and Massimo Salvadori, *Storia della Resistenza Italiana,* 1955.
41. Richard N. Coudenhove-Kalergi, *Die Europäische Nation,* 1953. Cf. also George Liska, *Europe Ascendant–The International Politics of Unification,* 1964, pp. 64 ff.
42. Max Weber, *Wirtschaft und Gesellschaft,* 1922, pp. 627 ff. Cf. also his article, cited by Hans Kohn, *The Idea of Nationalism,* 1944, ch. I, fn. 16.
43. Rupert Emerson, *From Empire to Nation,* 1961, esp. pp. 3 ff., 89 ff., and 188 ff.; and the work of Hans Kohn cited in the preceding note, esp. pp. 187 ff. Dempf, *op. cit.* (note 4 above), is also relevant.
44. Karl W. Deutsch, "The Growth of Nations: Some Recurrent Patterns of Political and Social Integration," *World Politics,* Vol. V (1953), pp. 168 ff. Cf. also his *Political Community and the North Atlantic Area: International Organization in the Light of Historical Experience,* 1957, which he edited and co-authored. See his *The Nerves of Government,* 1962, esp. chs. 12 and 13. Cf. my *Man and His Government,* ch. 8, for a full development.
45. Ernst B. Haas, "International Integration–The European and the Universal Process," *International Organization,* Vol. XV (1961), pp. 366 ff., argues against the myth of a "natural and inevitable reemergence." Very true. But the existence of historical antecedents is *politically* relevant, precisely because it makes such "myths" possible, and these are powerful factors in political development. Cf. Friedrich,

Man and His Government, ch. 5, where the function of the political myth is systematically explored. Incidentally, Haas defines political community, rather inadequately, as existing when "there is likelihood of internal peaceful change in a setting of contending groups with mutually antagonistic claims." Such a state is surely compatible with community, but is surely not its core. Cf. also Vol. II of *Nomos,* entitled *Community,* C. J. Friedrich (ed.), 1959, where many approaches are found.

2. European Consensus and Community Structure: A Federal Potential?

1. See Chapter 1 of the present book.
2. Edward McWhinney, *Comparative Federalism: States Rights and National Power,* 1962, offers an explicit treatment of federal loyalty (*Bundestreue*) under the heading of "federal comities." Another able recent treatment is in Peter Hay, *Federalism and Supra-national Organizations: Patterns for New Legal Structures,* pp. 194–201, where the more accurate translation "fidelity" is used.
3. Robert Bowie and Carl J. Friedrich, *Studies in Federalism,* 1954, ch. 15, pp. 765 ff.
4. For the problem of nullification, compare my *Philosophy of Law in Historical Perspective,* 2nd ed., 1965, ch. 22; and my *Man and His Government–An Empirical Theory of Politics,* 1963, pp. 279 ff. and 635 ff.
5. See for the general problems my *Trends of Federalism in Theory and Practice,* 1968, esp. ch. 23.
6. See my *Constitutional Government and Politics,* 1937, p. 176.
7. *Ibid.,* p. 184. Instead of the word "league" the term "confederation" is used.
8. In earlier versions of the theory I overstated the issue by insisting that the dynamic aspect of "federalizing" replaced the static aspect of patterning and structuring; the present formulation appears more appropriate.
9. For the Commonwealth, cf. Frank H. Underhill, *The British Commonwealth–An Experiment in Cooperation among Nations,* 1956; for the Soviet Union, Klaus von Beyme, "Federal Theory and Party Reality in the Soviet Union," *Public Policy,* Vol. XIII (1964), pp. 395–412; for Prussia see Arnold Brecht, *Federalism and Regionalism in Germany,* 1945, pt. III.
10. Dusan Sidjanski, *Fédéralisme en Amphictyonique–Elements de Système et tendance internationale,* 1956, where the author describes the truly federal tendencies in such organizations as the Council of Europe.
11. See Burke Marshal, *Federalism and Civil Rights,* 1964, pp. 8–9.

12. See William H. Rikes, *Federalism,* 1964, *passim.*
13. *Ibid.*
14. Richard N. Coudenhove-Kalergi, *Paneuropa,* 1923.
15. Coudenhove-Kalergi, *Die europäische Nation,* 1953.
16. Alexis de Tocqueville, *De la démocracie en Amérique, 1835–1840;* English edition by P. Bradley, 1948, chs. 7 and 8, esp. pp. 171, 451–452.
17. *Ibid.,* p. 414.
18. Ernst B. Haas, *The Uniting of Europe—Political, Social and Economic Forces 1950–1957,* 1958. For the earlier phases see Arnold J. Zurcher, *The Struggle to Unite Europe, 1940–1958,* 1958.
19. Thus the oath taken by mayors of French and German towns entering into partnership invariably refers to peace as a major reason for such fraternization. See Rolf-Richard Grauhan, "Die Verschwisterungen deutscher und französischer Gemeinden," in *Politische Dimensionen der europäischen Gemeinschaftsbildung* (1967), esp. pp. 58 ff.
20. Ronald Inglehart, "An End to European Integration?" *APSR,* Vol. LXI, No. 1 (March 1967), pp. 91–105. Cf. also the similar figures and graphs in J. R. Rabier, *L'information des Européennes et l'integration de l'Europe,* Brussels, 1965, pp. 36 ff.
21. Karl W. Deutsch, Lewis B. Edinger, Roy C. Macridis, and Richard L. Merritt, *France, Germany and the Western Alliance—A Study of Elite Attitudes on European Integration and World Politics,* 1968, pp. 218 and 230. The first sentence cited is from an article by Deutsch entitled "Integration and Arms Control in the European Political Environment," summarizing these findings and published in the *APSR,* Vol. LX (1966), p. 355.
22. Deutsch *et al., op. cit.,* p. 1.
23. Friedrich, *Man and His Government,* pp. 317 ff.; Deutsch *et al., op. cit.,* esp. chs. 4–8. See also *Changing Perspectives of the European Elites* by Daniel Lerner and Morton Gordon, 1969, for massive evidence in support of positions similar to those taken in the text above.
24. Deutsch *et al., op. cit.,* p. 215.
25. *Ibid.,* p. 219.
26. For the data on which the arguments of Deutsch and his associates are based, see Donald C. Puchala, "European Political Integration: Progress and Prospects," New Haven: Yale University Political Science Research Library, mimeographed, 1966, as cited by Deutsch, *op. cit.,* p. 220.
27. See tables 13.1 and 13.2 on pages 222 and 228 of Deutsch *et al., op. cit.*
28. The first statement was made in an article by Deutsch entitled "Integration and Arms Control in the European Political Environment," *APSR,* Vol. LX (1966), pp. 354 ff. and p. 355.
29. Deutsch *et al., op. cit.,* p. 229.

30. *Ibid.*, 230.
31. For these figures see Statistisches Bundesamt, *Statistisches Jahrbuch für die Bundesrepublik Deutschland* for the years 1963–1967 as tabulated in tables 7 and 8 on p. 44 of *Die deutsche Wirtschaft und die EWG*, published by the German CEPES–group, 2nd ed., 1968.
32. See Richard L. Merritt, *Symbols of American Community*, New Haven: Yale University Press, 1966, pp. 735–775.
33. Haas, *op. cit.;* for a useful assessment see the articles by Paul van Ypersele de Strihou, Roger Morgan, and Mary Forsyth in *European Community*, No. 115 (August 1968).
34. *Sondages*, 1963.
35. *Ibid.*, p. 21.
36. *Ibid.*, pp. 23–24.
37. Rabier, *op. cit.* (note 20 above), *passim.*
38. For this, see Arnold Rivkin, *Africa and the European Common Market–A Perspective*, Denver, Colo.: Social Science Foundation of the University of Denver, 2nd rev. ed., 1966. esp. pp. 48 ff.
39. Phrases such as these occasionally appear in the writings of ardent Europeans, though they are usually formulated more politely. See for instance Denis de Rougemont, *Vingt-huit siècles d'Europe*, 1961.
40. Rabier, *op. cit.*, p. 19, who nonetheless on p. 21 takes a more flexible view: "Peut-être vaudrait-il mieux à avancer pas à pas en favorisant la formation d'un consensus européen, d'une conscience politique européenne, par des techniques d'information, d'éducation et de consultation populaire, en renforçant ce consensus. . . ." It is too often forgotten that the national consensus is also quite defective and far from the "unanimity" and "agreement on fundamentals" which totalitarians and conservatives have always longed for.
41. Press Conference of March 25, 1959.
42. Friedrich, *Man and His Government*, chs. 9 and 30.
43. *Ibid.*, ch. 33.
44. This position resembles that of Edward Shils, as set forth in his article in the *IESS*, where he states: "Consensus is a particular state of the belief system of a society. It exists when a large number proportion of the adult members of a society, more particularly a large proportion of those concerned with decisions regarding the allocation of authority, status, rights, wealth and income, and other important and scarce values about which conflict might occur, are in approximate agreement in their beliefs about what decisions should be made and have some feeling of unity with each other and with the society as a whole." It is obvious that in no national community such consensus is perfect; indeed in Western democratic states there is usually a sharp conflict on a fairly large range of values and their allocation. I therefore believe the formulation in the text to be more realistic; in any case the fluidity of consensus and its increase and decrease are rather important features of it. Cf. also the article on the study of con-

sensus by Lewis Lipsitz in the *IESS,* where he distinguishes four different uses of the idea of consensus.

3. The Business Community: Enterprises

1. This chapter is based on the primary researches of M. Henri Schwamm. More detailed references to his study are given below. It has very recently been significantly implemented by Jean Meynaud and Dusan Sidjanski, *L'Europe des Affaires–Rôle et Structure des Groupes,* Paris, 1967. For the background, cf. Leon N. Lindberg, *The Political Dynamics of European Economic Integration,* 1963, where the quotation is found on p. 170.
2. Friedrich, *Man and His Government,* ch. 12.
3. Deutsch and Associates, *France, Germany and the Western Alliance,* 1967, p. 10.
4. Statistics as reported in *CE,* No. 118 (May 1968), p. 23.
5. Jean Halperin, *"L'organisation internationale agite-elle sur la pensée et les Politiques Economiques Contemporaines?"*; paper read at the Grenoble Round Table of IPSA, 1965, p. 12.
6. *Rapport de la Troisième Assemblée Générale de l'Organisation C.I.S.L.,* cited in J. Meynaud, *L'Action Syndicale et la Communauté Européenne,* 1962, p. 67.
7. Pierre Gerbet, *"La Modification des structures politiques et administratives Françaises en fonction de la coopération économique internationale"*; paper read at the Grenoble Round Table of IPSA, 1965, p. 11.
8. Jean-Jacques Servan-Schreiber, *Le Défi Américain,* 1967, ch. 2; also available in English, 1968; a summary extract appeared in *Harper's* (July 1968).
9. Lindberg, *op. cit.* (note 1 above), p. 96.
10. *Communautés Européennes* (February 1965).
11. Alessandro Silj, *L'industrie européenne,* Lausanne, 1966, p. 14. Cf. also Christopher Layton, *Trans-Atlantic Investments,* published by Atlantic Institute, Paris (presumably 1966), esp. ch. II and pp. 119 ff.
12. Michel Falise, in Schwamm.
13. For further detail see Schwamm, pp. 243 ff., and the statistics on pp. 287 ff.; cf. also the statistics in Silj, pp. 16/17.
14. Study by Deutsche Bank, May 1965. A similar study was made by the French Ministry of Industry in the summer of 1965. Cf. also the references in Silj, *op. cit.*
15. H. P. Drucker, in *EC* (June 1968), pp. 4 ff.
16. H. J. von Hake, in a lecture on "Deutsch-franzoesische Wirtschaftsbeziehungen" given October 19, 1965, before the International Chamber of Commerce at Berlin, and published in *Documents Révue des Questions Allemandes* (August 1966).
17. Cf. Schwamm, pp. 227–231.
18. Cf. as examples, Arnaud Man-Lipanski, *"L'Echéance du 1er juillet,"*

in *Europe-en-Formation,* No. 99 (June 1968), and the article by Drucker, cited above, note 15, where the quoted statement is found.

19. *Phoenix Gummi 1967, Bericht ueber das 96. Geschaeftsjahr,* Phoenix Gummiwerke AG, Hamburg-Harburg, esp. pp. 13 ff.
20. Cf. H. J. von Hake as cited in note 16 above.
21. Schwamm, p. 270.
22. Analyses such as the one by Servan-Schreiber, cited above, note 8, suggest this clearly.
23. *Die Europäischen Gemeinschaften,* 1968, p. 28.
24. *Euroforum,* 1968, Saarbrücken; see also therein the paper by G. Petrilli, pp. 34 ff.
25. Herbert J. Spiro, *The Politics of German Co-determination,* 1958. Concerning the more recent developments consult Viggo Graf Bluecher, *Integration und Mitbestimmung–Hauptergebnisse einer Untersuchung des EMNID–Instituts für Sozialforschung,* Sennestadt, 1966, und Goetz Briefs, *Mitbestimmung, Beitraege zur paritaetischen Mitbestimmung in der Wirtschaft,* Stuttgart, 1967.
26. "*La Participation: bouleversement où évolution?,*" in *Le Figaro* (Paris), July 3 and 4, 1968, offers a good illustration, with four different standpoints, including that of René Capitant, Minister of Justice.
27. Opposing viewpoints inform two other recent contributions: Roland Tittel, *Mitbestimmung in der Bundesrepublik Deutschland,* published by the Deutsches Industrieinstitut, 1966; and Heinrich Streithofen, *Wertmasstaebe der Gewerkschaftspolitik–Ein Beitrag zur Theorie der Gewerkschaft,* Heidelberg, 1967.
28. *Presseveröffentlichung* of the BDI of October 1, 1965, cited in Neunreither, in *Politische Dimensionen der europäischen Gemeinschaftsbildung,* 1967, p. 434.
29. Schwamm, p. 277, gives a number of specific statements on this issue.
30. A report and model statute have been published by the European Community under the title "*Projet d'un statut des Sociétés anonymes européennes,*" as Competition Series No. 6. Professor Sanders (Rotterdam) was chairman.
31. Schwamm, p. 284.
32. *European Communities,* No. 114, p. 5. Cf. also the more recent analyses by Commissioner Guido Colonna di Paliano, and by Alan Parker in the same periodical, No. 116, 1968, pp. 3 ff.
33. Schwamm, pp. 278–282; Silj, *op. cit.* The issue has been dramatized by Servan-Schreiber, *op. cit.*
34. We pass over the special arrangements for "joint enterprises" (*entreprises communes*) under Euratom. For these see Schwamm, pp. 273 ff.
35. For this decision see Cour de Justice des Communautés Européennes, *Recueil de la Jurisprudence de la Cour,* Vol. XII (1966), pp. 429–561, "Establissements Consten S.A.R.L. et Grundig-Verkaufs-C.m.b.H.

contre Commission de la C.E.E." The previous decision of the Commission is reproduced in Eric Stein and Peter Hay, *Law and Institutions in the Atlantic Area—Readings, Cases, Problems,* 1963, 1967, pp. 624–649. The decision was based upon a principle first enunciated in the Bosch case. Cf. Oberdorfer, Gleiss, and Hirsch, *Common Market Cartel Law,* 1963, pp. 86 ff.; and the commentary in Werner J. Feld, *Minnesota Law Review,* Vol. 501 (1966), pp. 423 ff.

36. Feld, *loc. cit.*, p. 433.
37. Astrid Lulling, in *EC* (No. 113), pp. 11/12.
38. Louis Kriesberg, in *Social Science* (April 1960).

4. The Business Community: Associations

1. See *European Community* (July 1968), No. 114, p. 5.
2. Besides the references given in the footnotes, this chapter is built on the study by Karl-Heinz Neunreither in *Politische Dimensionen* (cited in full in Chapter 2 above, note 19), pp. 358–444. In addition see particularly Jean Meynaud and Dusan Sidjanski, *L'Europe des Affaires—Rôle et Structures des Groupes,* 1967, and Haas, *op. cit.* (Chapter 2 above, note 18), chs. 5 and 9. The latter analysis is still useful, but does not deal with developments of the Common Market. See also Lindberg, *op. cit.* (Chapter 3 above, note 1).
3. Friedrich, *Constitutional Government and Democracy,* 1968, ch. 21; Neunreither, *op. cit.*, sec. III.
4. Haas, *op. cit.*, chs. 5 and 8; Lindberg, *op. cit.*, pp. 96 ff.
5. *Ibid.*, p. 354.
6. *Jahresbericht* of the *BDI,* 1956/57, pp. 33–34.
7. Neunreither, *loc. cit.*, p. 362.
8. See the statistics in Chapter 3 of the present book.
9. See the *Eighth General Report on the Activities of the EEC,* 1965; and *Fourth General Report on the Activities of the EEC,* p. 94.
10. *Jahresbericht* of the *BDI*, 1960–61, p. 31.
11. University of Caen, *La Grande Bretagne et le Marché Commun,* 1967, pp. 57 ff.; see also the excellent monograph of Gerhard Braunthal, *The Federation of German Industry,* 1965.
12. Cf., for example, the annual reports of the *BDI* and of the *CNPF.*
13. *Tätigkeitsbericht* of the *Deutsche Industrie-und Handelstag* (*DIHT*), 1964, pp. 235 ff.
14. Besides the chapter in Friedrich, *Constitutional Government and Democracy,* 1968, see S. E. Finer, *Anonymous Empire: A Study of the Lobby in Great Britain,* 1958; V. O. Key, Jr., *Political Parties and Pressure Groups,* 5th ed., 1958; and Jean Meynaud, *Les Groupes de Pression Internationaux,* 1961.
15. See Braunthal, *op. cit.*, note 11 above.
16. For a panorama of these interest groups, cf. Neunreither, in *Dimensionen,* pp. 388 ff.; but see also the thorough study by Fritz Fischer,

Die institutionalisierte Vertretung der Verbände in der Europäischen Wirtschaftsgemeinschaft, Kiel, 1965; and Meynaud-Sidjanski, *"Les Groupes Européennes,"* in *Science Politique et Intégration Européenne,* Geneva, 1965, pp. 58 ff.

17. Dr. Neunreither notes that such "recognition" is involved in whether an association was included in the *Verzeichnis,* or list. This, entitled *Verzeichnis der gemeinsamen Organisationen die in der Europäischen Wirtschaftsgemeinschaft von Industrie-, Handwerks- und Handelsvergaenden der sechs Länder geschaffen wurden,* was published by the general directorate "Internal Market" in 1960 and contains the names of 219 associations or interest groups exclusive of agriculture. A new list is in preparation and will be published soon. This list gives a good general idea on the range of interest groups involved.
18. See for this, Neunreither, in *Dimensionen,* p. 408.
19. Cf. *Tenth General Report,* EEC (June 1967), pp. 295 ff. A good general evaluation is found in Roberto Aliboni and Riccardo Perissich, "The Common Commercial Policy of the EEC," in *Lo Spettatore Internazionale,* vol. II (1967), pp. 318 ff. (English ed.). On p. 332, the authors justly remark: "On the whole, the EEC has given proof of a desire for liberalization not inferior to that of its partners, and occasionally superior."
20. Neunreither, *loc. cit.,* p. 409. See also Meynaud-Sidjanski, *op. cit.* (footnote 16 above), ch. 3.
21. Neunreither, *ibid.*
22. Werner Feld, "National Economic Interest Groups and Policy Formation in the EEC," in *Political Science Quarterly,* Vol. 81 (1966), pp. 392 ff.; at p. 408 Feld advances this claim, which probably was justified in 1965.
23. Concerning the problems of political influence, see my *Man and His Government,* ch. 11.
24. D. Sidjanski, "Pressure Groups and the European Community," in *Government and Opposition,* Vol. II (1967), pp. 397–416.
25. Neunreither, *Dimensionen,* p. 413. Cf. for the Eurocrats also below, Chapter 10.
26. E. P. Herring, *Public Administration and the Public Interest,* 1936. See also *Nomos,* vol. V (ed. Friedrich), ch. 13, "The Public Interest," by Glendon Schubert, esp. pp. 167 ff. See also David Truman, *The Governmental Process: Political Interests and Public Opinion;* and Henry Ehrmann, *Interest Groups on Four Continents,* 1958.
27. Feld, *op. cit.* (note 22, above), pp. 408/9.
28. Neunreither, *Dimensionen,* pp. 417–419.
29. Gerda Zellentin, *Der Wirtschafts-und Sozialausschuss der EWG und Euratom—Interessenrepräsentation auf übernationaler Ebene,* Leyden, 1962, who thinks that it is more important than the European Parliament. This view has been rejected by Hallstein. Cf. Fischer (note 16 above), pp. 99 ff.

30. See my *Constitutional Government and Democracy,* 4th ed., pp. 468 ff. On the corporative state see Gaetano Salvemini, *Under the Axe of Fascism,* 1936; and Carl D. Schmidt, *The Corporate State in Action,* 1939. More recently a participant's conception was furnished by Guiseppe Bottai, *Vent'anni e un Giorno,* Rome, 1946.
31. See my *Man and His Government,* ch. 3. See also my introductory essay to *Dimensionen,* pp. 13 ff.
32. The following mimeographed papers may be noted here as especially pertinent: M. Alting von Geusau, *Les sessions Marathon du Conseil des ministres de la Communauté Européenne;* Nadine Bernard, *Le Règlement No. 17 et la politique commune des transports* (an interesting case study of the interaction of Commission, Council of Ministers, Parliament and Economic and Social Council); Stephane Bernard, *Pouvoir et Influence—Contribution à l'étude de la décision politique dans le domaine interne et dans le domaine communautaire;* Robert de Bruin, *La préparation de la décision au niveau national néerlandais;* Jean Buchmann, *La valeur de la décision;* Guy de Carmoy, *L'inscription de l'aluminium sur la liste des exceptions dans les nègociations du Gatt;* Louis Cartou, *Le rôle de la Commission;* Jean-Marie Cotteret, *L'élaboration des budgets de fonctionnement dans le cadre des Communautés Européennes;* Pierre Duclos, *Comparaison des procedures de décision suivant le Conseil de l'Europe et suivant les procedures communautaires;* M. Dierick, *Le règlement No. 17 et l'élaboration de la decision communautaire;* Maurice Flory, *Irreversibilité et point de non retour;* Pierre Gerbert, *La préparation de la décision au niveau national français;* Theodor Holtz, *La préparation des décisions dans le cadre national de la R.F.A.;* Leon Lindberg, *The European Community as a Political System: Notes toward the Construction of a Model;* François Luchaire, *L'extension de la décision;* Jacques Megret, *Les Conseils des Communautés Européennes en tant que pouvoir de décision;* Karlheinz Neunreither, *Le rôle du parlement dans la formation de décision des communautés européennes;* Lucien Nizard, *Le modèle économique européen;* Emile Noel and Henri Etienne, *Quelques aspects des rapports et de la collaboration entre le Conseil et la Commission au cours de l'élaboration des décisions* (interesting report by two high officials of the Commission); Daniel Pepy, *La Négociation de la deuxième convention de l'association des états africains et malgaches à la CEE;* J. A. Salmon, *Le rôle des représentations permanentes dans la décision communautaire;* Guy Sautter, *Le controle de la décision communautaire: la cour de justice;* Dusan Sidjanski, *L'action des groupes de pression;* J. R. Verges, *L'élaboration du système de financement de la politique agricole commune;* François Visine, *Le pouvoir de décision à l'organisation de coopération et de développement économique;* Daniel Vignes, *Le secrétariat des Conseils.* These are papers presented to the *Colloque International sur la décision dans les organisations européen-*

nes, held at Lyon, November 11–12, 1966, under the auspices of the *Association pour le développement de la Science politique européenne* (concerning this organization, see Chapter 9 of the present book).

33. D. Sidjanski, *loc. cit.,* note 20 above.
34. See my article "Public Policy and the Nature of Administrative Responsibility" in *Public Policy,* I (1940); and *Nomos,* III (1960) (Responsibility), "The Dilemma of Administrative Responsibility," pp. 189 ff.
35. Fischer, *op. cit.* (note 16 above), pp. 200–201.

5. The Agricultural Community

1. This chapter is based on Yves Tavernier and Hélène Delorme Louët, *Les Paysans Français et l'Unité Européenne,* which will soon appear in both French and English. References are to the MS.
2. Cf. Benjamin Schwartz, *Chinese Communism and the Rise of Mao,* 1951. See also Mao, "On the New Democracy," as cited in *A Documentary History of Chinese Communism,* edited by Conrad Brandt, Benjamin Schwartz, and John Fairbank.
3. Cf. C. J. Friedrich, "The Agricultural Basis of Emotional Nationalism," *Public Opinion Quarterly,* 1 (1937); "The Peasant as Evil Genius of Dictatorship," *Yale Review,* 26 (1936), pp. 727–740; see also *Totalitarian Dictatorship and Autocracy,* 2nd ed., 1965, ch. 20.
4. The vast literature on the peasant cannot be reviewed here. Pathfinding were William I. Thomas and F. Znaniecki, in *The Polish Peasant in Europe and America* (1918–20); the quotation in this paragraph is from P. Sorokin and C. C. Zimmermann, *Principles of Rural-Urban Sociology,* 1929, pp. 407 ff. For the relation to Communism in France and Italy, see Mario Einaudi's (and Associates) *Communism in Western Europe,* 1951; and for an earlier insightful assessment, André Siegfried, *De la IIIe à la IVe République,* 2nd ed., 1952. Very illuminating and not only for Southern Italy, Edward C. Banfield, *The Moral Basis of a Backward Society,* 1958. A valuable corrective, though perhaps overdone, is provided by Barrington Moore, Jr., *Social Origins of Dictatorship and Democracy—Lord and Peasant in the Making of the Modern World,* 1966, esp. ch. IX, pp. 453 ff.
5. For a detailed list see Neunreither, *Dimensionen* (note 1, Chapter 4 above), p. 394.
6. See the documents published by the General Directorate for Parliamentary Documentation and Information of the European Parliament on a number of ordinances, e.g. Ordinance No. 19 (Cereals), No. 20 (Pork), No. 21 (Eggs), No. 22 (Chicken), No. 23 (Fruit and Vegetables), No. 24 (Wine). These documents show in three columns

the proposal of the Commission, the position taken by the Parliament, and the actual ordinance as issued. Considerable differences between the Commission draft and the final ordinance are said to be due to the influence of COPA and the national associations. Cf. Fischer, *op. cit.* (note 16, Chapter 4 above), pp. 55 ff.

7. Neunreither, *Dimensionen*, p. 397; Fischer, *op. cit.*, pp. 194 ff.
8. The Internal Regulations (*Règlement Interne*) of COPA contains a single sentence regarding the composition of the general assembly as follows: *"L'Assemblée, composée de représentants des organisations professionelles agricoles membres, est l'organe suprême du C.O.P.A."* (Art. 7)
9. A further discussion of this point is found in Neunreither, *Dimensionen*, pp. 407–409.
10. Neunreither, *loc. cit.*, p. 409. We noted in the last chapter that the same holds for UNICE.
11. See the documentary publication cited in note 6 above, ordinances Nos. 23 and 24, 1962. See also the work cited below in note 12, pp. 16–17.
12. *Agrarmarkt und Agrarpolitik* (November 1967), published by Presse- und Informationsdienst der EC, p. 7. What follows is based on this publication. It contains, of course, much additional statistical and other factual detail.
13. See EEC Commission, *Tenth General Report on the Activities of the Community* (June, 1967), ch. 1 and pp. 183 ff.
14. Cf. *loc. cit.* (note 12), pp. 54–55.
15. Here we follow Tavernier/Delorme as cited in note 1 above, hereafter cited as Tavernier. Cf. also Michel Gervais, Claude Servolin, and Jean Weil, *Une France sans Paysans*, 1965.
16. Tavernier, *op. cit.*, p. 4.
17. Tavernier, *op. cit.*, ch. 1.
18. Tavernier, *op. cit.*, ch. 2.
19. President F. Guillaume in *Le Monde* (October 8, 1963).
20. For more detail, see Tavernier, *op. cit.*, ch. 3.
21. For more detail, see Tavernier, *op. cit.*, ch. 6.
22. Tavernier, *op. cit.*, Mouvement International de la Jeunesse Agricole et Rural Catolic (MIJARC), *8000 Jeunes Ruraux d'Europe Nous Disent . . .* (no date), pp. 201–202.
23. Tavernier, *op. cit.*, ch. 7.
24. Miriam Camps, *European Unification in the Sixties—From the Veto to the Crisis*, 1966, pp. 55 ff.; Neunreither, *Dimensionen*, pp. 428 ff.
25. Tavernier, *op. cit.*, ch. 7.
26. *Le Marché Commun et l'Agriculture—Livre Blanc des Organisations Professionels et Agricoles* (October, 1965).
27. *Ibid*, p. 48.
28. *Ibid.*, p. 6.

29. *Agence d'Europe* (July 29, 1965), as cited by Neunreither. See also report on the Council in *Journal Officiel* (October 14, 1965). For French planning see P. Bauchet, *Economic Planning: The French Experience,* 1964 (a translation of *La Planification Française,* 1962); and John and Annemarie Hackett, *Economic Planning in France,* 1963. A more recent assessment is found in two papers given at the 1968 IPSA meeting in Salzburg: J. Hayward, *Projection, Political Choice and the Preparation of the Fifth French Plan;* and L. Nizard, *La Planification comme facteur d'intégration sociale.* MSS can be secured from the secretariat of IPSA (Brussels).
30. *Journal Officiel* (October 14, 1965).
31. Banfield, *op. cit.,* ch. 5 (see note 4 above).

6. The Labor Community in the Factory and the Guest Worker

1. Besides the material cited in the notes, this chapter is based on Hans-Viktor Schierwater, "Der Arbeitnehmer und Europa–Integrationstendenzen und –strukturen im Sozialbereich des Gemeinsamen Marktes," in *Politische Dimensionen, op. cit.* (cited in full in note 19, Chapter 2 above), pp. 294–357, especially pp. 330–351; and Stefano Passigli's study on the Italian guest workers, *Emigrazione e comportamento politico* (Bologna: Società editrice il Mulino, 1969), which will be published soon in English. Very basic besides these is Charles P. Kindleberger, *Europe's Post-War Growth–The Role of Labor Supply,* 1966.
2. See the article "Migration: Social Aspects," in *IESS;* and Oscar Handlin, *The Uprooted,* 1951.
3. Kindleberger, *op. cit.*
4. The article entitled *Le Caratteristiche dell'emigrazione italiana in Belgio . . . di Milano,* by Luciano Barbieri, in *Rivista Internazionale di Scienze Sociali,* LXIX (1961), pp. 227 ff., gives interesting detail on what happens to such guest workers, but without attention to their political outlook.
5. Cf. the classical study by Alfred Weber, *The Theory of the Location of Industries* (ed. C. J. Friedrich), 1929.
6. See EEC, *Tenth General Report* (June 1967), p. 241. For an earlier assessment see Xavier Lannes, "L'Emigration de travailleurs entre les Pays du Marché Commun," in *Population,* XVII (1962), pp. 29–50.
7. See Treaty, Articles 48 and 49.
8. For this see *Tenth General Report,* p. 245.
9. See *EC,* No. 116, p. 12.
10. Cf. the study by Stefano Passigli, cited in note 1, above. The French workers are dealt with by Schierwater, *loc. cit.*
11. See *Tenth General Report,* p. 246.

12. See the Commission's Special Report of 1967.
13. See, for comparison, Francesco Alberoni and Guido Baglioni, *L'integrazione dell'immigrato nella società industriale,* 1965.
14. Passigli, *op. cit.*, p. 104, and table VI (see note 1 above).
15. *Ibid.*, pp. 112–113.
16. *Les Jeunes Ruraux,* as cited in Chapter 5 above, note 22, pp. 211–217.
17. Passigli, *op. cit.*, pp. 136–137.
18. For the concept of anomie see Sebastian de Grazia, *The Political Community—A Study of Anomie,* 1948, who bases his analysis on Durkheim. Cf. also Friedrich, *Man and His Government,* pp. 144 ff.
19. Mattei Dogan, "Comportment politique et condition sociale en Italie," in *Revue française de sociologie,* Vol. VII (1966), pp. 700–734. The quote is found on p. 732 (italics in the original).
20. Edward C. Banfield, *The Moral Basis of a Backward Society,* 1958.
21. Samuel Henry Barnes, *Party Democracy—Politics in an Italian Socialist Federation,* 1967.
22. Passigli, *op. cit.*, pp. 136–137.
23. *Ibid.*, pp. 138 ff.
24. On October 31, 1964, there were 21,115 Frenchmen in Germany, as compared with 23,620 Germans in France. These and other relevant data are taken from Schierwater, *op. cit.*, pp. 330 ff.
25. Tables showing the precise distribution by cities are found in Schierwater, *loc. cit.*, p. 331.
26. A special study is nearing completion under our research program dealing with the actions and reactions of the German trade unions to the crisis of 1965; it has been undertaken by Mr. Rudolf Steiert.
27. See pp. 115 ff. of the present book.
28. See note 3 above.
29. See note 5 above.
30. Cf. EEC, *Tenth General Report,* pp. 245 ff.
31. *Joint International Seminar on adaptation of rural and foreign workers to industry,* OECD, 1965, containing a contribution by Heinz Richter, "Foreign Workers in Germany," pp. 121 ff.; see also Schierwater, *loc. cit.*, pp. 342–343
32. These researches have been undertaken by Mr. Henri Schwamm, but had not been completed by the time this study was concluded; however, I have benefited from the draft materials M. Schwamm has furnished, and which will eventually be published under the title *La Coopération des Travailleurs en Europe.*
33. There is considerable difficulty in giving actual figures; a rough estimate would be related to the percentage of businesses if migratory labor is not included. If it is, the figures would be raised by several percentage points.
34. FIOM, *Nouvelles* (June 1966); Bulletin FIOM (August 1966); the same, (May 1968). These problems will be more fully dealt with by Mr. Schwamm, *op. cit.* (note 32 above).

7. The Trade Union Labor Community

1. This chapter is based upon Hans-Viktor Schierwater, "Der Arbeitnehmer und Europa–Integrationstendenzen und-strukturen im Sozialbereich des Gemeinsamen Marktes," in *Politische Dimensionen, op. cit.* (note 2, Chapter 4 above), pp. 294 ff; and the works cited in his bibliography, more especially Jean Meynaud, *L'Action syndicale et la Communauté Européenne,* 1962. A more detailed investigation is in process under our program by Henri Schwamm, and provisionally entitled *La Coopération des Travailleurs en Europe.*
2. DGB, Bundespressestelle, *Nachrichtendienst,* Bd. 23, 1967, p. 212. The president of DGB, Ludwig Rosenberg, had declared similar sentiments repeatedly; cf. Bd. 21, 1965, pp. 264–265, *loc. cit.*
3. Merle Fainsod, *International Socialism and the World War,* 1935.
4. R. Colin Beever, *European Unity and the Trade Union Movements,* Leyden, 1960. This is a recurrent theme in the speeches of European Labor leaders. Cf. *Europa 1970. Politische und gesellschaftliche Folgen der wirtschaftlichen Integration.* For the *DGB,* edited by Karl Brauckmann, Koeln-Duetz, 1967. The discussion took place June 28–29 of that year. Note esp. pp. 87 ff., 94 ff., 118.
5. Cited by Meynaud, *op. cit.,* p. 21. This again is a recurrent theme in all kinds of manifestations. Cf., for example, besides reference in note 6 below, the following: Jean Fohrmann, of the High Authority, as reported in *Metallpressdienst,* 1967, p. 34; Erich Kitzmueller in *Europa 1970,* pp. 69–70; Buiter, *ibid.* p. 192; Rosenberg, *Informations Syndicales et Ouvrières,* 1968, Nr. 1, pp. 11 ff. (reports a resolution of the *Intersyndicale* of the Miners and metalworkers); this publication is by the *Service de Presse* of CE.
6. *Informations Syndicales et Ouvrières,* 1968, Nr. 3, pp. 7 ff. The resolution is found on p. 15. The CCN itself resolved at a meeting held May 3–5, 1968, that "*sur le plan Européen, le CCN se prononce fermement pour que l'action engagée en vue de renforcer les structures syndicales des organisations libres de l'Europe des Six soit concrètement poursuivie. . . .*" *ibid.* p. 8.
7. *Entscheidungen des BVG,* vol. V, 1956, pp. 85 ff. The case was translated and published in its entirety by W. P. von Schmertzing, *Outlawing the Communist Party,* 1957. A new Communist party has been organized recently, however, and so far has not been challenged by the government.
8. For these and the statistics that follow, cf. Schierwater, *op. cit., passim.*
9. Samuel H. Barnes, *Party Democracy: Politics in an Italian Socialist Federation,* 1967, p. 193.
10. Cf. Raymond Aron and Daniel Lerner (with others), *La Querelle de la C.E.D.,* 1956.

11. Ernst Haas, *op. cit.* (Chapter 2, note 18, above) pp. 363–373.
12. *Nouvelles FIOM*, Nr. 31, December 1968.
13. Schwamm has undertaken such an examination, which will be published in his forthcoming study.
14. Cf. the articles, based on speeches at the Rome Congress of the free trade unions, held in November 1966, by Ludwig Rosenberg, "Europa —Partner der Freien Welt"; and Otto Brenner, "Für ein Grundsatzprogramm der europaeischen Gewerkschaftsbewegung!" in *Gewerkschaftliche Monatshefte*, publ. by the DGB, vol. XVIII, 1967, pp. 1 ff. and 6 ff., resp.
15. See Otto Brenner, "Die Aufgaben der Gewerkschaftsbewegung in einem integrierten Europa," in *Materialien zu Grundsaetzen und Politik der europäischen Wirtschaftsgemeinschaft*, 1964, p. 12; on p. 13 we find the following statement: "*Wenn wir nicht wollen, dass sich in Europa ein Gewerkschaftsdschungel entwickelt, dann müssen wir alles tun, um in der nächsten Zeit eine gemeinsame Konzeption für die gewerkschaftliche Zusammenarbeit zu entwickeln.*" Cf. also note 14.
16. *Informations Syndicales*, 1968, Nr. 3, pp. 7 ff. This feeling is widespread and not limited either to union circles or to the Six. Thus Charles F. Ducommun, who is the general director of PTT at Bern, has stated that the unions, if they do not adopt new approaches but continue a sclerotic policy, may save themselves temporarily, but will lose in the long run. Cf. *AGEFI*. Geneva, October 10, 1968.
17. *Informations Syndicales*, 1968, Nr. 3, p. 15.
18. See for this, Gerda Zellentin, *Der Wirtschafts- und Sozialausschuss der EWG*, 1962; and Haas, *op. cit.*, ch. 10, esp. pp. 355 ff.; as well as Jean Meynaud, *L'Action syndicale et la CEE*, Lausanne, 1962.
19. André Renard (Belgium), as quoted in Haas, *op. cit.*, p. 384. Many similar statements are found in the papers and speeches cited above, notes 2, 4, 14.
20. See for this the publication of the European Trade Union Sekretariat of April 28, 1965, p. 8: "A spirit of collaboration has gradually developed with these bodies of the communities, particularly with those members of the European Commission who are ideologically close to the Free Trade Union Movement."
21. Haas, *op. cit.*, p. 387 (see note 18, Chapter 2 above).
22. Schierwater cites a *Rundgespräch über Wirtschaftsfragen* of January 7, 1965, between four members of the Commission and trade union leaders, which is reported in *EWG Gewerkschafts-und Arbeitnehmerinformationen*, 1 (1965), p. 20.
23. Zellentin, *op. cit.*, p. 192, who, however, overestimates its importance and as a result made an erroneous prediction, as noted above, Chapter 4, note 29, of the present book.
24. For the general literature see the work cited above, Chapter 4, note 11.

25. This thought was reiterated in 1967 by M. Louis Major, the new chairman; cf. *Tenth General Report of the EEC*, 1967, p. 379.
26. W. Hallstein, "Der USA als Faktor der europäischen wirtschafts-und sozialpolitischen Integration," in: *Gewerkschaft, Wirtschaft, Gesellschaft*, 1963, pp. 381 ff. See also Fischer, *op. cit.* (Chapter 4 above, note 12), who sharply criticizes Zellentin's view.
27. Fritz Fischer, *op. cit.*, pp. 135–136 (see note 16, Chapter 4 above).
28. W. P. Maddox, *Foreign Relations in British Labour Politics*, 1934, pp. 53 ff. and throughout; Fischer, *op. cit.*, p. 142.
29. *EEC Treaty*, Article 194.
30. *EEC, Fourth General Report*, 1963. Cf. also Zellentin, *op. cit.* (above, note 18); and Fischer, *op. cit.* (note 16, Chapter 4 above), pp. 99 ff.
31. Schierwater, in *Dimensionen*, pp. 317 ff.
32. Though there are exceptions, see F. Fischer, *op. cit.*, p. 100.
33. Cf. Zellentin, *op. cit.*, ch. 3, for the complex process of equilibration.
34. Schierwater, *op. cit.*, pp. 317–318.
35. *Tenth General Report of the EEC Commission*, 1967, p. 249.
36. For the activities of these committees see the Annual Reports of the Commission and more especially the *Tenth Report*, pp. 245–248.
37. Schierwater, *op. cit.*, pp. 223–224.

8. A Community of Communities: Grass-roots Integration

1. Cf. John Dewey, *The Public and Its Problems*, 1927.
2. See my *Constitutional Government and Democracy*, 1968, ch. XII, and the literature cited there, among it more recently William A. Robson, *Local Government in Crisis*, 1966; Robert A. Dahl, *Who Governs?*, 1961; and Edward C. Banfield and James Q. Wilson, *City Politics*, 1963.
3. Edward C. Banfield, *Political Influence*, 1961.
4. This conference was held under the auspices of the Istituto per la Scienza dell'Amministrazione Pubblica of Milan. The proceedings have been published under the title *Le Collectività locali e la Costruzione dell'Unità Europea*, 1963. The discussions were built around four major reports: (1) G. Miglio, giving a historical outline of the topic; (2) P. Biascaretti, discussing the juridical and administrative aspects; (3) A. Scotto, developing the economic aspects; and (4) B. Leoni, addressing himself to the cultural, political, and sociological aspects.
5. Cf. Biascaretti, in volume cited in note 4, above.
6. This speech has often been reproduced in the publications of the Conseil des Communes d'Europe.
7. Adolf Gasser, *L'Autonomie Communale et la réconstruction de l'Europe*, 1946. Cf. also his *Geschichte der Volksfreiheit und Demokratie*, 1939, in which the importance of local community is stressed.

8. For the preceding and the principles of the early group see Hans Muntzke, "Die Gründung und die Ziele des Rates der Gemeinden Europas," in *Der Europäische Gemeindetag*, IV, 1 (1961), pp. 5 ff.
9. Cf. *L'Ordine Politico delle Communità dello Stato secundo le leggi dello spirito*, 1946, esp. pp. 3–21. The *Communità* appear to be subdivisions of a province; decisive is the question of human contact: "Un organismo è armonico ed efficiente soltanto quando gli uomini preposti e determinati compiti possone esplicarli mediante contatti diretti." The commune, by contrast, is either too small or too large (p. 6), provinces are artificial creations, the great cities are incapable of providing genuine community. Typically, a *communità*, depending upon circumstances, would have between 65,000 and 150,000 inhabitants.
10. The student of the history of political thought cannot help but recall the close points of contact between these ideas and the outlook of Althusius and Rousseau; cf. for a sketch of the history my paper "Origin and Development of the Concept of Federalism in the United States," 1959–60, and ch. 32 in my *Man and His Government*, 1963.
11. The organization is described in the publication cited in note 4 above, pp. 223 ff.; cf. also my "The Grass-roots Base of the Unification of Europe," *Public Policy*, Vol. XII (1963), pp. 23 ff.
12. Resolution 76 of October 14, 1955.
13. See for the plan of reform Pierre Duclos, *La Réforme du Conseil de l'Europe*, 1958, pp. 124–125, who comments that "assurement, la réforme serait d'importance en mettant à égalité de dignité, sinon d'influence politique dans la Communauté Européenne, less États et les collectivités locales que ceux-ci tiennent généralement dans une tutelle étroite." Ernst Haas, in his otherwise comprehensive study *Uniting Europe*, 1958, overlooked the local communities which for Duclos ranked ahead of economic interests and parties. All three he considers "Sources d'autorité extra-nationales," which reinforce the original conception of the Council as simply an association of states; *ibid.*, pp. 122 ff.
14. The material on these goings-on is widely scattered and hard to come by. Little pamphlets with pictures are issued, such as that of the "fête du jumelage de Boulogne-Billancourt" (near Paris) with Anderlecht (Belgium), Hammersmith (England), Neukölln (Germany) and Zaandamm (Netherlands), featuring the motto: "L'Europe commence dans les Communes." Cf. for an overview *Communes d'Europe* (the official publication of the CCE, for August–September 1960, entitled "Jumelages de A jusqu'à Z," and the special issue of *Der Europäische Gemeindetag*, Vol. IV, April 1961. English publications also speak of these partnerships or "twinnings."
15. *Communes d'Europe, loc. cit.*, pp. 5 ff. Cf. also the issue of *Der Europäische Gemeindetag* for April 1961, pp. 42 ff.
16. Dr. Grauhan's report in *Dimensionen* contains numerous specific examples.

17. Cf. Rolf-Richard Grauhan's study *Die Verschwisterungen deutscher und französischer Gemeinden,* in *Dimensionen,* pp. 35–104.
18. As reported by the *Union Internationale des Maires,* 1968.
19. Dr. Grauhan's study is based upon the results obtained by means of this questionnaire; he also visited a number of French towns including Nancy, Avignon, Amiens, and Lille besides some smaller towns, and interviewed various persons on the subject of these partnerships. Interesting data were also supplied by Michael Fingerhut in the seminar paper dealing with the development of relations between the French town Lagny and the German town Haslach between 1964 and 1966. Very important information was provided by M. Jean Bareth, administrative secretary of the *Association Française pour le Conseil de Communes d'Europe* and Herr Hans Muntzke, the corresponding German official.
20. According to statistics of the Fédération Mondiale des Villes Jumelées, in their Annuaire Officiel des Villes Jumelées, Cités Unies, No. 39 Special (July 1964), 398 French communities had partnerships with communities in other countries. Of these 176 were communities of the Federal Republic, 142 were British, 76 were Belgian, and 68 Italian. In the case of Germany the partnerships with France are predominant. See for these statistics Grauhan, in *Dimensionen,* pp. 40/41.
21. Research on this is now going forward. See for a general review Burton Paulu, *Radio and Television Broadcasting on the European Continent,* 1967.
22. Johan Huizinga, *Homo ludens—A Study of the Play-Element in Culture,* 1949; and Sebastian de Grazia, *Of Time, Work and Leisure,* 1962.
23. Further research on the subject of the evolving pattern of intermarriage in the European Community is urgently needed.
24. As cited by Grauhan, in *Dimensionen,* p. 90, fn. 90: "Nos relations sont maintenant suffisamment intimes pour que nous puissions nous faire réciproquement des remarques sur certains détails qui peuvent laisser à desirer, sans pour cela nous froisser." The next quotation in the text is also found there.
25. Charles E. Merriam, *Political Power,* 1934, ch. IV.
26. M. Bareth, mentioned in note 19 above, in his address to the first Congress of the twin cities at Strasbourg, as cited in *Communes d'Europe* (August/September), 1964, p. 10.
27. Brian Chapman, *The Prefects and Provincial France,* 1955.
28. For a further development of this problem see Biascaretti, cited in note 4 above.
29. Jean Maurice Chevalier, Conseiller Culturelle, "La Vague Allemande," in *Le Monde* (October 16, 1963).
30. He goes so far as to construct a parallel with *jumelages* between French and Algerian cities; see J. M. Bressand, "La Sixième Colonne," in *Témoinage Chrétien* (September 19, 1963).

31. Statement by Herr Weber, director of the City of Braunschweig, which maintains a French *jumelage*.
32. On this see Coudenhove-Kalergi, *Die europäische Nation*, 1956, and my criticism above, pp. 9 ff.
33. Grauhan, in *Dimensionen*, pp. 54 ff. and 70 ff.
34. *Ibid.*, pp. 82 ff.
35. Dr. Grauhan gives some cases, e.g. Buxtehude and Romilly-sur-Seine (Aube). The CEE maintained in 1966 national branches in Belgium, the Netherlands, Luxembourg, Great Britain, France, Switzerland, Italy, Greece, Austria, the Federal Republic, and Denmark.

9. The Academic Community

1. Charles E. Merriam, *The Making of Citizens*, 1931.
2. Merriam, *op. cit.*, p. 23; but the discussion is not detailed.
3. This research was carried on by Professor Dusan Sidjanski of the University of Geneva. Besides the references given in the notes, this chapter is built on the study by Sidjanski in *Politische Dimensionen*, pp. 105–224.
4. S. d'Irsay, *Historie des Universités*, 2 vols., 1933–1934, and the same author's article on the universities in the *IESS*. For the original, see C. H. Haskins, *The Rise of the Universities*, 1923; H. S. Denifle, *Die Entstehung der Universitäten des Mittelalters bis 1400*, 1885–1956; and H. Rashdall, *The Universities of Europe in the Middle Ages*, 3 vols., 1895–1958. It is astonishing how limited is the scholarly literature on the relation of universities to public life prior to the 20th century.
5. A good survey of all these activities is provided by a recent publication of the Centre Européen de la Culture, *Bilan des Activités Culturelles au Service de l'Europe, 1949–1964* (no date, but presumably 1965), hereafter cited as *Bilan*.
6. L'Office Franco-Allemand pour la Jeunesse, *Rapport d'Activité 1963–1968*.
7. The structure and process of French and German universities are at present undergoing so much change that particular references do not seem very useful. Cf. for a general statement *Bilan*, p. 77.
8. See for this estimate Sidjanski, in *Dimensionen*, pp. 108–109.
9. Sidjanski, *loc. cit.*, gives a list of these agreements.
10. "Gesetz zu der Gemeinsamen Erklärung und zu dem Vertrag vom 22. Januar 1963 zwischen der Bundesrepublik Deutschland und der Französischen Republik über die deutsch-französische Zusammenarbeit" of June 15, 1963, in *Bundesgesetzblatt*, 1963, part II, pp. 705–710.
11. See *Bilan*, as cited in note 5 above.
12. The author himself has conducted such seminars.
13. Sidjanski, in *Dimensionen*, p. 113.

14. Cf. *Bilan*, p. 78. See also *Une Université Européenne?*, in Bulletin du CEC, Geneva, 1958; and *L'Università Europea*, in Documentazioni dell'Istituto Affari Internazionali, entitled *Problemi dell'Europa Communitaria*, No. 13, 1968.
15. Cf. *L'Università Europea*, as cited in note 14 above.
16. G. Guéron, R. Cohen, and J. Meyer, *Education sans Frontières*, 1967. Cf. also *Statut de l'École Européenne*, without date or publisher.
17. *Bilan*, pp. 22–60, discusses these and others in a semiofficial way.
18. Cf. Sidjanski, in *Dimensionen*, pp. 119–125.
19. Sidjanski, *loc. cit.*, pp. 126–134.
20. Cf. e.g. *Gesetzblatt für Baden-Württemberg*, E 3235, March 26, 1968, pp. 81–100, for the text of such a law. Cf. also the *Protokoll* of the 118th Session of the *Landtag* (February 15, 1968).
21. Cf. the list of such institutes given in *Bilan*, pp. 37–41. It includes, however, some whose program is much more general and others that are too specialized. About 25 are *bona fide* institutes of European political studies.
22. Cf. the statistics given in *Bilan*, pp. 41–42.
23. This association publishes a yearbook with much interesting information.
24. On this association see Sidjanski, in *Dimensionen*, pp. 232 ff.
25. Cf. *Bilan*, pp. 94 ff.
26. Sidjanski has indicated, *loc. cit.*, pp. 135 ff., the difficulties which he encountered in securing adequate references. For what follows, cf. Sidjanski, pp. 140 ff.
27. Note 5th Annual Report, as cited above, note 6.
28. Cf. Sidjanski, *loc. cit.*, p. 170.
29. Sidjanski, *loc. cit.*, pp. 172–173.
30. Sidjanski, *loc. cit.*, pp. 170–224.
31. See my *Man and His Government*, ch. 21. See also Harald Ofstad, *An Inquiry into the Freedom of Decision*, 1961.
32. Concerning assimilation see the article by Simpson in the *IESS* and earlier by Park in *ESS* and the literature cited there.
33. Cf. Yvon Bourdet, *Préjugés français et préjugés allemands*, no date. Regarding this see Jacques-René Rabier, "Préjugés français et préjugés allemands," in *Revue de Psychologie des Peuples*, 1968, pp. 186–202.

10. Trends and Prospects

1. *Die Zeit*, October 26, 1968—Editorial by Becker.
2. Gerd Wilcke in *The New York Times*, November 24, 1968.
3. *Ibid.*
4. Hans Joachim Arndt, *Politik und Sachverstand im Kreditwährungswesen*, 1963.

5. Concerning this, see the article by H. Parker Willis in the *ESS* and his work *The Federal Reserve System,* 1923, as well as Paul M. Warburg's, the architect's, classic two-volume work with the same title, 1930.
6. A study on this problem is under way; it is being done by Gerhard Glotz.
7. *Tenth General Report* of the EEC, 1967, p. 13. Cf. also the speech by President Rey, cited below, note 13. For the widespread demand for this development, cf., for instance, the conference at Saarbrücken, cited above, Chapter 3, note 24.
8. Guy Héraud, *L'Europe des Ethnies,* 1963.
9. *Treaty,* Arts. 2; 39, 2; and 49. Cf. also Arts. 92 and 226.
10. Riccardo Petrella, "The regional policy of the EEC," in *Lo Spettatore Internazionale,* English ed., vol. II, 1967, pp. 340 ff. The quote occurs at p. 343. The article contains rich documentation. Cf. also President Rey's speech as quoted below, note 13, pp. 18 ff. Cf. also Sergio Barzanti, *The Underdeveloped Areas in the Common Market,* 1965, for a comparative analysis in the economic perspective.
11. "First Memorandum on Regional Policy in the European Economic Community," May 11, 1965, as discussed in the *Ninth General Report on the Activities of the Community,* published in June 1966.
12. Documents of the European Communities, September 1965, No. 15, p. 6, as cited in Petrella, *loc. cit.,* p. 345.
13. Cf. e.g. the May 1968 session of the European Parliament and President Rey's speech before it; it was separately published by the CEE as Doc. 8238; 5/V/1968/5.
14. Rey, *loc. cit.,* p. 18.
15. On the British entry, cf. Miriam Camps, *Britain and the European Community 1955–1963,* 1964; for a more recent assessment of the Continental perspective see *La Grande Bretagne et le Marché Commun,* Report of a Colloque held at Caen on December 9 and 10, 1966, which includes, on pp. 97 ff., an assessment of future prospects by Richard Mayne. See also *L'Adhésion de la Grande Bretagne au Communautés,* Brussels, 1968 (Institut d'Études Européennes).
16. Cf. my "Selected Trends and Issues in Contemporary Federal and Regional Relations," in *Selected Background Studies Prepared for the United States–Puerto Rico Commission on the Status of Puerto Rico,* 1966, pp. 471 ff.
17. Cf. Arnold Rivkin, *Africa and the Common Market—A Perspective,* Monographs in World Affairs, Graduate School of International Studies, University of Denver, 1966; A. Kazancigil, *L'Association de la Turquie à la Communauté Économique Européenne,* FNSP, Paris, 1967; Communautés Européennes, *Le Marché Commun et la Grèce à travers les textes, 1959–1967.* Cf. also Daniel Pepy, "La Négociation de la Deuxième convention de l'association des Etats Africains et Malgaches à la Communauté Économique Européenne," and Bridget

Bloom, "The Agreement between the European Economic Community and the Republic of Nigeria," both papers read at the Lyon Conference of the *Association pour le Développement de la Science Politique Européenne,* November 11 and 12, 1966.
18. See my *Trends of Federalism in Theory and Practice,* 1968, ch. 11.
19. *Constitutional Government and Democracy,* 1968 (4th ed.), ch. 2.
20. Cf. Karl W. Deutsch and William J. Foltz (eds.), *Nation-Building,* 1963, esp. pp. 1–32. See also my *Man and His Government,* 1963, ch. 30.
21. See Lawrence Scheinman, "Some Preliminary Notes on Bureaucratic Relationships in the European Economic Community," in *International Organization,* vol. XX (1966), pp. 750 ff. Scheinman is writing a more comprehensive study, tentatively entitled *Patterns of Power: Bureaucracy and the Integrative Process.* See also Etienne Hirsch, "Relations between the Officials of the European Commission and the Governments of the Member States," in *Government and Opposition,* vol. II (1967), pp. 436 ff. Altiero Spinelli, in his *Rapporto Sull'Europa,* 1965, ch. 4, pp. 75 ff., also deals with the bureaucracy.
22. See Scheinman, *loc. cit.*, p. 751, for a definition.
23. See my article "Public Policy and the Nature of Administrative Responsibility," in *Public Policy,* I (1940), pp. 3 ff., recently reissued in Alan Altshuler, *The Politics of Federal Bureaucracy,* 1968, pp. 414 ff.
24. *Der Europäische Offentliche Dienst,* ed. Burns and Langrod, 1957; cf. for background Egon Ranshofen-Wertheimer, *The International Administration of the International Secretariat,* 1946.
25. Treaty, Art. 157, 2.
26. For this problem see my *Man and His Government,* ch. 11.
27. See for this Etienne Hirsch, *loc. cit.* (fn. 2), pp. 437 ff. The problem was also developed by Altiero Spinelli in ch. 4 of his *Rapporto Sull'Europa,* 1965.
28. Hirsch, *loc. cit.* (note 21 above), pp. 440–441.
29. Spinelli, *op. cit.*, p. 101. Cf. also for the preceding quotation Margot Lyon in her paper "Reshuffling the 'Eurocrats,'" in *EC* No. 111, April 1968, pp. 10 ff.
30. Cf. Burton Paulu, *Radio and Television Broadcasting on the European Continent,* 1967, ch. III, esp. at pp. 58 ff., gives a good overall analysis. Cf. also the interesting debate in the *Assemblée Nationale*'s Chamber of Deputies on May 26, 1964, *Journal Officiel,* pp. 1376–1379.
31. Paulu, *op. cit.*, ch. III, pp. 63 ff.
32. See Donald R. Reich, "Court, Comity and Federalism in West Germany," *Midwest Journal of Political Science,* Vol. VII (1963); this article is based on the author's unpublished doctoral dissertation at Harvard, dealing with this controversy; cf. also Gerard Braunthal, "Federalism in Germany–The Broadcasting Controversy," *Journal of Politics,* Vol. XXIV (1962), and W. Phillips Davison, in *West*

German Leadership and Foreign Policy (ed. Speier and Davison), 1957.

33. For Italy see RAI Radiotelevisione Italiana, *This is RAI*, 1963, and the evaluation by Cesare Mannucci, "Structure and Policy of the RAI–TV," in *Gazette*, Vol. XI (1965), pp. 57–65.
34. Interview of January 24, 1966.
35. Contrary to promise, 102 of the 281 journalists of ORTF had been dismissed by August 7, and similarly drastic action hit other responsibles; cf. *Die Welt*, August 8 (report by H. Weissenberger). To be sure, the ORTF was overstaffed, very costly, and honeycombed with patronage; the French press had criticized it bitterly for many years, but more especially for the government's excessive influence, which has become even more pronounced after the recent overhaul.
36. *Les Cahiers Luxembourgeois: Radio Télé Luxembourg*, 1961. European governments have been trying to regulate these activities; cf. "European Agreement for the Prevention of Broadcasts transmitted from Stations outside national Territories," *European Treaty Series*, No. 53, Council of Europe, Strasbourg, 1965. Cf. also the Protocol, *ibid.*
37. As did Deutsch and Associates in their study, cited above (Chapter 2, note 21) and discussed further on pp. 35 ff.
38. A study of these developments is being developed under our Project.
39. A thorough study of this development is urgently needed.
40. The reduction in social distance makes Frenchmen and Germans see each other no longer as aliens. "Aliens are felt to be not individuals but men of a particular type . . . ," Simmel, *Soziologie*, 2nd ed. 1922, pp. 510 ff. See also in this connection Dolf Sternberger's suggestive essays in *Gefuehl der Fremde*, 1958.
41. "L'Europe des Couples," in *Vers la Vie Nouvelle*, II (1968), p. 8 (by R. and J. P. Guerend).
42. D. Lerner and M. Gordon, *A Decade of Challenge—The Response of European Leaders*, ch. VII (MS); cited with permission.
43. Karl Deutsch and Associates, *op. cit.* (Chapter 2, note 21 above), p. 298.
44. Leon N. Lindberg, "The European Community as a Political System: Notes toward a Model," *Journal of Common Market Studies*, Vol. V (1967), pp. 344 ff. A book on the subject is forthcoming. Lindberg outlined it in an unpublished paper (April 1967, Center for International Affairs, Harvard).
45. David Easton, *A System Analysis of Political Life*, 1965, and *A Framework for Political Analysis*, 1965; cf. also Dennis Thompson's critical analysis in *Political Science Quarterly*, 1968.
46. Lindberg, *op. cit.*, p. 348, where the quotation from Easton, *Framework*, p. 86 is found.
47. Lindberg, *op. cit.*, e.g., p. 359.

48. *Nation-Building,* ed. Karl Deutsch and William J. Foltz, 1963, p. 31. The definition is more fully elaborated in *Annales de la Philosophie Politique,* 1968. Cf. also my *Man and His Government,* ch. 30, for background.
49. *First General Report on the Activities of the European Community 1967,* Brussels, 1968. Cf. in this connection Karlheinz Neunreither, *Das Europa der Sechs ohne Aussenpolitik,* 1964.
50. Raymond Aron, in *Le Figaro,* 1967. For the growth of regionalism, Bruce M. Russett, *International Regions and the International System; A Study in Political Ecology,* 1967, has explored the problem of regionalism in the world-wide perspective rather than regionalism within countries; for these the earlier work done in the U.S., France, and other countries is more relevant. On international regionalism—in terms of which the CM or Europe or both would be regions—cf. also the interesting collection of essays, some cited earlier, edited by Joseph S. Nye, Jr., *International Regionalism,* 1968.
51. J. A. R. Marriott, *Federalism and the Problem of the Small State,* 1943.
52. John Stuart Mill, *Considerations on Representative Government* (1861), Liberal Arts Press, 1958, ch. 17, p. 246; see for this my *Trends of Federalism in Theory and Practice,* 1968; the quotation is found on p. 183.

List of Abbreviations

AEDE	Association Européenne des Enseignants (European Association of Teachers)
AELE (EFTA)	L'Association Européenne de Libre Exchange (European Free Trade Association)
AFL–CIO	American Federation of Labor and Congress of Industrial Organizations
AIEE	Association des Institutes d'Etudes Européennes (Association of Institutes of European Studies)
BDA	Bundesvereinigung der Deutschen Arbeitgeberverbände (Federal Union of German Employers' Associations)
BDI	Bundesverband der Deutschen Industrie (Federal Union of German Industry)
BENELUX	Belgium, Luxembourg, and the Netherlands
BGB	(Board of the German Union of Trade Unions)
BLEU	Belgium-Luxemburg Economic Union
BVG	Bundesverfassungsgericht (German Federal Constitutional Court)
CCC	Council for Cultural Cooperation, of the Council of Europe
CCE	Conseil des Communes d'Europe (Council of the Communes [local communities or municipalities] of Europe)
CCN	National committee of the CGT–FO, France
CE	Conseil de l'Europe (Council of Europe)

CEC	Centre Européen de la Culture (Center for European Culture)
CECA (ECSC)	Communauté Européenne du Charbon et de l'Acier European Coal and Steel Community
CEE (EEC)	Communauté Economique Européenne European Economic Community
CEPES	Comité Européen pour le Progres Economique et Social (European Committee for Economic and Social Progress)
CES (ESC)	Comité Economique et Social Economic and Social Committee
CESR	Comité de l'Enseignment superieur et de la Recherche (Committee of Higher Learning and Research)
CFCE	Conseil des Fédérations Commerciales d'Europe (Council of Federations of Commerce of Europe)
CFDT	Confédération Française et Démocratique du Travail (Catholic Trade Union—France)
CGIL	Confederazione Generale Italiana del Lavoro (General Confederation of Italian Workers)
CGT	Confédération Général du Travail (General Confederation of Labor—France)
CIFE	Centre International de la Formation Européenne (International Center for European Education)
CISC	Confédération Internationale des Syndicats Chrétiens (International Confederation of Christian Trade Unions)
CISL	Confédération Internationale des Syndicats Libres (International Confederation of Free Trade Unions)
CM	The Common Market
CNJA	Centre National des Jeunes Agriculteurs (National Center of Young Farmers)
CNMCCA	Confédération Nationale de la Mutualité, Coopération, et Crédit Agricole (National Confederation of Farmers' Mutuals, Cooperatives, and Credit Organizations)

CNPF	Conseil National du Patronat Français (National Council of French Employers)
COCCEE	Comité des Organisations Commerciales des Pays de la CEE (Committee of the Commercial Organizations of the Countries of the European Economic Community)
COGECA	Comité Général de la Coopération Agricole des Pays de la Communauté Economique Européenne (Committee for the Agricultural Cooperatives in the Six Countries of the European Economic Community)
CONFINDUSTRIA	Confederazione Generale dell'Industria Italiana (General Confederation of Italian Industry)
COPA	Comité des Organisations Professionelles Agricoles des Six Pays de la Communauté Economique Européenne
DAG	Deutsche Angestelltengewerkschaft (German Union of Office Workers)
DBB	Deutscher Beamtenbund (Union of German Civil Servants)
DBV	Deutscher Bauernverband (German Farmers' Union)
DGB	Deutscher Gewerkschaftsbund (German Union of Trade Unions)
EC	European Communities
ECSC	European Coal and Steel Community (see CECA)
EEC	European Economic Community (see CEE)
EFTA	European Free Trade Association (see AELE)
ELEC	European League for Economic Cooperation (see LECE)
EP	European Parliament (See PE)
ERO	European Regional Organization—of the International Union of Free Trade Unions
ESC	Economic and Social Committee (see CES)
EURATOM	European Atomic Energy Community
EUROCRAT	European Bureaucrat

FEOGA — Fonds Européen d'Orientation et de Garantie Agricoles
European Agricultural Fund

FIB — Fédération des Industries Belges
(Federation of Belgian Industries)

FIOM — Fédération Internationale des Ouvriers sur Metaux
(International Federation of Metal Workers)

FMVJ — Fédération Mondiale des Villes Jumelées
(World Council of [Paired] Municipalities)

FNSEA — Fédération Nationale des Syndicats d'Exploitants Agricoles
(National Federation of Agricultural Organizations)

FO — Force Ouvrière
(Workers' Force)

GD — General Directorate—group of 3 or 4 commissioners

IFOP — Institut Français d'Opinion Publique
(French Institute for Public Opinion)

IPSA — International Political Science Association

ISCI — International Secretariat of the Chemical Industry—of the EEC

LECE — Ligue Européenne de la Coopération Economiquo (see ELEC)

MODEF — Mouvement de Défense des Exploitations Familiales
(Movement for the Defense of Family Farms)

MRP — Mouvement Républican Populaire

NSU — Neckarsulm—Location in Württemberg, Germany, of NSU Werke, automobile manufacturer

OCDE — Organisation pour la Coopération et le Développement Economique
(See OECD—formerly the OECE/OEEC)

OECD — Organization for Economic Cooperation and Development (see OCDE)

OECE — Organisation Européenne de Coopération Economique (see OEEC)

OEEC — Organization for European Economic Cooperation (see OECE)

ORTF	Office de Radiodiffusion et Television Française (Office of French Television and Radio Broadcasting)
PE	Le Parlement Européen (see EP)
PSI	Partita Socialista Italiana (Italian Socialist Party)
RAI	Radiotelevisione Italiana (Italian Television and Radio Broadcasting)
SOFRES	Societé Française d'Enquêtes par Sondages—conducts public opinion polls
UACEE	Union de l'Artisanat de la CEE (Union of the Craftsmen of the EEC)
UAEE	Union des Associations Européennes d'Etudiants (Union of European Student Associations)
UNESCO	United Nations Educational, Scientific, and Cultural Organization
UNICE	Union des Industries de la Communauté Européenne (Union of Industries of the European Community)
WEU	Western European Union—founded in 1954

Index

Aberdeen, 176
Abs, Hermann, 48
academic community, 175 ff.
academic degrees, 45
"Action by Pressure Groups," 87–88
Action des groupes de pression, L', 228
Action syndicale et la Communauté Européenne, L', 233, 234
"added value tax," 58
Adenauer, Konrad, xi
Adhésion de la Grande Bretagne au Communautés, L', 240
adult education, 76
advancement, 125, 127–128
Advisory Committee of the CSC, 145
AEDE, 181, 183
AELE, *see* EFTA
AFL–CIO, 138
Africa, 10, 18, 45, 114, 201
Africa and the European Common Market–A Perspective, 223, 240
AGEFI, 234
Agence d'Europe, 231
Agrarmarkt und Agrarpolitik, 230
"Agreement between the European Economic Community and the Republic of Nigeria, The," 241
agreements, economic, 59–62
"Agricultural Basis of Emotional Nationalism," 229
agricultural community, 90 ff.
agricultural policy, 45
agriculture, 204
AIEE, 186–187
Aix-Tübingen, 192, 193
Albania, 19
Alberoni, Francesco, 232
Alexander I of Russia, 7
Aliboni, Roberto, 227
Althusius, 236
Altshuler, Alan, 241
America, *see* USA
American Federation of Labor and Congress of Industrial Organizations, *see* AFL–CIO
amoral familism, 121–122
Anciens Combattants, 171
Anciens Déportés, 171
Anglo-German group, 153
Annales de la Philosophie Politique, 219, 243
Annuaire Officiel des Villes Jumelées Cités Unies, 237
Anonymous Empire: A Study of the Lobby in Great Britain, 226
Anthropology Today, 219
APSR, 33*n.*
Aquinas, Thomas, 2
Arab world, 10, 114
Arabia, 18
"Arbeitnehmer und Europa–Integrationstendenzen und -strukturen im Sozialbereich des Gemeinsamen Markets, Der," 231, 233
Aristotle, 4

Armand, Louis, 48, 55
Arndt, Hans Joachim, 239
Aron, Raymond, 219, 233, 243
Artisanat, 70
Asia, 10
Assemblée Nationale, 241
Association de la Turquei à la Communauté Economique Européenne, L', 240
Association des Institutes d'Etudes Européennes, *see* AIEE
Association Européene de Libre Exchange, *see* AELE
Association Europénne des Enseignants, *see* AEDE
Association for the Development of a European Political Science, 87, 187
Association Française pour le Conseil de Communes d'Europe, 237
Association of Institutes of European Studies, *see* AIEE
Association pour le Développement de la Science Politique Européenne, 229, 241
Aubenas, 157
"Aufgaben der Gewerkschaftsbewegung in einem integrierten Europa, Die," 234
Aufsichtsrat, 64
Austria, 2, 3, 158, 177, 185
Autonomie Communale et la réconstruction de l'Europe, L', 235
auxiliaries, 205

Baglioni, Guido, 232
"balance of power," 8
Banfield, Edward C., 113, 121–122, 229, 231, 232, 235
"barbarian threat," 18
Barbieri, Luciano, 231
Bareth, Jean, 165, 237
Barnes, Samuel Henry, 137, 232, 233
Barzanti, Sergio, 240
Bauchet, P., 231
Bavaria, 3–4
BDA, 70
BDI, 70, 74, 77, 78, 79, 226
Beever, R. Colin, 233
Bekaert, M., 79
Belgium, 2, 19, 32, 44, 45, 47, 67, 91, 93, 114, 147, 155, 157, 185, 188–189
see also Benelux
Belgium-Luxembourg Economic Union, *see* BLEU
Bell, Daniel, 219
Benelux, 59, 73, 96, 137, 150, 184, 204
Berg, Fritz, 79
Berlin, 171
Bernard, Nadine, 228
Bernard, Stephane, 228
Bernhard, H., 220
Betriebsordnungsgesetz, 63
Beyme, Klaus von, 221
Biascaretti, P., 235, 237
Bilan, 238, 239
Bilan des Activités Culturelles au Service de l'Europe, 1949–1964, 238
Bilotte, Gen., 168
Bismarck, 25
BLEU, 52
Bloom, Bridget, 240–241
Bleucher, Viggo Graf, 225
Board of the German Union of Trade Unions, *see* DGB
book publishing, 208, 209
Bottai, Guiseppe, 228
Bourdet, Yvon, 239
Bowie, Robert R., xii
Bradley, P., 222
Brandt, Conrad, 229
Brauckmann, Karl, 233
Braunthal, Gerhard, 226, 241
Brecht, Arnold, 221
Brenner, Otto, 142, 234
Bressand, J. M., 237
Briand, Aristide, xi, 20
Briefs, Goetz, 225
Brinton, Crane, 218
Britain, *see* Great Britain
Britain and France Between Two Wars, 218
Britain and the European Community, 240
British Commonwealth, 1, 18, 28
see also Great Britain and England
British Commonwealth, The—An Experiment in Cooperation among Nations, 221
British Dominions, 8
see also British Commonwealth
British Empire, 10, 28
broadcasting, 205–208
Bruin, Robert de, 228

Brundsatzfragen der europäischen Integrätion, 218
Brzezinski, Zbigniew, 219
Buchmann, Jean, 228
Buddhism, 12
Buiter, Harm G., 140, 233
Bull Electric, 131
Bundesgesetzblatt, 238
Bundestreue, 221
Bundesverband der Deutschen Industrie, *see* BDI
Bundesvereinigung der Deutschen Arbeitgeberverbände, see BDA
Bundesverfassungsgericht, *see* German Federal Constitutional Court
bureaucratic interpenetration, 203
Burma, 19
"By and with estates," 86

Caen, University of, 226
Cahiers Luxembourgeois, Les: Radio Télé Luxembourg, 242
Camps, Miriam, 230, 240
Canada, 32, 40
capital, 45
capitalism, 17
Capitant, René, 225
Caratteristiche dell'emigrazione italiana in Belgio . . . di Milano, Le, 231
Caribbean, 19, 25–26
Carmoy, Guy de, 228
Cartou, Louis, 228
Cassirer, Ernst, 218
Catholic Party of France, *see* MRP
Catholic Trade Union–France, *see* CFDT
CCC, 179–180
CCE, 154–156, 157–158, 236
CCN, 142, 233
CE, 155, 178, 179, 182, 184, 187, 224, 233
CEA, 93 ff.
Ceausescu, Nicolae, 14
CEC, 183, 186, 187
CECA, 135, 139
see also ECSC
CEE, 135, 182, 238
see also EEC
Center for European Culture, *see* CEC
Center for International Affairs, xii
Centre Européen de la Culture, 238
see also CEC
Centre International de la Formation Européenne, *see* CIFE
Centre National des Jeunes Agriculteurs, *see* CNJA
Centrifugalism in the Caribbean, 218
CEPES, 223
Cervantes, 4
CES, *see* ESC
CESR, 184–185
CFCE, 70
CFDT, 142
CGIL, 134–135
CGT, 134–135, 136, 138
CGT–FO, 142
Chambers of Agriculture, 101
Chambers of Commerce of the Six, 78
Changing Perspectives of the European Elites, 222
Chapman, Brian, 237
Chateaubriand, François de, 31
Chevalier, Jean Maurice, 237
Cheylard, Le, 161
China, 1, 16, 18, 21
Chinese Communism and the Rise of Mao, 229
Christian Trade Unions, 136, 141
Christianity, 12
Churchill, Winston, 16
Cicero, 4
CIFE, 76, 183, 208
CISC, 140–141, 142
CISL, 140, 142
Citröen, 61, 131
"City air makes free," 3
City Politics, 235
civitas Christiana, 176
Claessens, Hilde, 65, 69
CM, *see* Common Market
CNMCCA, 101
CNJA, 101, 103
CNPE, 70
CNPF, 70, 72, 76, 77, 78, 226
Coal and Steel Authority, 66, 72
Coal and Steel Community, 71, 133, 138, 201
Coal and Steel Treaty, 73
coal and steel unions, 139
COCCEE, 77–78
Code Civil, 7
Code Napoléon and the Common Law World, The, 218
coexistence, 17

COGECA, 94
Cohen, R., 239
Cohn-Bendit, Daniel, 178
"cold war," 15
Collectività locali e la Costruzione dell'Unità Europea, 235
Colloque International sur la décision dans les organisations européennes, 228–229
Cologne and Clermont-Ferrand, 190–191
Columbia University, 37
Coming World Civilization, The, 217
Comité de l'Elysée, 53
Comité de l'Enseignment superiur et de la Recherche, *see* CESR
Comité des Organisations Commerciales des Pays de la CEE, *see* COCCEE
Comité des Organisations Professionelles Agricoles des Six Pays de la Communauté Economique Européenne, *see* COPA
Comité des syndicaux métaux des pays du Marché Commun Européen, 131–132
Comité Economique et Social, *see* CES
Comité Européen pour le Progres Economique et Social, *see* CEPES
Comité Général de la Coopération Agricole des Pays de la Communauté Economique Européenne, *see* COGECA
Comité Métal, 131–132
comity, 26–27
Commissariat du Plan, 111–112
Commission, *see* EEC
Committee for Civic Education, 183
Committee for the Agricultural Cooperatives in the Six Countries of the European Economy Community, *see* COGECA
Committee for the Social Fund, 148
Committee of Higher Learning and Research, *see* CESR
Committee of Permanent Delegates, 85
Committee of Presidents, 140
Committee of Professional Agricultural Organizations, 93–94
see also COPA
Committee of the Commercial Organizations of the Countries of the European Economic Community, *see* COCCEE
Committee of 21, 139, 140, 143
Committee on Free Circulation of Labor, 135
"Common Commercial Policy of the EEC, The," 227
Common Market, xiii, 19, 30, 35–36, 38–39, 41, 44, 46, 47, 49 ff., 69, 90, 91, 94, 95, 100 ff., 114 ff., 133 ff., 156, 166, 177, 179, 183, 184, 185, 186, 193, 196 ff., 226
Common Market Cartel Law, 226
Common Market Treaty, 67–68, 73
Communauté Economique Européenne, *see* CEE
Communauté Européene du Charbon et de l'Acier, *see* CECA
communauté naissante, 190
Communauté universitaire européenne, 190
Communautés Européennes, 224
communes, 177, 188, 189
Communes d'Europe, 236, 237
Communism, 17, 25, 92, 103, 106, 114, 118–119, 130, 134 ff., 168–169, 172, 178, 195
Communism in Western Europe, 229
Communist China, 15, 21
see also China *and* Red China
Communist Manifesto, 134
communità, 154, 236
Community, 221
Community of the Six, 37, 38, 44, 47, 58, 142, 155, 181, 182
Comparative Federalism: States Rights and National Power, 221
Comparison des procedures de décision suivant le Conseil de l'Europe et suivant les procedures communautaires, 228
"Comportment politique et condition sociale en Italie," 232
"concert of Europe," 7
Conciliar Movement, 3
Confédération Française et Démocratique du Travail, *see* CFDT
Confédération Général du Travail, *see* CGT

Confédération Internationale des Syndicats Chrétiens, *see* CISC
Confédération Internationale des Syndicats Libres, *see* CISL
Confédération Nationale de la Mutualité Coopération, et Crédit Agricole, *see* CNMCCA
Confederazione Generale dell'Industria Italiana, *see* CONFINDUSTRIA
Confederazione Generale Italiana del Lavoro, *see* CGIL
Conference of European Rectors and Vicechancellors, 184
Conference of French and German Rectors, 180, 185
Conference of Rectors, 187, 192–193
Conference of the Communes of Europe, *see* CCE
CONFINDUSTRIA, 70
Confucianism, 12, 16
Conseil des Communes d'Europe, 153–154, 235
see also CCE
Conseil de l'Europe, *see* CE
Conseil des Fédérations Commerciales d'Europe, *see* CFCE
Conseil National du Patronat Français, *see* CNPF
Conseils des Communautés Européennes en tant que pouvoir de décision, Les, 228
consensus evolution, 38
Considerations on Representative Government, 243
Consten, *see* Grundig-Consten case
Constitutional Government and Democracy, 235, 241
Constitutional Government and Politics, 221
Consultative Assembly, 179
Consultative Committee of the High Authority of the Coal and Steel Community, 133, 143
contacts outside work, 125, 129–130
Controle de la décision communautaire, Le: la cour de justice, 228
Coopération des Travailleurs en Europe, La, 232, 233
COPA, 70, 79, 80, 83–84, 93 ff., 145, 230
Copenhagen, 176
Corporate State in Action, The, 228
Cotteret, Jean-Marie, 228
Coudenhove-Kalergi, Richard N., xi, 9–10, 20, 21, 30, 32, 218, 220, 222, 238
Council for Cultural Cooperation of the Council of Europe, *see* CCC
Council of Communes of Europe, *see* CCE
Council of Europe, *see* CE
Council of European Communities, 159, 166, 168, 173
Council of Federations of Commerce of Europe, *see* CFCE
Council of Ministers, 78, 82, 85, 86, 95, 97, 98, 99, 100, 106–107, 108, 112, 125, 128, 134–135, 146–147, 182
Council of Permanent Representatives, 27
Council of Presidents, 70, 78, 79, 80
Cour de Justice des Communautés Européennes, 225
"Court, Comity and Federalism in West Germany," 241
co-workers, 125, 126–127
Cracow, 176
Cravatte, Henri, 156
Cuba, 19
Cultural Convention, 179
cultural relations, 44, 183
Cummings, Rosalind, xiii
currency, 197–198
customs, 45, 58, 107
Customs Union, 60, 64, 69, 74, 75, 107, 128, 148, 198
Czechoslovakia, 2, 17, 219

DAG, 137
Dahl, Robert A., 235
Dante, 25
Darmstadt, 157
da Vinci, Leonardo, 4, 25
Davison, W. Phillips, 241–242
DBB, 137
DBV, 96, 97
Decade of Challenge, A—The Response of European Leaders, 242
"decision-makers," 37
decision-making in European organizations, 87, 228 (m.32)
Défi Américain, Le, 220, 224

"Definition fonctionelle de l'idéologie et le problème de la 'fin du siècle de l'idéologie,'" 219
De Gaulle, Charles, 14, 18, 42, 46, 97, 102, 108, 110, 166, 167, 186, 195, 196, 197, 206, 207
Dehio, Ludwig, 217
De la IIIe à la IVe République, 229
Delorme, H., 104
  see also Louït, H. D.
Démocracie en Amérique, De la, 222
Dempf, Alois, 217
Denifle, H. S., 238
Denmark, 2, 155, 185
Descartes, 4, 25
Deschamps, E., 142
De Tocqueville, Alexis, 31, 222
Deutsch, Karl W., 35, 37, 211, 218, 220, 222, 224, 241, 242, 243
"Deutsch-franzoesische Wirtschaftsbeziehungen," 224
Deutsche Angestelltengewerkschaft, *see* DAG
Deutsche Bank, 57, 224
Deutsche-Franzoisches Jugendwerk, 180
Deutsche Wirtschaft un die EWG, Die 223
Deutscher Bauernverband, *see* DBV
Deutscher Beamtenbund, *see* DBB
Deutscher Gewerkschafsbund, *see* DGB
Deutsches Industrieinstitut, 225
Dewey, John, 235
DGB, 133, 136, 137, 139, 233, 234
Dierick, M., 228
DIHT, 77, 226
"Dilemma of Administrative Responsibility, The," 229
Dimensionen, see Politische Dimensionen . . .
direct investments, 59
d'Irsay, S., 238
Documentary History of Chinese Communism, A, 229
Documents Révue des Questions Allemandes, 224
Dogan, Mattei, 232
dollar deficit, 56
dosage principle, 204
Drucker, H. P., 224, 225
Dubček, Alexander, 14
Duclos, Pierre, 228, 236
Ducommun, Charles F., 234
Dürer, Albrecht, 4
Duroselle, Jean Baptiste, 217
Durkheim, Emile, 232
Dutch, *see* Netherlands
Dutschke, Rudi, 178

Eastern European Communists, 168–169
Easton, David, 212, 242
EC, 83, 98, 99, 100–101, 111, 146, 147, 149, 150, 187, 198, 205, 211, 231
  see also European Communities
Echéance du 1er juillet, L', 224
economic advantages, 44
Economic and Social Committee, *see* ESC
Economic and Social Council, 86, 112
Economic Planning: The French Experience, 231
Economic Planning in France, 231
Economic Union, 60, 74, 75, 128, 198
ECSC, 47, 83, 143, 178
  see also CECA
Edinger, Lewis B., 35, 222
education, 125, 126, 175–176
Education sans Frontières, 239
EEC, 39, 43, 48, 50, 52, 53, 54, 55, 57, 61, 63, 65, 70, 74, 75, 78, 83, 84, 87, 89, 90, 94, 95, 96, 102, 103, 106, 108, 109, 112, 114, 115, 117, 125, 133, 140, 141, 143–145, 146, 148, 178, 227, 231, 232, 235
EFTA, 38–39, 185
  see also AELE
Ehrmann, Henry, 227
Eighth General Report on the Activities of the EEC, 226
Einaudi, Mario, 229
Elaboration des budgets de fonctionnement dans le Cadre des Communautés Européennes, L', 228
Elaboration du système de financement de la politique agricole commune, 228
ELEC, *see* LECE
"elite concept," 36–38
Emerson, Rupert, 220
Emigration de travailleurs entre les Pays du Marché Commun, L', 231

Emigrazione e comportamento politico, 119*n.*, 231
End of Ideology, The, 219
"End to European Integration?, An," 33*n.*, 34*n.*, 222
Engels, Friedrich, 134
England, 3, 184
  see also Great Britain
Enlightenment, Age of, 6
"Enquête Internationale," 43
entreprises communes, 225
Entscheidungen des BVG, 233
Entstchung der Universitäten des Mittelalters bis, Die, 238
Entwicklungslaender, 201
Erhardt, L., 108
ERO, *see* International Union of Free Trade Unions
ESC, 80, 86, 89, 94, 98, 133, 135, 144–145, 146–148
ESS, 239, 240
Esso Europe, 56
"establishment," 37
  see also "elite concept"
"Establissements Consten S.A.R.L. et Grundig-Verkaufs-C.m.b.H. contre Commission de la C.E.E.," 226
Etienne, Henri, 228
Euratom, 83, 143, 178, 181, 205
Euratom Treaty, 181
Eurocrat, 83, 202, 203–204, 205, 227, 241 (n.29)
Euroforum, 63
Euroforum, 225
"Europa—Partner der Freien Welt," 234
Europa der Sechs ohne Aussenpolitik, Das, 243
Europa 1970, Politische und gesellschaftliche Folgen der wirtschaftlichen Integration, 233
Europabild und Europagedanke—Beiträge, 217
Europäische Gemeindetag, Der, 236
Europäische Nation, Die, 220, 222, 238
Europäische Offentlinche Dienst, Der, 241
Europäischen Gemeinschaften, Die, 225
Europäischen Revolutionen, Die, 218
Europe Ascendant—The International Politics of Unification, 220
"Europe commence dans les Communes, L'," 236
Europe des Affaires, L', 30, 47, 224, 226
"Europe des Couples, L'," 242
Europe des Ethnics, L', 240
Europe-en-Formation, 225
"Europe of Businessmen," 30
Europe of the Seven, 2
Europe of the Six, 1–2, 40
Europe of the Thirteen, 2
"European Agreement for the Prevention of Broadcasts transmitted from Stations outside national Territories," 242
European Agricultural Fund, *see* FEOGA
European Assembly, 156
European Association of Teachers, *see* AEDE
European Atomic Energy Community, *see* Euratom
European Bureau for Popular (Adult) Education, 183
European Bureaucrat, *see* Eurocrat
European Chamber of Commerce, 78
European Coal and Steel Community, *see* ECSC
European Commission, 143, 234
European Committee for Economic and Social Progress, *see* CEPES
European Committee of Agriculturalists, 93
  see also CEA
European Committee of the International Metals Federation, 131
European Communities, 43, 63, 69, 109, 135, 140, 142–143, 180–181
  see also EC
European Communities, 225
European Community, xi–xii, 1 ff., 42, 87, 116, 134, 194, 201, 213, 214, 237
European Community, 223, 226
European Community as a Political System, The, 228, 242
European Defense Community, 138
European Economic Community, *see* EEC and CEE

European Free Trade Association, *see* EFTA
European Fund for Agriculture, 99
European Investment Bank, 201
European League for Economic Cooperation, *see* LECE
"European Political Integration: Progress and Prospects," 222
European Social Fund, 115
European Trade Union Sekretariat, 234
European Treaty Series, 242
European Unification in the Sixties—From the Veto to the Crisis, 230
"European Union in the Resistance," 220
European Union of Trade Unions, 140
European Unity and the Trade Union Movements, 233
European University Center, 195
European university community, 190
Europe's Post-War Growth—The Role of Labor Supply, 231
EWG Gewerkschafts-und Arbeitnehmerinformationen, 234
Extension de la décision, L', 228

Fabre-Luce, Alfred, 220
Fainsod, Merle, 233
Fairbank, John, 229
Falise, Michel, 56, 224
federal comity, 26–27
federal loyalty, 26, 27
Federal Republic, 38, 54, 91, 93, 96, 124, 136, 168, 169
  see also Germany *and* West Germany
Federal Reserve System, The, 240
federal spirit, 26, 27, 29
Federal State of the Italian Communities, 154
"Federal Theory and Party Reality in the Soviet Union," 221
Federal Union of German Employers' Associations, *see* BDA
Federal Union of German Industry, *see* BDI
federalism, 10, 11, 25–27, 214–215
Federalism, 222
Federalism and Civil Rights, 221
Federalism and Regionalism in Germany, 221
Federalism and Supra-national Organizations: Patterns for New Legal Structures, 221
Federalism and the Problem of the Small State, 243
"Federalism in Germany—The Broadcasting Controversy," 241
Fédéralisme en Amphictyonique—Elements de Système et tendance internationale, 221
Fédération Internationale des Ouvriers sur Metaux, *see* FIOM
Fédération Mondiale des Villes Jumelées, *see* FMVJ
Fédération Nationale des Syndicats d'Exploitants Agricoles, *see* FNSEA
Federation of German Industry, The, 226
Feld, Werner J., 226, 227
FEOGA, 102, 103, 104, 107
Ferro, Marc, 219
Fiat, 131
fidelity, 221
Figaro, Le, 225, 243
Finer, S. E., 226
Fingerhut, Michael, 237
Finland, 185
FIOM, 131, 132, 232, 234
First Communication, 199–200
First General Report on the Activities of the European Community, 243
"First Memorandum on Regional Policy in the European Economic Community," 240
Fischer, Fritz, 226, 227, 229, 230, 235
Flanz, G. H., 219
Flory, Maurice, 228
FMVJ, 168, 237
FNSEA, 101–102, 109–110, 111
FNSP, 240
FO, 136
Fohrmann, Jean, 233
Foltz, William J., 218, 241, 243
Fonds culturel, 179
Fonds Européen d'Orientation et de Garantie Agricoles, *see* FEOGA
food, 125, 127
Force Ouvrière, see FO
foreign aid, 44
Foreign Relations in British Labour Politics, 235
"Foreign Workers in Germany," 232

Forsyth, Mary, 223
Fourth General Report, EEC, 226, 235
Framework, 242
Framework for Political Analysis, A, 242
France, 1, 2, 3, 8–9, 20, 30, 32, 33, 34, 37, 38, 40, 42, 43, 44, 45, 48, 50 ff., 72, 74, 76, 81, 83, 91 ff., 114 ff., 133 ff., 151, 155 ff., 175 ff., 204, 207, 209, 210–211, 213, 229, 237
France, Germany and the Western Alliance—A Study of Elite Attitudes on European Integration and World Politics, 35, 222, 224
Franck, Thomas M., 219
Franco-German Chamber of Commerce, 59
Franco-German Office for Youth Exchanges, 165
Franco-German Treaty of Friendship, 165
Franco-German Youth Office, 178–179, 189
Franco-German Youth Work, 180
Frankfurt-Lyon, 192, 193
Fraser, James Fitzroy, 218
Frederick II of Prussia, 5, 176
Free Trade Union Movement, 143, 234
Free Trade Union Organization, 141
Freiburg-Grenoble, 192
French Institute of Public Opinion, *see* IFOP
French language, 204–205
French Ministry of Industry, 224
French Prefects, 167
French Revolution, 25, 92–93
Friedrich, Carl J., 218, 220–221, 222, 223, 224, 226, 227, 229, 231, 232
Friendship Treaty, 178
From Empire to Nation, 220
"Function and Process of Political Ideology, The—The Revival of Ideology in the United States," 219
"Für ein Grundsatzprogramm der europaeischen Gewerkschaftsbewegung," 234

Gasser, Adolf, 154, 235
Gazette, 242
Gefuehl der Fremde, 242
Geibel, Emanuel, 219
General Confederation of Italian Industry, *see* CONFINDUSTRIA
General Confederation of Italian Workers, *see* CGIL
General Confederation of Labor—France, *see* CGT
General Directorate, 84
general directorates, 82–83
General Electric, 131
generation conflict, 101
Gerbet, Pierre, 224
German Democratic Republic, 136, 168–169, 172
German Farmers' Union, *see* DBV
German Federal Constitutional Court (BGV), 206
German Peasants Union, 96
see also DBV
German Union of Industry and Trade, 76
German Union of Office Workers, *see* DAG
German Union of Trade Unions, *see* DGB
Germany, 1, 2, 7, 8, 19, 20, 22, 30, 32, 33, 34, 37, 38, 40, 41, 42, 43, 44, 50 ff., 72–73, 74, 76, 81, 83, 96, 99, 105–106, 108, 112 ff., 133 ff., 155 ff., 175 ff., 200, 204, 207, 209, 210–211, 213, 237
see also Federal Republic, Weimar Republic, *and* West Germany
Gervais, Michel, 92*n.*, 230
Geschichte der Volksfreiheit und Demokratie, 235
Gesetzblatt für Baden-Württemberg, 239
Geusau, M. Alting von, 228
Gewerkschaft, Wirtschaft, Gesellschaft, 235
Gewerkschaftliche Monatshefte, 234
Geyl, Pieter, 195
Glasgow, 176
Gloeilampenfabrieken, 131
Glotz, Gerhard, 240
Goebbels, Joseph, 206
Goethe, 209
Gollwitzer, Heinz, 217, 218
Gordon, Morton, 211, 222, 242

Government and Opposition, 84*n.*, 88*n.*, 220, 227, 241
Governmental Process, The: Political Interests and Public Opinion, 227
Grand Design, 5
Grande Bretagne et le Marché Commun, La, 226, 240
"Grass-roots Base of the Unification of Europe, The," 236
grass-roots integration, 151 ff.
Grauhan, Rolf-Richard, 162, 163, 222, 236, 237, 238
Grazia, Sebastian de, 232, 237
Great Britain, 2, 7, 8–9, 18, 30, 50, 74, 83, 146, 166, 177, 185, 188, 196–197, 201, 202, 206, 213
Greece, 2, 4, 114, 179, 185, 201
Groupes de Pression Internationaux, Les, 226
Groupes Européennes, Les, 227
"Growth of Nations; Some Recurrent Patterns of Political and Social Integration," 220
Grundig-Consten case, 67
"Gründung und die Ziele des Rates der Gemeinden Europas, Die," 236
Guérend, J. P., 242
Guérend, R., 242
Guéron, G., 239
"guest workers," 114 ff.
Guillaume, F., 230
Gustav Stresemann's Vermächtnis—Der Nachlass in drei Bänden, 220

Haas, Ernst B., 71–72, 220–221, 222, 223, 226, 233, 234
Hackett, Annemarie, 231
Hackett, John, 231
Hague Conferences, 8
Hake, H. J. von, 59, 224, 225
Hallstein, Walter, 146, 199, 227, 235
Halperin, Jean, 224
Hamburg, 19
Handlin, Oscar, 231
Handwerk, 70
Hansa cities, 19
Harmel Plan, 197
Harper's, 224
Haskins, Charles Homer, 217, 238
Hay, Peter, 221, 226
Hayward, J., 231
"heartland," 2
Heidelberg, 176
Heidelberg-Montpellier, 192, 193
Henry IV of France, 5
Héraud, Guy, 240
Herring, E. P., 227
Herriot, Edouart, 153–154
High Authority, 82, 140, 143, 149
High Commission, 82, 83, 85, 102
Hindus, Maurice, 219
Hirsch, Etienne, 205, 226, 241
Historie des Universités, 238
Hitler, Adolf, 18, 20–21, 28, 92, 160, 206
Hocking, William Ernest, 217
Holmes, Oliver Wendell, 23
Holy Alliance, 7–8
Homer, 4
Homme et la Sociéte, L'; Revue Internationale des recherches et de synthèses sociologiques, 219
Homo ludens—A Study of the Play-Element in Culture, 237
housing, 125, 129
Huizinga, Johan, 237
Hungary, 2
Huntington, Samuel P., 219

Iceland, 185
Idea of Nationalism, The, 220
Idée d'Europe dans l'Histoire, 217
Idee zu einer allgemeinen Geschichte in weltbürgerlicher Absicht, Werke, 218
"Ideological and Philosophical Background, The," 218
IESS, 223, 224, 231, 238, 239
IFOP, 49, 104, 105, 106, 107
India, 1, 18, 21, 30, 32, 214
Indonesia, 19
Inevitable Peace, 218
Information Agricole, L', 111
Information des Européennes et l'intégration de L'Europe, 222
Information Service of the Communities, 49
Informations Syndicales et Ouvrières, 233, 234
Inglehart, Ronald, 33*n.*, 34*n.*, 222
Inquiry into the Freedom of Decision, An, 239

Inscription de l'aluminium sur la liste des exceptions dans les négociations du Gatt, L', 228
Institut d'Etudes Européennes, 240
Institut Français d'Opinion Publique, *see* IFOP
Institut International de la Philosophie Politique, 219
Institutionalivierte Vertretung der Verbände in der Europäischen Wirtschaftsgemeinschaft, Die, 227
Integration, 10–12, 115, 118 ff., 139, 144, 146, 151 ff., 193–195, 203, 208, 210, 212, 213
"Integration and Arms Control in the European Political Environment," 222
Integration und Mitbestimmung-Hauptergebnisse einer Untersuchung des EMNID–Instituts für Sozialforschung, 225
Integrazione dell'immigrato nella società industriale, L', 232
Interest Groups on Four Continents, 227
intermarriage, 209–210
Internal Federation of Europe Houses, 183
"Internal Market," 227
International Administration of the International Secretariat, The, 241
International Center for European Education, *see* CIFE
International Chamber of Commerce, 78, 224
International Confederation of Christian Trade Unions, *see* CISC
International Confederation of Free Trade Unions, *see* CISL
International Federation of Metal Workers, *see* FIOM
"International Integration–The European and the Universal Process," 220
International Organization, 220, 241
International Political Science Association, *see* IPSA
International Regionalism, 243
International Regions and the International System: A Study in Political Ecology, 217, 243
International Secretariat of the Chemical Industry–of the EEC, *see* ISCI
International Socialism and the World War, 233
International Union of Free Trade Unions, 138, 139
International Union of the Hague Conferences, The, 218
internationalism, 134
interpenetration, 61
Intersyndicale, 233
IPSA, 224, 231
Iran, 19
Ireland, 2, 185
ISCI, 88
Israel, 19
Istituto per la Scienza dell'Amministrazione Pubblica of Milan, 235
Italian Socialist Party, *see* PSI
Italian Television and Radio Broadcasting, *see* RAI
Italy, 1, 2, 7, 8, 22, 41, 45, 52, 60–61, 73, 91, 92, 93–94, 99, 100, 101, 113, 114, 116, 117, 118, 120, 121, 122, 126, 134, 137, 139, 147, 150, 155, 158, 178, 182, 184, 185, 188–189, 200, 201, 204, 207, 213, 229, 242

Jacobins, The–An Essay in the New History, 218
Jahresbericht of the *BDI*, 226
Japan, 10, 19
Jeunes Ruraux, Les, 232
"joint enterprises," 225
Joint International Seminar on Adaptation of rural and foreign workers in industry, 232
"joint production," 61
Journal of Common Market Studies, 242
Journal of Politics, 241
Journal Officiel, 112, 231
jumelages, 156, 159, 184, 186, 188 ff., 208, 237, 238
"Jumelages de A jusqu'à Z," 236

Kaiser, Edith, xiii
Kant, Immanuel, 5, 6, 25, 218
Kazancigil, A., 240
Kennedy, Robert F., 37
Kennedy Round, 81, 100, 109

Key, V. O., Jr., 220, 226
Kindleberger, Charles P., 231
King, Martin Luther, 37
Kissinger, Henry, 218
Kitzmueller, Erich, 233
Kluckhohn, Clyde, 219
Kohn, Hans, 218, 220
"Konzept regionaler Friedensorganisation, Das—Resistance und europäische Einigungsbewegung," 220
Koster, H. J. de, 79
Kriesberg, Louis, 226
Kroeber, A. L., 219

L-terms, 49–52
labor, 45
language, 125, 126, 129, 204–205
Lannes, Xavier, 231
Latin America, 10, 14, 18
Law and Institutions in the Atlantic Area—Reading, Cases, Problems, 226
"laws of power," 145
Layton, Christopher, 224
LECE, 70
League of Nations, 5–6, 8–9
Lenin, Nikolai, 16, 219
Leoni, B., 235
Lerner, Daniel, 211, 222, 233, 242
levée en masse, 7
Levi-Sandri, M., 133
Ligue Européenne de la Coopération Economique, *see* ELEC
Lindberg, Leon N., 35, 212, 224, 226, 228, 242
Lipgens, Walter, 220
Lipsitz, Lewis, 224
Liska, George, 220
"little Europe," 1
Local Government in Crisis, 235
Locarno—The Reality, 220
Locarno sans Rèves, 220
Locarno Treaty, 20
Louët, Hélène Delorme, xiii, 104, 229, 230
Löwenthal, Richard, 219
Luchaire, François, 288
Lulling, Astrid, 226
Luther, Martin, 25
Luxembourg, 2, 45, 93, 99, 147, 155 *see also* Benelux
Lyon, Margot, 241
Macridis, Roy C., 35, 222
McWhinney, Edward, 221
Madariaga, Salvador de, 217
Maddex, W. P., 235
magazines, 208
Magna Charta, 25
Magnus, Albert, 2
"Main Agreement of All the Reich Deputies," 7
Major, Louis, 234
Making of Citizens, The, 175, 238
Man-Lipanski, Arnaud, 224
"Man and His Government," 219, 243
Man and His Government, 218, 220–221, 222, 223, 224, 227, 228, 232, 236, 239, 241, 243
Man and His World, 219
Mannucci, Cesare, 242
Mansholt, S., 94, 95, 97–98
Mao Tse-tung, 16, 91, 229
Marché Commun et la Grèce à travers les textes, 240
Marché Commun et l'Agriculture—Livre Blanc des Organisations Professionels et Agricoles, 230
Marriott, J. A. R., 243
Marshal, Burke, 221
Marx, Karl, 134
Marxist-Leninist ideology, 16
mass communications, 205 ff.
Materialien au Grundsaetzen und Politik europäischen Wirtschaftagemeinschaft, 234
Mayne, Richard, 240
Mayors' Union, 170
Medieval Mind, The, 217
Megret, Jacques, 228
Merriam, Charles E., 175, 237, 238
Merritt, Richard L., 35, 222, 223
Metallpressdienst, 233
Metternich, 7
Meyer, J., 239
Meynaud, Jean, xiii, 224, 226, 227, 233, 234
Michelin Co., 58
Middle Ages, 2–3
Midwest Journal of Political Science, 241
Miglie, G., 235
migrant workers, 114 ff.
"Migration: Social Aspects," 231
MIJARC, 230

Mill, John Stuart, 215, 243
Mind of Modern Russia, The, 218
Minnesota Law Review, 226
Mirror for Man, 219
mission civilisatrice, 6, 13
Mitbestimmung, Beitraege zur puritaetischen Mitbestimmung in der Wirtschaft, 225
Mitbestimmung in der Bundesrepublik Deutschland, 225
MODEF, 103
Modèle économique européen, le, 228
Modification des structures politiques administratives Françaises en fonction de la coopération économique internationale, 224
Mohammedanism, 12
Monde, Le, 230, 237
Moore, Barrington, Jr., 229
Moral Basis of a Backward Society, The, 229, 232
Morgan, Roger, 223
Mother Russia, 219
Mouvement de Défense des Exploitations Familiales, *see* MODEF
Mouvement International de la Jeunesse Agricole et Rural Catolic, *see* MIJARC
Mouvement Républican Populaire, *see* MRP
Movement for the Defense of Family Farms, *see* MODEF
MRP, 167
Muntzke, Hans, 236, 237
Murville, Couve de, 107, 108
Mussolini, Benito, 92

Nachrichtendienst, 233
Naples, 176
Napoleon Bonaparte, 6–7
Napoleon III, 8
Nation-Building, 218, 241, 243
National Center of Young Farmers, *see* CNJA
National committee of the CGT–FO, *see* CCN
National Confederation of Farmers' Mutuals, Cooperatives, and Credit Organizations, *see* CNMCCA
National Council of French Employers, *see* CNPF
"National Economic Interest Groups and Policy Formation in the EEC," 227
National Federation of Agricultural Organizations, *see* FNSEA
nationalism, 31–32, 92–93
nationes, 176
NATO, 203
Neckarsulm, *see* NSU
Négociation de la deuxième convention de l'association des états Africains Malgaches à la CEE, 228, 240
Nenni, Pietro, 135
Nerves of Government, The, 220
Netherlands, 2, 33, 34, 44, 45, 52, 56, 79, 91, 93–94, 99, 100, 113, 131, 147, 155, 185, 211
    see also Benelux
Neue Freie Presse, xi
Neunreither, Karl-Heinz, xii, 75*n.*, 74, 76, 77, 81, 83, 85–86, 95, 109, 225, 226, 227, 228, 229, 230, 243
New Belief in the Common Man, The, 220
"New Messianism, The," 218
New York Times, 219, 239
newspapers, 208
Niebuhr, Rheinhold, 217
Nigeria, 25–26
Nijhoff, Martinus, 217
Ninth General Report on the Activities of the Community, 240
Nizard, Lucien, 228, 231
Noel, Emile, 228
Nomos, 221, 227, 229
North Africa, 114
Norway, 2, 185
Nouvelle Revue Française, La, 209
Nouvelles, 232, 234
NSU, 132
Nye, Joseph S., Jr., 243

OCDE, 178
    see also OECD
OECD, 232
    see also OCDE
OECE, 178, 179
OEEC, *see* OECE
Of Time, Work and Leisure, 237
Office de Radiodiffusion et Television Française, *see* ORTF

Office Franco-Allemand de la Jeunesse, 178–179
Office of French Television and Radio Broadcasting, *see* ORTF
Ofstad, Harald, 239
Olivetti, Adriano, 154
On Eternal Peace, 5
"On the New Democracy," 229
Opium des Intellectuels, 219
Ordine Politico delle Communità State secunde le leggi dello spirite, L', 236
Organisation Européenne de Coopération Economique, *See* OECE *and* OEEC
Organisation internationale agite-elle sur la pensée et les Politiques Economiques Contemporaines?, 224
Organisation pour la Coopération et le Développment Economique, *see* OCDE
Organization for Economic Cooperation and Development, *see* OCDE *and* OECD
Organization for European Economic Cooperation, *see* OEEC *and* OECE
"Origin and Development of the Concept of Federalism in the United States," 236
ORTF, 206, 207, 242
Out of Revolution—Autobiography of Western Man, 218
Outlawing the Communist Party, 233

Pakistan, 19
Paliano, Guido Colonna di, 225
Pan-Africanism, 11
Pan-Americanism, 11
Pan-Arabism, 11
Pan-Europa, 9, 218
Paneuropa, xi, 222
Paneuropean Union, 9
pan-movements, 10
Panslavism—Its History and Ideology, 218
Parker, Alan, 225
Parsons, Talcott, 218
partenaires sociaux, 52–53
participation, 125, 128
Participation, La: Bouleversement où évolution, 225
Partita Socialista Italiana, *see* PSI
Party Democracy—Politics in an Italian Socialist Federation, 232, 233
Passigli, Stefano, xii–xiii, 117–118, 119*n.*, 120, 122, 231, 232
Patronat Français, 76
Patterns of Power: Bureaucracy and the Integrative Process, 241
Paulu, Burton, 237, 241
"Paysans," 91*n.*
Paysans Français et l'Unité, Les, 229
Peace of Utrecht, 5
Peace of Vienna, 7
"Peasant as Evil Genius of Dictatorship, The," 229
peasants, 90–93
Pepy, Daniel, 228, 240
Perissich, Riccardo, 227
Permanent Committee of CE, 155–156
"Permanent Conference," 78
Petrella, Riccardo, 240
Petrilli, G., 225
Phillips, N. V., 131
Philosophy, Religion and the Coming World Civilization—Essays in Honor of William Ernest Hocking, 217
Philosophy of Kant, The, 218
Philosophy of Law in Historical Perspective, 221
Phoenix Gummi 1967, Bericht ueber das, 96, 225
Pipes, Richard, 219
place of work, 125, 126
Planification comme facteur d'intégration sociale, La, 231
Planification Française, La, 231
Plato, 4
Poland, 2, 3, 17, 22, 91
Polish Peasant in Europe and America, The, 229
Political Community, The—A Study of Anomie, 232
Political Community and the North Area: International Organization in the Light of Historical Experience, 220
political consensus, 46
Political Dynamics of European Economic Integration, The, 224
Political Influence, 235
Political Parties and Pressure Groups, 226

Political Power, 237
Political Power: USA/USSR, 219
Political Science Quarterly, 227, 242
Politics of Federal Bureaucracy, The, 241
Politics of German Co-determination, The, 225
Politik und Sachverstand im Kreditwährungswesen, 239
Politische Dimensionen der Europäischen Gemeincshaftsbildung, xii, 222, 226, 227, 228, 229, 230, 231, 233, 235, 236, 238, 239
Pompidou, Georges, 110
Population, 231
Portrait of Europe, 217
Portugal, 2, 114, 185
Pouvoir de décision à l'organisation de coopération et de développment économique, Le, 228
Pouvoir et Influence–Contribution à l'étude de la décision Politique dans le domaine interne et dans le domaine communautaire, 228
Powicke, F. M., 217
Prague, 176
Precarious Balance, The, 217
Prefects and Provincial France, The, 237
"Préjugés français et préjugés allemands," 239
Préparation de la Décision au Niveau national néerlandais, 228
Préparation des decisions dans le cadre national de la R.F.A., 228
Press and Information Service, 180–181
Presseveröffentlichung, 225
"Pressure Groups and the European Community," 227
price stabilization, 102
Principles of Rural-Urban Sociology, 229
Problemi dell'Europa Communitaria, 239
Problems of Communism, 219
"Problems of the Historical Approach, 219
Projection, Political Choice and the Preparation of the Fifth French Plan, 231
Projet d'un statut des Sociétes anonymes européennes, 225
Projet pour rendre la Paix perpetuelle en Europe, 5–6
Prussia, 3–4, 28, 221
PSI, 137
PTT, 234
Public Administration and the Public Interest, 227
Public and Its Problems, The, 235
"Public Interest, The," 227
Public Opinion Quarterly, 229
Public Policy, 221, 229, 236, 241
"Public Policy and the Nature of Administrative Responsibility," 229, 241
Puchala, Donald C., 222

Quelques Aspects des rapports et de la collaboration entre le Conseil et la Commission au Cours de l'élaboration de décisions, 228
Querelle de la C.D.D., La, 233

Rabier, Jacques-René, xiii, 222, 223, 239
radio, 206
Radio and Television Broadcasting on the European Continent, 237, 241
Radio Luxemburg, 208
Radiotelevisione Italiana, *see* RAI
RA Index, *see* "relative acceptance index"
RAI Radiotelevisione Italiana, 242
Ranshofen-Wertheimer, Egon, 241
Rapport d'Activité 1963–1968, 238
Rapport de la Troisième Assemblée Générale de l'Organisation C.I.S.L., 224
Rapporto Sull'Europa, 241
Rashdall, Hastings, 217, 238
Raymond VII of Toulouse, 176
Rectors of European Universities, 178
Recueil de la Jurisprudence de la Cour, 225
Red China, 16–17
  see also China
Réforme du Conseil de l'Europe, La, 236
regional policy, 199
"Regional policy of the EEC, The," 240

Règlement Interne, 230
Règlement No. 17 et la politique commune des transports, 228
Règlement No. 17 et l'elaboration de la décision communautaire, 228
Rehwinkel, E., 112
Reich, Donald R., 241–242
Reichsdeputationshauptschluss, 7
"Relations between the Officials of the European Commission and the Governments of the Member States," 241
"relative acceptance index" (RA Index), 36, 39
religion, 12, 13
Rembrandt, 4
Renard, André, 234
Representative Government, 215
"Reshuffling the 'Eurocrats,'" 241
Responsible Electorate, The, 220
Revolutionary Russia, 219
Revue de Psychologie des Peuples, 239
Revue française de l'opinion publique (Sondages), 45
Revue française de sociologie, 232
Rey, Jean, 200, 240
Richter, Heinz, 232
Rights of Man, 6
Riker, William H., 222
Rise of the Universities, The, 217, 238
Risorgimento, 25
Rivista Internazionale de Scienze Sociali, 231
Rivkin, Arnold, 223, 240
Robson, William A., 235
Roche, Emile, 145
Roi soleil, Le, 25
Rôle de la Commission, Le, 228
Rôle des représentations permanentes dans la décision communautaire, Le, 228
Rôle du parlement dans la formation de des communautés européennes, Le, 228
Rome, 4
Rome Treaty, *see* Treaty of Rome
Roosevelt, Franklin D., 21
Rosenberg, Ludwig, 233, 234
Rosenstock-Huessy, Eugen, 218
Rougemont, Denis de, 217, 223
Rouner, Leroy S., 217
Rousseau, Jean-Jacques, 5, 7, 236
Rubel, 219
Rumania, 2
Rundfunk-and *Fernseh,* 207
Rundgespräch über Wirtschaftsfragen, 234
Russett, Bruce M., 217, 218, 243
Russia, 1, 8, 90–91
see also Soviet Union *and* USSR
Russian Empire, 10
Russian Revolution, 10

sabotage, 26
Sacrum Imperium, 3, 217
St. Andrews, 176
Saint-Cloud, 169
Saint-Pierre, Abbé, 5, 7
Sakharov, Andrei D., 16, 219
Salmon, J. A., 228
Salvadori, Massimo, 220
Salvemini, Gaetano, 228
Sanders, Prof., 225
Sautter, Guy, 228
Saxony, 3–4
Scandinavia, 40, 177, 201, 202
Schadenfreude, 64
Schaff, Adam, 219
Scheinman, Lawrence, 241
Schierwater, Hans-Viktor, xii, 125, 129, 150, 231, 232, 233, 234, 235
Schleswig, 167
Schmertzing, W. P. von, 233
Schmidt, Carl D., 228
Schöndube, Claus, 218
"school for democracy," 152
Schubert, Glendon, 227
Schücking, Walter, 218
Schumann, Robert, xi
Schumann Plan, 139
Schwamm, Henri, xii, 62, 149, 224, 225, 232, 233
Schwartz, Benjamin, 229
Schwarzenbach, 157
Science Politique et Intégration Européenne, 227
Scotto, A., 235
secession, 26
Secrétariat des Conseils, le, 228
security, 43
Segré, Claudio, 65

Selected Background Studies Prepared for the United States–Puerto Rico Commission on the Status of Puerto Rico, 240
"Selected Trends and Issues in Contemporary Federal and Regional Relations," 240
self-regulation, 212
Serafini, Umberto, 154
"serment du jumelage," 156
Servan-Schreiber, Jean-Jacques, 220, 224, 225
Servolin, Claude, 92*n.*, 230
Sessions Marathon du Conseil des ministres de la Communauté Européenne, Les, 228
Shakespeare, William, 4, 25
Shils, Edward A., 218, 223
Sidjanski, Dusan, xii, xiii, 84*n.*, 87–88, 181, 189, 190, 192, 193, 194, 221, 224, 226, 227, 228, 229, 238, 239
Siegfried, André, 229
Silj, Alessandro, 224, 225
Simmel, 242
Sino-Soviet Conflict, 1956–1961, The 219
Sirre, 157
Six, *see* Community of the Six
"Sixième Colonne, La," 237
Social Origins of Dictatorship and Democracy–Lord and Peasant in the Making of the Modern World, 229
"social partners," 52
Social Science, 226
Social Science Foundation of the University of Denver, 223
social security, 45, 117, 124, 125, 128, 149
Social System, The, 218
social workers, 127
Socialism, 17, 92, 137
Società editrice il Mulino, 231
société commerciale, 65–66
Societé Française d'Enquêtes par Sondages, *see* SOFRES
SOFRES, 106
"Some Preliminary Notes on Bureaucratic Relationships in the European Economic Community," 241
Sondages, 43, 45*n.*, 105*n.*, 107*n.*, 223
Sorokin, P., 229
Soviet Union, 1, 9, 10, 12, 17, 21, 130, 169, 221
see also Russia *and* USSR
soviets, 90–91
Sozialbetreuer, 127
Soziologie, 242
Spain, 2, 3, 7, 114, 185, 188, 213
Speier, Hans, 241–242
Spengler, Oswald, 13
Spettatore Internazionale, Lo, 227, 240
Spinelli, Altiero, 205, 220, 241
Spiro, Herbert J., 225
Springer press, 208
Stalin, Joseph, 16, 21
standard of living, 43, 44
Standard Oil Company of New Jersey, 56
Ständestaat, 86
Statistisches Jarbuch für die Bundesrepublik Deutschland, 223
Statut de l'Ecole Européenne, 239
Steiert, Rudolf, xiii, 232
Stein, Eric, 226
Sternberger, Dolf, 242
Storia della Resistenza Italiana, 220
Streithofen, Heinrich, 225
Stresemann, Gustav, xi, 20
Strihou, Paul van Ypersele de, 223
"Structure and Policy of the RAI–TV," 242
Structure of Nations and Empires, The, 217
Struggle to Unite Europe, The, 1940–1958, 222
Studies in Federalism, 221
Sully, Minister, 5
Sweden, 3, 185
Switzerland, 2, 19, 21, 32, 57, 114, 117, 155, 157, 158, 177, 185, 204
System Analysis of Political Life, A, 242

Tableux de l'agriculture Française, 91*n.*
Taoism, 16
tariff, 57–58
Tätigkeitsbericht of DIHT, 226
Tavernier, Yves, xiii, 104, 106, 229, 230

taxes, 117
Taylor, Henry O., 217
television, 206, 207
Témoinage Chrétien, 237
Tenth General Report, EEC, 52*n*., 227, 230, 231, 232, 235, 240
Terreur, 6
Theory of the Location of Industries, The, 231
"third estate," 6
Third Internationale, 134
This is RAI, 242
Thomas, William I., 229
Thompson, Dennis, 242
"Thoughts on Progress, Peaceful Coexistence and Intellectual Freedom," 219
Tito, 14
Tittel, Roland, 225
Togliatti, M., 139
Tolstoy, Leo, 18
Totalitarian Dictatorship and Autocracy, 229
"Totalitarianism: Recent Trends," 219
tourism, 44, 160, 210
see also travel
Toward a General Theory of Social Action, 218
Toynbee, Arnold, 13
trade unions, 121, 122, 133 ff.
"transactions," 36, 38
Trans-Atlantic Investments, 224
travel, 40–41, 44, 61
Treaty of Rome, 66–67, 72, 78, 86, 109, 110–111, 112, 115, 133, 138, 199, 200–201
Treaty on Franco-German Cooperation, 180
Trends of Federalism in Theory and Practice, 218, 221, 241, 243
Troyes, 157
Truman, David, 227
Tsarist Empire, 28
Turkey, 2, 19, 114, 179, 185, 201
"twinnings," 236

UACEE, 70, 78
UAEE, 188
Under the Axe of Fascism, 228
Underdeveloped Areas in the Common Market, The, 240
underdeveloped countries, 201
Underhill, Frank H., 221
Une France sans Paysans, 92*n*., 230
Une Université Européenne, 239
UNESCO, 49
UNICE, 65, 69, 70, 77, 78–79, 80, 82, 83–84, 88, 93, 95, 96, 109, 140, 145, 230
Union de l'Artisanat de la CEE, *see* UACEE
Union des Associations Européennes d'Etudiants, *see* UAEE
Union des Industries de la Communauté Européenne, *see* UNICE
Union Internationale des Maires, 237
Union of European Student Associations, *see* UAEE
Union of Free Trade Unions, 143
Union of German Civil Servants, *see* DBB
Union of Industries of the European Community, *see* UNICE
Union of Soviet Socialist Republics, *see* Russia, Soviet Union, *and* USSR
Union of the Craftsmen of the EEC, *see* UACEE
Unions d'Etudiants de l'Europe des Six, 187
United Nations, 5–6, 19, 203, 214
United Nations Educational, Scientific, and Cultural Organization, *see* UNESCO
United States of America, *see* USA
Uniting Europe, 236
Uniting of Europe, The—Political, Social and Economic Forces, 1950–1957, 222
Università Europea, L', 239
universities, 175–176
Universities of Europe in the Middle Ages, The, 217, 238
Uppsala, 176
USA, 1, 8–9, 10, 12 ff., 29–31, 37, 38–39, 40, 54, 58, 60, 63, 65, 74, 83, 118, 131, 138, 170, 179, 188, 204, 211
"USA als Faktor der europäischen wirtschafts-und sozialpolitischen Integration, Der," 235
Usine Nouvelle, L', 111
USSR, 13 ff., 28

"Vague Allemande, La," 237
Valeur de la décision, La, 228
Vent'anni e un Giorno, 228
Verfassungstheorie und Verfassungspolitik, 218
Verges, J. R., 228
Vers la Vie Nouvelle, 242
Verschwisterungen (sisterhoods), 156
"Verschwisterungen deutscher und französischer Gemeinden, Die," 222, 237
Verzeichnis der gemeinsamen Organisationen die in der Europaeischen Wirtschaftsgemeinschaft von Industrie-, Handwerks- und Handelsvergaenden der sechs Länder geschaffen wurden, 227
Vienna, 176
Vierteljahrshefte für Zeitgeschichte, 220
Vietnam, 14
Vignes, Daniel, 228
Vingt-Huit Siècles d'Europe—La Conscience Européenne a travers les Textes dé Hesiode à nos jours, 217, 223
Virgil, 4
Visine, François, 228
Vorstand, 63–64

Warburg, Paul M., 240
Weber, Alfred, 231
Weber, Max, 16, 220, 238
Weill, Jean, 92*n.*, 230
Weimar Republic, 28
Weissenberger, H., 242
Welt, Die, 48, 242
Werke, 219
Wertmasstaebe der Gewerkschaftspolitik—Ein Beitrag zur Theorie der Gewerkschaft, 225
West German Leadership and Foreign Policy, 241–242
West Germany, 48, 169
see also Germany
"West Indian Federation," 219
Western European Union, *see* WEU
WEU, 184, 197
Wolfers, Arnold, 218
Wheare, K. C., 29
Who Governs?, 235
Why Federations Fail—An Inquiry into the Requisites for Successful Federalism, 219
Wilcke, Gerd, 239
Willis, H. Parker, 240
Wilson, James Q., 235
Wilson, Woodrow, 8
Wirtschaft und Gesellschaft, 220
Wirtschafts-und Sozialausschuss der EWG und Euratom, Der—Interessenrepräsentation auf übernationaler Ebene, 227, 234
Workers' Force, see FO
World Communism—The Disintegration of a Secular Faith, 219
World Congress at Strasbourg (1964), 169
World Council, 168, 169
World Council of (Paired) Municipalities, *see* FMVJ
World Peace Restored, A: Metternich, Castlereagh, and the Problem of Peace, 218
World Politics, 220

Yale Review, 229
Yugoslavia, 2, 17, 19, 91, 114

Zagoria, Donald S., 219
Zeit, Die, 239
Zellentin, Gerda, 227, 234, 235
Zelzate, 157
Zimmermann, C. C., 229
Znaniecki, F., 229
Zurcher, Arnold J., 222

CARL J. FRIEDRICH is Eaton Professor of the Science of Government at Harvard University. For twelve years he also held the professorship in political science at the University of Heidelberg, where he founded and directed the Institut für Politische Wissenschaft.

During World War II Professor Friedrich directed the School for Overseas Administration at Harvard. From 1946 to 1949 he served as government affairs advisor to the U.S. Military Governor in Germany and participated in the research for the drafting of the constitution of the Federal Republic of Germany.

Professor Freidrich has been actively concerned with the problems of European unification for over forty years. At present he is directing a major research project on "The Political Implications of Informal Community Formation in Europe" (which was begun in 1963) under the auspices of the Center for International Affairs, Harvard University, and is also an active participant in the International Political Science Association's Research Committee on European Integration.

Considered one of the world's leading political scientists, Professor Friedrich is currently president of the International Political Science Association and of the Institut International de Philosophie Politique. He is a past president of the American Political Science Association.

69 70 71 72 73 8 7 6 5 4 3 2 1

Emory & Henry College - Kelly Library
3 [illegible]36 0012 7106 3